THE PRACTICAL ANARCHIST

AMERICAN PHILOSOPHY

Douglas R. Anderson and Jude Jones, series editors

THE PRACTICAL
ANARCHIST

Writings of Josiah Warren

Edited and with an Introduction by
CRISPIN SARTWELL

FORDHAM UNIVERSITY PRESS   NEW YORK   2011

Fordham University Press has no responsibility for the persistence or accuracy of URLs for external or third-party Internet websites referred to in this publication and does not guarantee that any content on such websites is, or will remain, accurate or appropriate.

Fordham University Press also publishes its books in a variety of electronic formats. Some content that appears in print may not be available in electronic books.

Library of Congress Cataloging-in-Publication Data

Warren, Josiah, 1798–1874.
    The practical anarchist : writings of Josiah Warren / edited and with an introduction by Crispin Sartwell.—1st ed.
        p. cm.— (American philosophy)
    Includes bibliographical references and index.
    ISBN 978–0-8232–3370–0 (cloth : alk. paper)
    ISBN 978–0-8232–3372–4 (epub)
    1. Warren, Josiah, 1798–1874.   2. Anarchism—United States.
3. Utopian socialism—United States.   I. Sartwell, Crispin, 1958–
II. Title.
    HX843.7.W27   2011
    335′.83092—dc22

                                                           2011013452

Printed in the United States of America
13 12 11   5 4 3 2 1
First edition

Contents

Acknowledgments

A summer grant from Dickinson College helped to fund research in collections and to obtain photocopies. I thank Dickinson for that and many other forms of support. My work on Warren has piggybacked on the exemplary research of Shawn Wilbur. Dana Ward's "Anarchy Archives" website gave me my first real contact with Warren's texts, and earlier versions of some of texts reprinted here, including versions typeset by Warren, can be found there. The Wisconsin Historical Society, the Indiana Historical Society, the Labadie Collection at the University of Michigan, the Houghton Library at Harvard University, and the Working Men's Institute at New Harmony, Indiana, were of extraordinary aid in obtaining the materials contained in this book. Finally, I want to express my admiration for Josiah Warren: a half-cracked monomaniac but also an omni-competent human being. I admire his style of anti-leadership, based on anti-charisma: too reticent to tell you how to live. Rarely have extreme idealism and extreme realism been so idiosyncratically or so compellingly combined. It is a combination we may require yet.

INTRODUCTION

The early- and mid-nineteenth-century United States produced a bewildering variety of individualists, in the sense of people who advocated the primacy of the human individual politically and of the particular thing metaphysically, and in the sense of seriously idiosyncratic persons who followed their own odd genius wherever it dragged them. It was, in many ways, a religious revival, but it soon sacrificed God on the altar of nonconformity. It produced undoubted geniuses of the caliber of Emerson, Fuller, Thoreau, Melville, Whitman, and Hawthorne. It produced social reformers as pure and intense as any that the world has known—such as William Lloyd Garrison, Elizabeth Cady Stanton, and Captain John Brown. And it produced utopians who thought they could found a new social order—including Adin Ballou, John Humphrey Noyes, Amos Bronson Alcott, and Josiah Warren.

Like almost all of these astonishing and exasperating people, Josiah Warren hailed from New England. Like Garrison (and Ben Franklin,

Pierre-Joseph Proudhon, and Albert Parsons) he was a printer. Like John Brown he was a revolutionist, though Brown was violent and Warren, by his own declaration, peaceful. Like Emerson and Whitman, he sang, or in his case lectured, about free individuality and connected it to an understanding of the universe. Like Thoreau he loved simplicity and skill, and displayed them prodigiously as qualities of character and thought throughout his life. And like Ballou— and the rest of these people at one time or another—he loathed the state and took steps to fashion a life without it.

You could think of Warren as an Emersonian avatar, someone who lived what "The American Scholar," "Self-Reliance," "Nature," and even "Fate" taught at the very same time that Emerson was formulating those fundamental statements of the American character. He practiced wilderness self-sufficiency, anticapitalist economy, radical democracy that entailed extreme decentralization of decision making, and a metaphysics of particulars. In short, his philosophy was "transcendentalism," and he practiced it as early as Emerson did. But unlike Emerson, he was devoted not to stating this philosophy beautifully, but to realizing it practically.

Josiah Warren was both a genius and a crank of nearly the first order. He has often been called the first American anarchist, though he called himself a "Democrat." And though I am certain he wasn't the first American anarchist (since every state breeds skeptics, and since radical Protestants of all sorts had vowed to live outside or against the state in the previous two centuries), it is not an entirely inapt characterization. In the usual histories of anarchist thinking, only William Godwin comes earlier, and Warren's *Peaceful Revolutionist* (1833) has plausibly been called the first anarchist periodical. Through Stephen Pearl Andrews and Benjamin Tucker—also extremely idiosyncratic thinkers—Warren became known as the founder of "individualist" anarchism. Though "first American anarchist" is an appropriate reflection of his importance, it would be more accurate to say that he was the first American to publish his views whose anarchism was not primarily religious.[1]

He was also—until now, I believe—nearly unreadable. He himself never regarded writing as his most important work, but rather his practical experiments in living. His prose is undoubtedly that of a man who developed a less expensive and time-consuming process for manufacturing his own type and printing his own books, pamphlets, and periodicals. Warren's is some of the most typographically perverse writing produced before surrealist poetry. For example, he often uses several sizes of small caps for different degrees of emphasis, tossing in a half dozen exclamation marks for effect. I calculate informally that among his works about a third of the sentences end in at least one exclamation point; in his notebooks, the percentage is far higher. He introduced marginal indexing systems and tables of reference so that one could either follow a single theme through a book or read in different thematic orders, a kind of hyperlink typesetting that yields perverse organizations worthy of Spinoza. In his handwritten journals he used a system of underlining meant to add absurd shades, degrees, and intensities of emphasis, building to a bathetic crescendo of hyperbole. Bracing and fundamentally original ideas are studded with mere enthusing, as in this typical sentence from his fundamental work, *Equitable Commerce*: "Consider on what foundation rest all customs, laws, and institutions which demand *conformity! They are all directly opposed to this inevitable individuality, and are therefore* FALSE!!! and the great problem must be solved with the broadest admission of the ABSOLUTE RIGHT OF SUPREME INDIVIDUALITY."[2] Even as American anarchists appealed to him as their founder and to his ideas as their solution, he was something of an embarrassment. The texts in this volume are edited to remove emphasis and to excise redundancies and expressions of mere enthusiasm. I hope that at least some of the texts can be scanned and placed online so that scholars may compare the edited to the original versions.[3] At any rate, the American literary and political figures mentioned above may or may not have been smarter or better human beings than Josiah Warren. They may or may not prove to be greater benefactors of humankind. But they were undoubtedly better prose stylists.

Why, then, revive the sage of . . . Utopia, Ohio? Warren developed and tried to put into operation practical plans for a complex society in which unity does not rest on coercion. He is our most practical anarchist. Further, his political philosophy derives from a set of profound insights that were astonishing and perverse when they were articulated, and which are perhaps even more astonishing and perverse today—but which also confront us with a fundamental and plausible theoretical possibility or alternative. For those reasons I have striven to produce readable texts of Warren's most important works.

Warren's Life and His Leading Ideas

Moncure Conway, describing an evidently sprightly sixty-year-old Josiah Warren in 1858, wrote, "He was a short, thick-set man about fifty years of age, with a bright, restless blue eye, and somewhat restless, too, in his movements. His forehead was large, descending to a good full brow; his lower face, especially the mouth, was not of equal strength, but indicated a mild enthusiasm. He was fluent, eager, and entirely absorbed in his social ideas."[4]

For someone who dedicated much of his life to writing and self-publishing, Josiah Warren revealed surprisingly little about himself. He was born in 1798 in Boston, and during the economic depression of 1819 he married (he and his wife, Caroline, eventually had a son, George, and at least one daughter who did not survive to adulthood), moved to Cincinnati, and set up shop as a performer and teacher of music. An inveterate tinkerer, he invented a lamp that burned lard as opposed to the more expensive tallow, for which he obtained a patent in 1821. In the mid-1820s, Warren established a concern to manufacture his invention. Inspired on hearing a lecture by Robert Owen— the great Welsh industrialist and utopian projector—Warren and his family removed to the socialist community of New Harmony, Indiana, where he served as the bandleader. Returning to Cincinnati after the failure of the initial New Harmony experiment in 1827, Warren established the first of his Time Stores, which gave rise to a small cooperative economy, illustrated the labor theory of value, and put into circulation the first version of Warren's currency, the labor note. In 1835, he established the first of his "trial villages" in Tuscarawas County, Ohio, which was followed by experiments at Utopia, Ohio, commencing in 1847, and the wild anarchist free-love paradise or hell of Modern Times, on Long Island, in 1851. Warren's priority in all cases was to make it possible for people with no means to build homes, and the communities were successful in that regard. In 1833, he published what is often termed the earliest anarchist periodical, *The Peaceful Revolutionist*, the first of a number of periodicals and pamphlet series he was to disseminate. Throughout his life, small-scale publishing ventures were conjoined with dramatic innovations in type production, typesetting, and printing, including what was perhaps the world's first continuous-feed press, which he perfected in the 1820s and 1830s. This is often seen as a precursor of—or as essentially identical to—the Hoe press that revolutionized publishing late in the nineteenth century. In 1844 he published the first version of his new "mathematical" system of musical notation. He moved to Modern Times in the 1850s, then to the Boston area by the 1860s, and was active in the nascent American labor movement of that era, as well as in a number of cooperative enterprises for ameliorating poverty. He died in 1874.[5] For more details, consult the timeline of his life (appendix A).

Throughout his adult life, Warren thought of his philosophy as easily captured in a few simple principles. He listed them in various enumerations. Here I give them in four: individualism, self-sovereignty, the cost limit of price, and the labor note as a circulating medium.

(1) *Individualism, as an ontology and as a science; that is, as a statement of what there is and of the principle for finding out what there is, by ever-finer appreciation of the specificities of every event, thing, or person.*

Warren is one of the most extreme of American individualists, a group that includes such iconoclasts as Emerson, Thoreau, Garrison, Lysander Spooner, and many great American reformers of the period, including feminists and advocates of peace. Though individualism is now associated primarily with the Right, it was the consensus position of radical American reformers of the first three quarters of the nineteenth century, that is, during Warren's lifetime. It is a political position, or at least it entails political positions, but it is also a metaphysics and an epistemology, developed systematically by the obscure American genius Alexander Bryan Johnson, and unsystematically by a great many other American radicals.

First, let us consider individualism as a metaphysical and epistemological system. The study of anything, as understood since the earliest Greeks, is the process of generalizing from particulars. That's the origin of the pre-Socratic cosmologies of Thales or Democritus, and it's the essence of Platonism, where generalities are the only truths, to say nothing of Augustine or Plotinus. Aristotle qualified but did not abandon this approach to disciplinary taxonomies and the actual nature of things in his physics, logic, metaphysics, ethics, poetics, and politics. Medieval Islamic and Scholastic philosophy displays the Aristotelian negotiation between the purity of ideas and the particularities of phenomena. Science—in its initial bloom in the hands of Bacon, for example, and certainly through the "scientistic" late nineteenth and early twentieth centuries—is sometimes thought of as a refinement of everyday induction: one makes a series of observations and draws generalizations from them. In this sense, we might say that science is the art of generalization, the practice of observing and capturing the shared qualities of phenomena in principles or laws. Newtonian physics is a good example, of course, but perhaps an even clearer one—and one closer to Warren's spirit and moment—is Darwin's theory of natural selection. Devising, refining, and defending the theory required that Darwin observe countless particular organisms in relation to the particularities of their environments. But its value became manifest at the moment a generalization emerged that encompassed and accounted for all the particularities. This generalization, in turn, could be used to understand and potentially control further particulars. The specific phenomena, we might say, were instrumental in the process of generalization, and were expunged into it, comprehended by it, and turned to useful work within it.

Warren formulates the opposite principle, which he himself called the first principle of all his work: "The Study of Individuality, or the practice of mentally discriminating, dividing, separating, or disconnecting persons, things, and events, according to their individual peculiarities" (*Equitable Commerce*, see below, p. 56). Provincial though he was, Warren was steeped in the rhetoric of modern science and in the atmosphere of British empiricism, and saw the world being continually demystified as principles yielded to observations. This tradition emerged from the revival of republicanism and skepticism and the rapid improvement of technology. Nevertheless, the goal of science was conceived to be an adequate taxonomy of nature (the primary project of eighteenth-century science, as in Linnaeus). To arrange the world by categories was to comprehend its laws, which opened the globe to navigation using ships and lenses, and thereby created prosperity.

Nevertheless, in complement, science thus conceived fundamentally involves unprecedented attention to the individual object and an attempt to account for the bewildering array of experience through a multiplication of specific categories. In *Equitable Commerce*, Warren argues that if you want to organize your correspondence or a box of tools, you individualize and separate them. But of course you also conflate them into categories. Indeed, the two processes are complementary and inseparable. It was Warren's goal to emphasize what we might call the subaltern moment in this dialectic.

In application to human beings, Warren's particularism takes the form of an affirmation of the irreducibility of subjectivity and a critique of language, in particular written language. For Warren, the problem at the heart of a political order is that it necessarily de-individualizes its subjects, treating them en masse or in classes. In his view, the worst imaginable approach would be to subject human beings to laws or constitutions, which are inevitably interpreted differently by each person, or even by the same person at different times. To freeze a dynamic social order into a document is mere folly: you simply launch into the interminable, and in principle insoluble, process of interpretation. Words are the tools of persons (as in the conception of the "rule of law"), and that cannot be changed until human subjectivity can be eradicated. The eradication of subjectivity—the dream or nightmare of Rousseau, Hegel, and Marx—would be the eradication of persons and the world they experience. In other words, subjectivity is a dimension of the massed specificities of each person, a human aspect of the pluralism and dynamism of the universe. Indeed, the political movement of modernity, which depends in almost any of its formulas on some system of combining interests and identities, is—according to Warren—simply a fantasy and a recipe for interminable conflict. In his view, people clash when their interests are the same, not when they are carefully distinguished, and conflict can be minimized by extricating people from one another, not by rolling them up in ever-larger human bales.

For Warren, one last move remains in the history of science considered as a program: total acknowledgment of and knowledge about specificity, in which the value and character of each incomparable object, event, and person becomes manifest. It is a hyper-nominalist fantasy, and it potentially re-mystifies experience. In the Western tradition it has antecedents in Heraclitean flux, Cynicism, medieval nominalism, and Scottish commonsense philosophy. And surely this is also an idea scouted by Emerson, Nietzsche, and Heidegger. Particularism of this variety can look either like anti-scientism or the triumph of scientism over the Western tradition that returns us to the brute truth of reality, as the tradition shows, by its own epistemic standards, its own untruth. The truth lodges in particulars, not in principles. Every abstraction from the world is . . . an abstraction from the world, a digression or diversion from it, and a devaluation of it. For millennia, we have been bundling things together to try to comprehend them; now the point is to appreciate their strangeness, their resistance to categorization. Individualism is an attempt to remake the world by affirming it.

Indeed Warren, à la Saussure, treats symbol systems, including his own musical notation, as organizations of differences, and he points out that signs mean anything only because they are syntactically distinct and separated from one another spatially or temporally. The world is an indefinitely large plethora of particulars, and so are the representational systems by which we show it forth or grasp it.

The critique itself, of course, is self-refuting. As soon as Warren starts founding disciplines and capturing in a term ("individuality") the essence of the universe, or the basis of all justice and social arrangements ("self-sovereignty"), he is doing what the discipline he invented demands he not do. But his own discipline demands that he do it. In any event, Warren is located at the heart of this conceptual tornado. No one has flatly stated what he believed to be the truth more comprehensively in just a few sentences, and no one has inveighed more extremely against drawing any generalizations from experience. For precisely these reasons, he is both an extreme and emblematic figure, one who has delved as far into a certain dilemma as anyone the Western tradition has ever gone.

Two broad strands of religious/political individualism emerged from the Protestant Reformation. Both of them took with some literalness Luther's call for a "priesthood of all believers," a basic statement of religious individualism most emblematically expressed in the United States in Quakerism. Luther placed each person in charge of his or even her own relationship with God; there were to be no intercessors, none of Catholicism's layers of beings between the peasant and the Lord (though to some extent Luther thought that Scripture performed this function, a view Warren would utterly oppose). As Reformation Europe tried to throw off clerical institutions and remake political institutions, it focused on the individual believer and assigned to her the task of becoming apparent before God, as the Lutheran lay preacher and Warren contemporary Kierkegaard put it. Like many individualists, Warren almost ritually invoked Luther, though Warren was not a Christian: "We want a Luther in the political sphere, and another in the financial sphere, another in the commercial, another in the educational sphere, to rouse the people to use their own experience" (*True Civilization*, 155).

It is worth mentioning that the Reformation's aesthetic was minimalist and utilitarian. It held that a Catholic aesthetic of teeming imagery and encrusted decoration was a form of idolatry. Each more radical sect simplified further the principles of design. The aesthetic of Warren's system is extremely clear, simple, and consistent from the 1820s to the 1870s: a Shaker chair of a philosophy, and thus opposed temperamentally to, let us say, Hegel or even Emerson. Though Luther aligned himself with the secular state to ward off the Catholic Church, the political implications of his individualism became apparent in a variety of radical movements, many of which recognized no authority over the individual but God—that is, no human authority. This was important in the development of modern democratic political theory, and it is in my view the precursor of all modern forms of anarchism.

One form of individualism that emerged from the Reformation arose among the educated classes, especially in England, where it is called the "liberal tradition." We see it in Hobbes's notion that people can only be brought out of a state of nature by their own consent. This becomes, with an admixture of academic Thomism, the notions of natural rights and of government instituted by contractors or independent agents in something similar to a business transaction. The tradition is of course associated with republicanism as a political system, above all with Locke and Madison. And it is associated with capitalism as an economic system, the classic statements being made by Smith and Ricardo. It eventuates in British utilitarianism in the writings of Bentham and Mill (an admirer of Warren). It is empirical, this-worldly, emphasizing inalienable individual political and (above all) economic rights. By the time of its maturity in Hume or Gibbon, it loses even the veneer of theology (in Locke, God is still close at hand), and it leads as well to what are called the social sciences, in the works of Comte, Spencer, or Mead. It seeks limitations on government power without an actual descent into anarchy. Its real center is an elitist but civic-minded republicanism of a sort compatible with a Protestant monarchy or a representative republic.

The other strand was an individualism not of scholars and gentlemen but of half-mad enthusiasts or even fanatics. Consider the radical peasant movements of the German Reformation, such as radical Anabaptism, which eventually extended into North America. These

movements recognized no authority over the individual, either religious or temporal, because they asserted the unconditional obligation
each person was under to obey the commands of God as God was
manifest in the life and mind of that person, though they also practiced various forms of social discipline. We might mention radical
Protestant dissenters in England, including religious anarchists such
as the Diggers and, more mildly, the Quakers and their ilk. The earliest expression of this attitude of "antinomianism" on the American
continent is the movement of Roger Williams and Anne Hutchinson
to secede (or court expulsion) from Plymouth Colony and establish
communities of conscience. They did not conceive of their activities
as the effusion of reason and science, but as the direct inspiration of
God, His intervention into every aspect of life. It was an individualism among persons for the sake of the union with God: individualism
as the abandonment of individuality. Its mood was not genteel or
scholarly or commercial, but ecstatic. This is the idea that swept the
United States in a half-beautiful and half-farcical movement in the
early nineteenth century and led from an enthusiasm for God to an
enthusiasm for . . . enthusiasm, a hyper-provincial romanticism.

At any rate, these two strands of individualism—the genteel and
the ecstatic—conflict at times; they are as much temperaments as
opinions, and though in some ways the opinions dovetail, the temperaments are fiercely incompatible. But we might think, for example, of the American Revolution as patrician liberal individualists
leading ecstatic Protestant individualists. Certainly the average person
in western Pennsylvania or Virginia was not reading Locke. But he
was going to church. A good example of an authorship poised on this
borderline is that of Lysander Spooner. Never have liberal principles
(natural rights) been given a clearer exposition, or a more extreme
statement. Meanwhile, Spooner was founding an alternative postal
service and plotting to liberate John Brown with a raid into Virginia.
But as a scholar of English legal theory or of anything else, Warren is
no match for Spooner. Warren is a pure product of the American
utopian vision, drifting westward to make the lands bloom, a beautiful idealist and a semi-cracked enthusiast.

American ecstatic individualism reveals its essence in Warren's work, where it is thoroughly secularized. Warren has none of Emerson's and Thoreau's distance or erudition or poetry, none of Spooner's or Garrison's polemical mastery. But he delivers a central formulation of the motif of American reform, circa 1840, a political theory to match his pre-Thoreauvian ontology of particulars. And he states an extreme response to Western metaphysics even as he insists on a utopian vision.

One of the most interesting aspects of Warren's authorship is that he is an individualist and an advocate of liberty with no sophisticated notion of natural rights. He says the individuality of each person is ineradicable and hence in the strictest sense literally inalienable. Then the question is, how are we to deal politically and economically with this reality?

(2) *The sovereignty of the individual; that is, each person is to have absolute control over his own body and actions, at his own cost or responsibility.*

The ideal of self-sovereignty is central to the reform movements of early-nineteenth-century America, and it is a direct, secularist development out of religious conviction of the sovereignty of God. True commitment to the authority of God, according to the radical Reformation, meant that one could not come under any lesser authority. One must always be free to obey God's command, which is paramount over any lesser command, whether of ruler, priest, or master. You don't find Locke or even Jefferson talking about self-sovereignty: in their hearts these are republicans who are sensitive to the construction of civic identities, who urge us to identify ourselves with the interests of the polis. But the radical Reformation, represented, for example, by the preacher of the Great Awakening, George Whitefield, tore at even this fairly mild bundling of identities.

What crystallizes the idea of self-sovereignty as the pure expression of American individualism is the abolitionist movement. Along the same timeline as the life of Josiah Warren, this viewpoint emerged from an extreme ecstatic Protestantism to a fairly secular vision of universal freedom. The problem of slavery appeared to Garrison, Henry Clarke Wright, and the Grimké sisters as the overarching sin of their own nation and people. And the problem with slavery was not merely its cruelty, but the source of its cruelty: its claim to owner-ship of persons. This position appeared to be poised in precise oppo-sition to the teachings of Jesus, above all the Sermon on the Mount. Ownership of other people was conceived as the essence and acme of all evil, the justification of every violation. To say that this has anar-chist implications is overly mild. Government—with its authority that rests on coercion and a policy of expropriation of property, its conscription and use of people as cannon fodder, its pretensions to oversee the values of its citizens—is thoroughly incompatible with each person's ownership of herself.[6]

The key figures in the abolitionist movement simply asserted (a typical statement is Thoreau's in "Civil Disobedience") that gov-ernment cannot possibly impose actual duties on its citizens that they do not already possess, government or not. For one thing, the government of the United States, as embodied in the Constitution, recognized the institution of slavery, as did various Christian de-nominations. Since dominant institutions plainly can permit or en-courage the greatest of evils short of soul murder, it was obvious that governments could actually be satanic; Garrison famously called the Constitution a pact with the devil.

The ancients characterized forms of government by forms of sov-ereignty. Aristotle sorts regimes according to whether one person, a few persons, or all persons rule. Once you have the insight that free-dom means individual self-sovereignty—the rule, we may say, of each—it is evident that you cannot countenance human government. One might also reach this conclusion directly from Christian pacifism of the kind embodied by Garrison and Adin Ballou, later taken up by Tolstoy and King: if physical violence is wrong, human government is illegitimate. One way to capture the pacifist intuition is that to physically attack someone is to tear away their self-ownership, liter-ally to violate their humanity and hence one's own. Indeed, the early American anarchist movement—as it was constituted by such figures as Warren, Ezra Heywood, and a young Ben Tucker and Voltairine de Cleyre—was explicitly pacifist.

Eventually, the idea of self-sovereignty became something of a euphemism for license, and the residents of Modern Times in the 1850s were referred to with a bit of derision as "sovereigns." Under the tender ministrations of Stephen Pearl Andrews and Ezra Heywood, self-sovereignty came to be associated with extreme eccentricity and free love. But for Warren, self-sovereignty was as much about responsibility as liberty. One problem with social combination is that it tends to obscure the lines of responsibility, and surely we should say that modern government has brought this offloading of responsibility and hence personhood to near perfection. Warren was particularly concerned to emphasize individual productivity and responsibility—in short, self-reliance—early in his career, as in *The Peaceful Revolutionist*.

(3) *Cost as the limit of price; that is, the price of something should be fixed by the cost of producing it, measured by the labor or pain expended in producing it, rather than by what a given person is prepared to pay for it.*

Of the figures usually described as "utopian," only Warren actually founded a place called "Utopia," a town in Ohio that still exists by that name. It had some success, primarily because Warren's vision of how social living might be arranged was realistic, grounded in the basic skills and trades it took to keep people alive. Warren always concentrated on the circulation of commodities, improvement of standards of living, technological development, and pride in individual ownership. And yet there was to be no accumulation of capital or profit because business would be conducted according to Warren's doctrine of equitable commerce. This taught that the price of goods was to be fixed not by what they would bring on the open market, but by what they cost to produce.

Obviously, this is a radical conclusion in the face of Smith-style capitalist economics. Yet it is also strikingly simple as an economic law. According to Warren, the alternative—that demand fixes price—is morally and politically repellant: it explicitly authorizes blackmail and coercion. He always returns to the same reductio ad absurdum of the law of supply and demand: What is the value of a glass of water to a man dying of thirst? Everything he has. It would be contrary to self-interest, the supposed essence of all human motivation, not to take it all. At times people do take everything that someone has, justifying themselves by the supposed law that price is fixed by demand and the corollary of debt at interest, which treats money itself as a commodity. Ought they to, and must they? At the macro scale, one works on fleecing one or another segment of the economy, alternately underselling to destroy competitors and inflating prices to exploit local monopolies; prices are entirely capricious, as speculation rests on and exacerbates price fluctuations; economic crises inevitably result, and so on. This of course recalls Marx's analysis of capitalism, the common strand between Warren and Marx provided by Robert Owen's socialism (discussed below).

For Warren, the profit motive devours people and the economy. It is an indulgence in greed, not a natural condition of human beings. Speculation and lending at interest occur at every stage in the circulation of goods in a capitalist economy, and each person's greed provides a motivation and justification for the greed of everyone else. By the time a commodity arrives at use, it has layers of inflated and imaginary costs associated with it, and because one needs the wherewithal to obtain it, one must oneself seek to maximize profits from all activities. Great hoards of useless wealth coexist with grinding poverty, homelessness, starvation, and terrible exploitation. In a rational system where price is fixed by cost or value measured in labor, a modest industriousness would be enough, according to Warren, to provide each person with what she needs and even a bit more.

It is not entirely clear whether, for Warren, cost as what fixes price is a mere utopian ideal or an economic law. But it is not completely out of place as a description of mature, small-scale capitalist economies, even as a conclusion of the usual laissez-faire arguments. Warren actually proved time and again by practical experiment that businesses conducted on this principle would undersell businesses that operated on the motive of maximum profit. This seems obviously true in the sense that prices cannot fall short of costs without the concern failing, while a firm operating at a large profit will be undersold unless they can enforce a monopoly. It seems likely that in a situation of free competition, prices must approach costs, thereby eliminating profits.

The idea that price must be fixed by cost shows us why Warren cannot be annexed to the greed-is-good crowd of libertarian egoists (e.g., Ayn Rand) or to Smithian rational utility maximizers. In his history of American utopian movements, John Humphrey Noyes called them "American Socialisms." The word "socialism" is of course impossibly vague (actually, both words are), but it is meant to encompass Christian anarcho-communism of the sort that Noyes taught at Oneida and Warren's equitable communities. Possibly Robert Owen coined it while working on his projects. Eventually "socialism" just indicated plans for social improvement, and then was used in the sense of state projects for social amelioration and control of the economy. But Warren is one of the few thinkers ever to propose ownership, even of capital, without greed: a modified capitalism—deleting the profit motive—that could be based on a sober assessment of one's actual interests but could also be an inspiring ideal of a decent life of moderate ownership and useful work.

Warren, as should already be evident, was an adherent of the labor theory of value, which was already something of a commonplace when he wrote. Vernon Parrington, discussing the theory as propounded in the mid-eighteenth century by Benjamin Franklin, gives the notion the following pedigree. "In his *Treatise on Taxes*, written in 1662, Sir William Petty . . . clearly elaborated the principle of labor-value; it was restated by Vauban in 1707, . . . by Hume in 1752, and later by the Physiocrats; and when Adam Smith wrote it was pretty widely known."[7] One might remark that it is implied in Locke's account of property. Obviously it was an article of faith for Marx and later communist theorists. Indeed, one supposes that it is an ancient insight, a kind of inevitable conclusion. As an exclusive account of why things actually have the value they do, of course, it has its limitations. In Warren's version, however, the labor theory of value is an ideal: he asserts that expenditure of time and pain is the only rational and stable means of fixing price; that all other systems, in particular specie, entail arbitrary fluctuation of price, speculation, usury, and poverty.

His account was refined over the decades of his writing. Initially he argued that all labor was of equal worth: that one hour's work of a washerwoman was worth one hour of lawyering. As he went on, he came to think that cost was equal to pain, and hence, for example, that the work of a washerwoman was worth substantially more than that of a lawyer, and far, far more than that of a musician (such as himself), whose labor was for the most part an actual pleasure.

(4) *The labor note as circulating medium; that is, the only rational medium of exchange is a representation of a certain definite quantity of labor of a certain type, which is equivalent to a certain quantity of a commodity.*

This idea follows, according to Warren, from the labor theory of value, and formed the basis of Warren's Time Stores in Cincinnati, New Harmony, Utopia, and Modern Times. He admitted that a circulating medium was desirable for commerce. Warren attributes the idea of a labor-exchange economy to a few remarks by Robert Owen. Owen's biographer Frank Podmore credits Warren with the first practical trial of the idea (at New Harmony in 1827), and says that when Owen himself tried similar experiments, he had Warren's model in mind.[8]

Warren's account of economics is radical in its attack on money, and beautifully clear as a theory of economic representation and circulation. He argues that money, in the then-current capitalist economy, is a commodity like anything else: its price is fixed by its value, or what it will bring. For precisely this reason, money—regardless of whether it is backed by gold—is unsuited to be a circulating medium: one can never fix the value of money from one moment to the next. Currency and credit, like corn in an irrational capitalist economy, are subject to sudden inflation because of speculation or limits on the supply, and sudden deflation because of overproduction or people dumping hoarded supplies. A stable, rational circulating medium must be nothing but a representation of a certain amount of goods or labor, a sheer placeholder for things of intrinsic value. Goods are, in turn, resolvable into labor; the two are interchangeable.

Various collections preserve labor notes from different eras of Warren's career, and most of them are proposed to be negotiable for a certain amount of labor of a certain type (e.g., sewing) or good of a certain quantity (e.g., bushels of corn). Warren had from his earliest experiments devised a strategy for weaning people from currency to labor notes. At the Time Stores he established, one would pay for goods usually in legal tender, repaying the storekeeper for his time in purchasing, stocking, weighing, selling, and so on with a labor note, calculated by a large clock (hence "Time Store"). Eventually, if the cooperative became large enough, the labor notes of a variety of people would be desirable; goods could then be purchased with labor notes, or labor notes could be exchanged as people made their needs known to one another by posting them on a notice board at the Time Store. Thus the Time Store would eventually mutate into a labor bank that would be the basis of a local cooperative economy. This would be of inestimable help to the poor and homeless, who have wealth in this context if they dispose of their own labor; indeed, at Utopia and Modern Times people were able to build homes with almost no outlay of money by exchanging their labor with one another. In other words, Warren regarded this approach as a solution to homelessness and poverty.

In addition, the labor note as a circulating medium solves the problem that Warren came more and more to conceive as of central importance: securing for labor, which produces all wealth, its just reward. For each person to be self-sovereign entails that each person controls her own labor. If labor is equitably exchanged along the lines explored at the Time Stores, each individual will receive the equivalent of her actual production. This is Warren's "socialism," his way of addressing the emerging polarizations of class along the lines of

ownership in labor, which many American radicals of the era regarded as a mode of ownership in persons or a development of slavery (i.e., "wage-slavery").

There are many possible objections to a labor note economy. For
one thing, nothing apparently stops people from issuing an indefinite
number of labor notes, then absconding or failing to make good
when the labor is (or goods are) demanded. Further, there could be
speculation in labor notes (e.g., one might seek to monopolize an industry by buying up the notes of those who work in that industry).
But Warren (especially as elaborated by Heywood in the essay "Hard
Cash") argued that a credit system would evolve along with the labor-
note economy, so that people whose notes were not good would soon
find themselves unable to have their notes accepted.[9] Potential speculators, not having anything to begin with but their own notes, would
be unable to amass wealth in that form. The economy could in essence be self-regulating, the only coordination being provided by a
central clearinghouse of needs and abilities.

Another objection might be that such a system is appropriate only
to a small-scale economy: it is a craft or artisanal model of production
and could not work on an industrial scale. On the contrary, the
model is more plausible the larger the economy and the more specialized the tasks that people perform, because each such increase increases the likelihood that one will find in a labor exchange a person
able to perform the exact task one requires. Warren was an advocate
of division of labor, but he also hoped that each person could learn
several trades and thus be able to gravitate toward the productive sec-
tors of the economy. He evidently thought that seeking to cut labor
costs combined with sheer irrepressible human ingenuity would continue to produce technological innovations.

As mentioned above, at first Warren believed that all labor should
be valued at the same rate. Over time he came to believe that the
value of labor varied not only with time expended but also with the
onerousness of the task, so that the tasks people were least happy to
perform should be paid at the highest rate. That is, the labor note was
a calculation of pain. This too could be left to the free market in

notes, as the notes of those able to perform the most painful tasks would be the least common, and no one would be able to perform such tasks for many hours at a clip. Thus, if anything, the class order would be inverted, and those engaged in purely artistic or intellectual tasks would pay a (small and reasonable) price for the pleasantness of their professions.

Warren certainly believed that with his "experiments" he had demonstrated the practicality of labor notes as a circulating medium, and their effectiveness at pulling people out of poverty and realigning class interests.

New Harmony and American Utopias

Josiah Warren is a central figure in what is sometimes rather derisively termed the American "utopian" movement, or the attempt to set up ideal communities, often on the edge of the frontier. Though relative to the total populations of Europe or the Americas the movement was small, the utopians showed something essential about how America was conceived, particularly in the seventeenth, eighteenth, and the first half of the nineteenth centuries: as, precisely, a "new world," a place to begin again without the burdens of monarchy, rigid class structures, religious institutions, and irrational traditions. In short, it was seen as a place of freedom and possibility. Many, including the transcendentalists, toyed with the idea that America could be the salvation of humankind.

Warren's thought and projects fit with difficulty into the idea of utopia. As this is usually set out, from Plato's *Republic* to More to Fourier, a utopia consists of a form of society designed—often to a quite absurd level of detail—a priori and imposed on reality. Nothing could be further from Warren's thinking. He wanted to create the possibility of an open future, an unpredictable and uncontrolled development of human individuality. Whereas utopian projectors starting with Plato entertained the idea of creating an ideal species through eugenics and education, as well as a set of universally valid institutions inculcating shared identities, Warren wanted to dissolve such identities in a solution of individual self-sovereignty. His educational experiments, for example—possibly under the influence of the great Swiss educational theorist Johann Heinrich Pestalozzi (via Owen)—emphasized the nurturing of both the independence and the conscience of individual children, not the inculcation of preconceived values. In this, Warren is strikingly connected to the work of the transcendentalist pedagogue Bronson Alcott, though I know of no evidence of direct interchange.

Before Owen's community at New Harmony, Indiana, the American ideal communities were religious, organized by radical Protestants, and often included "primitive Christian communism" (i.e., community of property). We might mention in this regard Ephrata in Pennsylvania, the Shakers in a number of locations, and the "Rappites" or "Harmonists" who originally built Harmonie, Indiana, on the banks of the Wabash River and sold it lock, stock, and barrel in 1825 to Robert Owen, who renamed it New Harmony. The New Harmony experience was central to Warren's life and thought, and many of his ideas can be seen as attempts to understand and correct the failures of that community while retaining the energy and idealism that first drew him there.

It is difficult to know whether to write the story of Robert Owen as an inspiring tale of uplift or as a comedy. He made his fortune running a textile mill in New Lanark, Scotland, and in the context of a successful business venture had introduced a number of reforms, including a shorter workday, a reduction in child labor, and educational projects based on the work of Pestalozzi.[10] People came from all over Europe and the United States to see Owen's industrial paradise at New Lanark in the first two decades of the nineteenth century. But Owen quickly became a controversial figure due to his explicit atheism, which was perhaps one reason he decided to try a socialistic venture in the United States. New Harmony was something of a disaster, and persisted as an attempt to realize his initial vision for about two years, on the scale of thirty thousand acres and about nine hundred people.[11]

Owen must have been an extremely compelling speaker, because many people, including Josiah Warren, changed their lives entirely after hearing him. John Humphrey Noyes—the founder of Oneida and historian of American ideal communities—attributes Owen's communism to his contact with the Rappites; in any case, it is clear that by the time of the New Harmony experiment, Owen was no longer content with benevolent capitalism of the sort he practiced at New Lanark. As idealists and others gathered in New Harmony, Owen promoted the project relentlessly. It is a measure of the seriousness with which he was taken that he addressed a joint session of Congress and met President James Monroe, President-elect John Quincy Adams, and former president Thomas Jefferson. He proposed to make the whole of the United States into a system of "phalansteries," or square-shaped building-complexes surrounding courtyards, a style later advocated by Fourier, Owen's inheritor in utopian socialism.

The Owenite trend was based perhaps more on his personal charisma than on the soundness of his schemes. As he promoted New Harmony here and there, his young son William and others tried to set up a community based on his vague set of suggestions, in contrast to the meticulous contracts establishing a community of property that had been entered into by the Rappites. Property was to be held in common, but the terms under which resources were pooled led immediately to all sorts of disputes. One area of such disputes was the common store; people recorded credits for labor and debits for what they obtained at the store, which proved a matter of constant bickering.

Warren, then in his twenties, served as the leader of the band and a music teacher at the school, which, as Kenneth Rexroth points out, were "the community's only two successful institutions."[12] Observing the extreme difficulties surrounding the store, his sense of how this procedure could be improved led to his plans for the Time Stores, a much more practical approach to this particular set of problems. In particular, he believed that the whole project foundered on disputes originating in communal ownership of property.

The failure of one other feature of New Harmony left its mark on Warren. The community was filled with eccentrics, scientists, and poets inspired by Owen's vision. The founder's son Robert Dale Owen described the population as "that heterogeneous collection of radicals, enthusiastic devotees to principle, honest latitudinarians, and lazy theorists, with a sprinkling of unprincipled sharpers thrown in."[13] Conspicuously lacking were farmers, mechanics, laborers, artisans, carpenters, blacksmiths, and competent manufacturers. One of the many reasons the community failed was its lack of practical know-how, which is obviously entirely essential to establish a working economy on the frontier. Though Warren eventually faced a similar situation at Modern Times—the eccentrics of which made those of New Harmony look conventional—he set himself to acquire a set of practical skills and recruit for and inculcate them in the people with whom he worked.

By 1826, people were abandoning the town, and schismatic movements and rival villages were springing up. By early 1827, Owen sold property to the people occupying it, thereby ending the communism that in fact was based on the ownership of the area by Owen, and beginning the chaotic transition of New Harmony to a more conventional American community.[14] This failure is the origin of Warren's individualism and what we might term "anticommunism": he came to believe that people entered into conflict when their resources and interests were the same, not when they were different. Above all, he turned against the basic idea of utopian socialism, in which an a priori scheme (embodied above all in the phalanstery) was imposed on a group of people. His vision of an ideal community shifted to the idea of creating circumstances in which each person might be free to perform whatever experiments in living arrangement they saw fit.

Though Owen, Fourier, and others presented their schemes as "scientific," Warren held that they were just the opposite, in that they imposed a preexisting plan rather than relying on careful observation and continual adaptation. As William Wilson observes in his history of New Harmony, by 1826 Owen "had reached a point in his life from which he would thereafter never retreat, a point where, for him, the

truth was only what he wanted to believe and facts were of no importance."[15] And though Owen and Fourier presented their schemes as
liberatory or democratic, Warren detected in their ideas an element of
benevolent tyranny based on charismatic leadership. Such criticisms
certainly contained an element of truth. In such matters, Warren expresses a vision connecting radical democracy (or anarchism) with
science and practical technology that originates in the connections of
republicanism with science and technology in such figures as Franklin
and Jefferson and would be taken up in modified form by thinkers
such as John Dewey. But the element of radical individualism that
Warren appropriated from his contemporary atmosphere distinguished his ideas from those of his predecessors and successors.

One way into this issue is his observation that even if a utopian
plan could be perfectly formulated—for example, in a book or a
constitution—each person would interpret the plan differently.
Whatever your procedure, the individuality of the participants is
ineradicable, a hard fact to which any scheme—even the best of
them—must bend. The biographer William Bailie quotes Warren a
quarter century later, reflecting on his experience at New Harmony:
"If the world could only assemble on these hills around and look
down on us through all these experiences, what lessons they would
learn! There would be no more French Revolutions, no more patent
political governments, no more organizations, no more constitution-
making, law-making, nor human contrivances for the foundation of
society."[16] Indeed, two weeks after a constitution was adopted at New
Harmony, its application was so chaotic that the citizens requested
Robert Owen to assume dictatorial power. One might also say that
Warren formed his anti-charismatic style of leadership in response to
Owen. Charles Codman observed Warren at Modern Times thus:
"Mr. J. Warren was a poor leader. He had no magnetic qualities so
needful in persuasion or gaining converts. Also he was a timid man
and hated to wrangle."[17] Of course, this was Warren's actual personal-
ity, but it was also his principled approach to leadership. He didn't
want to inspire converts; he wanted each person to do what expressed

her individual personality. In short, it was in response to Owen's failure at New Harmony that Warren formulated his basic approach to philosophy, reform, and leadership style.

It is worth remarking, however, on one of the basic ideas that Warren retained from Owen. A remarkable feature of Warren's advocacy of individual liberty is that he takes it to follow from environmental determinism. Even more radically, and, one might think, oddly for an extreme individualist, Warren takes a deflationary attitude toward the human self; in his view, it has no core, but rather is an ever-changing bundle of experiences. In fact, that is precisely wherein individuality consists: in the incomparability of the experiences of each of us, and the pressure on each of us of a unique set of uncontrollable circumstances.

One correlate of this is that punishment for crime is wrong and ineffective. If one does not want people to commit some class of act, the environment that gives rise to that act must be altered. Controlling people under threat, trying to erase their individuality according to some text or model, is worse than hopeless. Facilitating the greatest possible flourishing of human variety and eccentricity is the only approach that respects the circumstances and hence the character of each individual, and it is the approach best suited to finding, by practical experiment, how to live. In all these positions, Warren strikingly resembles his contemporary John Stuart Mill, who credited Warren with lending him the idea of self-sovereignty.

Warren is notably reticent on matters of religion. It may be that, under the influence of Alexander Bryan Johnson, he believed that religious claims were literally senseless, or that they referred only to the emotional states of the speaker. Certainly, under the influence of Owen, he believed that religion had been a disaster for the social development of humankind. But he rarely addressed the matter explicitly, and in keeping with his basic philosophy he thought of religious beliefs as an individual prerogative. Nevertheless, I think it's fairly certain from a few stray remarks—notably very early, in *The Peaceful Revolutionist*—that Warren was an atheist or perhaps a deist. In *True Civilization* he defines "the Divine" as whatever is not human, or as the natural, a fascinating and extraordinarily problematic assertion that of course emphasizes his connections to thinkers such as Thoreau. At any rate, he never believed in the human soul, that kernel of inexplicable individual essence. Rather, he believed in the self as an ever-changing kaleidoscope of experiences, fragments of glass through which the world shone.

One other figure connected to New Harmony must be mentioned: Fanny Wright, one of the boldest and most radical reformers of the period. Scottish by birth, she was associated with Owen's reforms but was even more radical; as she toured the United States, she urged religious skepticism, equality of the sexes and races, and many other controversial positions. Anticipating the role of female lecturers in Garrisonian abolitionism, she was the first woman in the United States to lecture to audiences of mixed gender, which she did at New Harmony in 1828. She founded perhaps the most astonishing ideal community of the period: Nashoba, in Tennessee, a mixed-race community based to some extent on Owen's ideas, though Owen himself did not explicitly advocate race or gender equity. At the same time, she advocated miscegenation as the cure to the race problem, which was perhaps the most provocative position possible at that place and moment. With Robert Dale Owen, Wright edited the *New Harmony Gazette*, which later mutated into the *Free Enquirer*, a publication remarkable for its constant representation of views hostile to those of its editors. This provided Warren with some of his sense of the power of the printed word and the importance of free expression, which led to his later printing inventions. A poem he wrote on the death of her sister Camilla (see appendix A) suggests that they were friends. That puts Warren's work in a somewhat different perspective, positioning it as a direct result of radical British and American reform of the 1820s. Warren therefore came earlier than Garrisonian abolitionism but persisted well past it, as he had some connection to most of the reform causes undertaken into the 1870s.

Of Warren's Time Stores, Fanny Wright wrote, "Unaided by money, unbacked by influence, and unseconded save by his own conviction of the value of the principle he had seized and the beneficial

consequences of the practice he was prepared to explore, he succeeded in exhibiting to the understandings, and bringing home to the
worldly interests of thousands the perfect facility of living in plenty
with one third of the labor and without any of the anxiety inseparable
from the existing monied exchange of the world."[18] Warren, like Garrison, stands out for his advocacy of women's equality, and he treats
the individuality of women in precisely the same way he treats that of
men. One of the advantages of being an individualist is that it will
make you skeptical of racial and gender categories; Warren always argued that placing people into a few neat categories was fictional, and
that even words such as "man" or "woman" were ultimately too
crude to apply to particular persons.[19]

Shortly after the New Harmony period, both Warren and Wright
were exposed to the work of a remarkable philosopher, Alexander
Bryan Johnson, who emigrated from England as a teenager and set up
shop in Utica, New York. (This intellectual affinity again suggests that
Warren and Wright were in dialogue through the 1820s.) Johnson was
a successful banker and husband of a granddaughter of John Adams
who wrote numerous works in philosophy, political commentary, and
fiction, none of which seems to have made much of an impression on
anyone at the time, or indeed since. The one exception, for reasons
that remain a trifle obscure, occurred in Cincinnati in the late 1820s,
when Johnson's *Philosophy of Human Knowledge; or, A Treatise on
Language* received ecstatic reviews from Frances Wright and others.[20]

Johnson's philosophy of language would have been an influential
contribution to human thought had it been more widely read. It
looks back to and elaborates the classical empiricists and commonsense philosophers in one direction, and strikingly anticipates logical
positivism and pragmatism on the other. For Johnson, the meaning
of a statement or theory is the means that would be used to prove or
give evidence for it; a statement means the difference its truth would
practically make in experience. He attacked language on the grounds
that might be termed radically nominalistic. Nature, he said, appeared only in particulars, whereas the words applied to these particulars were always general. That is, in every instance of a different

thing to which a word refers or which falls into its extension, the same word is applied, but in each case the particular phenomenon is distinct. This leads philosophers and the rest of us into a massively fallacious interpretation of nature, in which it is viewed as a series of instantiations of universals. Rather, language should be adapted to the ever-more-precise delineation of particulars: "Individuality is characteristic of nature. Language unites under one name, as identities, what is only partially identical. Individuality is no anomaly of nature. It is nature's regular production, and boundless riches. No two parcels of calomel possess the perfect identity which the sameness of their name implies. No two men possess the perfect identity which the sameness of their manhood implies; nor possesses any one man, at all times, and under all circumstances, the complete identity with which language invests his individuality."[21]

Johnson was a phenomenalist: he believed that the fundamental data of experience were what Hume termed "sense impressions" (Johnson calls them sights, sounds, feels, smells, and tastes), and that what we term "individual objects" were composed of or identical with such impressions. Any term that could not be referred to a specific impression—someone's experience at some time—was asserted by Johnson to be without meaning: it was returned to nature as a pristine, blank sound. He did not follow this into a Berkeleyan idealism, however, but to a radical realism (which, to be fair, is one reading of Berkeley):

> My hand is red, hair is often red, the moon is sometimes red, fire is red, and Indians are red. These objects possess a congruity of appearance that entitles them to the appellation of red; but the precise meaning of the word in each application is the sight itself which the object exhibits. Whether an object shall or not be called red is a question which relates to the propriety of phraseology, and with which nature has no concern; but the meaning of the word red in each application, is a question which relates solely to nature, and with which language has no concern:—at least, language possesses over it no control.[22]

This is a remarkable doctrine, taken by Johnson to be a direct result of his nominalism: it returns us to nature and, explicitly, to language as a mirror of nature, albeit a dark mirror. Language is serviceable and sensible insofar as it reflects nature in its massed specificities. A perfect language would have a different name for each phenomenon of nature, but such a thing is beyond our power to wield. We must keep speaking in generalities, but we must also open ourselves to the specificities of reality: real knowledge would consist of a de-generalization or an ever-closer approximation to nature, which consists in nothing but unique particulars. Warren sought a politics that could thus respond to particularity—in other words, a nominalism of persons.

Throughout his career Warren also displayed an interest in notational systems and what we might call practical semantics, and his philosophy at its best is expressed in a notably precise style. He devised new systems of musical notation and stereotyping, and was followed by Stephen Pearl Andrews, whose first works introduced Pitman's phonetic shorthand to American audiences. The problem of reference and a critique of language were never far from Warren's mind. Warren absorbed Johnson's proto-pragmatism, his critique of language, his nominalism, and his celebration of individual things and moments as the reality underlying experience. Indeed, Warren's life can in some ways be read as the attempt to live out Johnson's anti-metaphysics, to make it into a social philosophy as well as a philosophy of language. Though he defines himself initially in opposition to Owen, he later defines himself by alliance with Johnson.

In any event, immediately after the experience of New Harmony, Warren launched on his series of experiments: Time Stores (the first of which was established in May 1827 at West Fifth and Elm streets in Cincinnati), ideal communities, and innovations in printing, all of them designed at once to reverse and to make good Owen's utopian vision. Noyes acutely observes, "The village of 'Modern Times,' where all forms of social organization were scouted as unscientific, was the electric negative of New Harmony."[23] In the initial presentations of his thought, for example in *The Peaceful Revolutionist*, it is obvious that his internal dialogue with Owen drove many of his ideas.

But he did not reject all of Owen's precepts. He retained Owen's determinism, translating it into a variety of individualism: if people are what their circumstances make them, their differences are ineradicable. He also retained Owen's religious skepticism. And he retained the secularized millennialism, a tone of limitless optimism, and the anticipation of a transfigured world. As a matter of personal style, we might speculate that Warren, in the face of Owen, rejected leadership in its entirety because of his enthusiasm for and then disappointment with Owen, his feeling that he and others had been seduced by Owen's passion. His own style of leadership was pointedly self-effacing. He did want followers of his compelling personality, or followers at all, but only people compelled both by the power of his ideas and inventions and by their own.

Transcendentalism and American Reform

More widely, we must connect Warren's work with the mania of reform sweeping the United States—particularly New England—during the three decades beginning around 1820. Emetic cures and spirit visitations, all the motley of apocalyptic cults, celibate saints, community-of-wives trigamists, primitive Christian communists, violent abolitionists, come-outers, hydropathists, absolute nonresistants, temperance fanatics, and so on, each with a vision from on high and a plan to redeem the world or abandon it completely: Adin Ballou and John Humphrey Noyes, Shakers and Mormons, mentally ill or divinely instructed. Some of these people were, in fact, cranks. Others were, in fact, saints, and William Lloyd Garrison and Nathaniel Peabody Rogers—beautiful souls by any standard—are as characteristic as anyone. Their ideas were entirely serious though no doubt extreme: immediate abolition of slavery; absolute nonresistance; anarchism, on the grounds that the state consists fundamentally in violence; feminism (Garrison insisted that women act as full participants and leaders in the abolitionist movement); and the inviolability of the human person. All of these positions emerged directly for Garrison from a reading of the Sermon on the Mount, and Garrison was in every sentence and every gesture a profoundly religious man. And even though Warren was not a religious man, he agreed with every one of these positions.[24]

On one level, Josiah Warren is about as levelheaded and practical a man as it is possible even for a backwoods philosopher to be. At heart, he's a pragmatist in the early sense and professes no interest in theory even as he writes it. On another, he's a pure second-revival millenarian, over the moon for the ecstasy at the imminent end of history. In this, Warren was in keeping with the mood of both secular and religious society, of scholars and fanatics, geniuses and dolts, as-cetics and libertines: it hovers over the era like a fog or a sun, depend-ing on your view. The divergent Protestant sects of Europe awaited the apocalypse, and they brought that expectation to North America. The Shakers anticipated the millennium, and John Humphrey Noyes said that it had already occurred. The Mormons taught a version of the rapture, and Owen and Fourier showed the way to a social para-dise. Marx and Hegel predicted the inevitable, paradisiacal end of his-tory. Emerson and Thoreau kept hinting that human beings were just about to get much, much better. The abolitionists, the transcenden-talists, the spiritualists: none was immune to the atmosphere.

I'm not sure that such a mood can be explained. We might think of the radical displacements and rapid economic and environmental changes of the late eighteenth or early nineteenth century, but one might say the same of practically any era. The typical millennial vi-sion participated in the optimistic implications of an apparently open continent or world: a penchant for starting over in a direction that would lead to perfection or salvation, a renewal of or return to the garden that would bring this sorry tale to a close, the ecstasy at the end or beginning of history. Warren is as close to the radical Protes-tant sects in this matter as he is to Owen, and the overflow of his typography is his ecstatic testimony, his shaking and quaking and speaking in tongues. Even late in his life he retains an optimism that arises from faith rather than reason, though his own mood is tem-pered (as is, by then, the mood of all the apocalyptic cults aside from those of Marx and Hegel).

What is remarkable about several of these figures—certainly Noyes, for example, and the Shakers (under the leadership of Frederick Evans, Warren's fellow veteran of New Harmony)—is their combination of extreme, eccentric faith with Yankee ingenuity and know-how. These were people with the ability to perform the practical tasks before them in an extremely effective manner. Indeed, Warren's paradise was above all a place where practical skills were inculcated, practiced, and valued to their fullest. These were people likely to clear the land, survey it, build structures on it and furnish those structures, and then build institutions or anti-institutions (e.g., Time Stores) of remarkable practical value. This highlights a key problem in the Owenite communities: whereas skill was a form of prayer for the Shakers, the Rappites, and Thoreau, the population of New Harmony was feckless.

By the time American philosophy transformed from transcendentalism to pragmatism, the mood of optimism had shifted from millennialist to meliorist. And meliorism would have been more than enough to fund Warren's experiments, and more in keeping with his experiences: small-scale, qualified successes, with a total transformation toward equity or self-sovereignty nowhere in sight. Warren's successes were modest, especially in relation to his world-transforming ambitions. Yet his faith, like that of many of those around him, remains touching, and he retained it more truly than most in the face of war and industrialization. The perversity and quixoticism with which he pursued his vision made him occasionally the object of ridicule, but it also, as with Quixote, retained an underlying nobility or even sublimity even as it occasionally threatened to lose contact with reality. And what ultimately redeemed the experience of the people he worked with and for was the element of the practical that we see accompanying the American dream of that era: the concerted economic practicality of the Rappites or Mormons—or for that matter Ben Franklin—growing rich on the frontier; Thoreau's pencil-making and surveying; Warren the pointedly practical economist and inventor, improbably inventing a vision of redemption for humankind.

By 1860, and after that, many of the surviving enthusiasts lost their idealism and descended into decadence, rolling from fad to fad, like Warren acquaintances Victoria Woodhull and Mary Gove Nichols. One might find oneself believing or at least trying to believe anything; precisely the implausibility of an idea became its compelling quality; individuality descended into mere eccentricity. But by the same token, Warren's presence in reform organizations—such as the New England Labor Reform League—increased in the postwar years, no doubt because after the establishment of Modern Times, the equity community on Long Island, he lived in New York and Boston rather than on the edge of civilization.

Indeed, it is not too much to say that in the decade before his death in 1874, he turned from trying to introduce small-scale models of social reform toward mass organizing. His influence in the American labor and banking reform movements around 1870 was pervasive. Many of the postwar reformers—people such as William Batchelder Greene, Ezra Heywood, and Stephen Pearl Andrews—had been abolitionists, and each of them claimed Warren as an inspiration of their views. A young Benjamin Tucker emerged from this environment and ended up as the most eminent American individualist anarchist. These figures themselves were soon superseded by leaders influenced by such European radicals as Marx, Stirner, and Bakunin. The Warren style of political activism—in particular, his individualism—had been superseded by 1880.

Emerson and Thoreau stand in fascinating relation to the American reform tradition. For Americans, they were the most cosmopolitan of Harvard men, casually dropping into ancient Greek. Yet they emerge in the culture of religious and political enthusiasm and in many ways crystallize it, even as they maintain a wry distance, seen with absurd clarity in Emerson's essay "New England Reformers." The radical history of the United States becomes, in them, an American literature. Thoreau was, despite his own oaths to swear off, more directly interested in political matters than was Emerson, as was made clear after

John Brown's raid. But the political themes are also visible throughout his books, journals, and correspondence. Both men expressed
themselves equivocally about engagement in reform movements,
though they wished them well and were willing to make contributions
from time to time of one sort or another.

Again, Warren could be regarded as an Emersonian avatar, and he
continually put into practice the idea of self-reliance as Emerson formulated it in his great 1841 essay. And Warren's great practical com-
petence, tendency to gravitate to the wilderness, basic individualism,
and rejection of government authority could all be thought of as Tho-
reauvian. But the connection is that they all emerged in the same atmosphere rather than that there was direct influence either way.
Emerson and Thoreau were younger than Warren, but I know of no
evidence that the transcendentalists were acquainted with Warren
until late in all their lives, and no evidence that he was acquainted
with them.

Perhaps the most important distinction between Warren and Em-
erson/Thoreau is that Warren was not, essentially, an intellectual, but
rather by his own account a practical projector. While Emerson, Thoreau, Fuller, and others were reading Carlyle and Coleridge, the *Tao
Te Ching* and the *Bhagavad Gita*, and rejecting eighteenth-century
empiricism in favor of more grandiose and spiritual orientations, including forms of pantheism, Warren was never influenced by these
developments. He retained a basically empiricist orientation, under
the influence of Alexander Bryan Johnson, and never speculated on
the nature of God, much less Emerson's "Oversoul." He was remarkably isolated from the intellectual currents of the day, even as he developed a system of thought that was related to them in complex
ways.

But that very fact confirmed Emerson's and Thoreau's ideas about
the United States in a variety of respects. Even as they speculated
about the birth of a characteristically American spirit or genius, the
transcendentalists remained engaged in the European debates and
taxonomies, though they also shifted them in various ways. That
Warren was operating in Ohio and Indiana in very much the way

they suggested, and with remarkably little intellectual history at his disposal, would have been a lovely confirmation of their sense of the American spirit, had they been aware of Warren's work. Emerson, Thoreau, Fuller, and Theodore Parker were engaged in learning for its own sake. Warren had little time or inclination for information that did not have a direct practical application, yet his activities strikingly mirrored their ideas.

In my view, however, the transcendentalists are less transcendent than they are sometimes portrayed as being. Thoreau's basic commitment is to the everyday world: labor, skill, and the close observation of nature. The transcendentalists are certainly not "idealists" in the grand German sense, à la Schelling, Hegel, and Schopenhauer. They intentionally had no systematic metaphysics. They were continuously attentive to the particular, and not merely as a sign of the general or as an expression of the Oversoul. Whatever Thoreau believed, he endeavored to put into practical operation.

The transcendentalists were, of course, examples of what came to be known as romanticism, and in particular were committed to the cult of nature most famously expressed in Wordsworth and now associated with Thoreau above all. Thoreau famously thought that wildness could redeem the world. But a man trying, with small groups of fellow travelers, to carve out a living in the semi-wilderness is likely to view nature, first, as a provider of resources and, second, as something to be overcome. Warren was more interested in how to make an efficient sawmill than in how to experience oneness with the trees.

Nevertheless, the commonalities between Emerson/Thoreau and Warren are striking. Emerson wrote many times of America as a new start for humankind, and there is an almost ecstatic tone in his speculations about what might be achieved socially and politically. In a typical passage, he writes, "The land is the appointed remedy for whatever is false and fantastic in our culture. The continent we inhabit is to be physic and food for our mind, as well as our body. The land, with its tranquilizing, sanative influences, is to repair the errors of a scholastic and traditional education, and bring us into just relations with men and things."[25] Indeed, many a European and

American regarded the United States in precisely this way: as a place where humanity could be created anew. Warren certainly regarded it that way, and as much as anyone set out to make it a reality. Emerson, Thoreau, Alcott, Whitman: all hinted that America would redeem the species. Warren tried to make it so.

Emerson taught that human individuality was sacred, or was a spark of the divine. It was our duty to cherish it, develop it, guard it in ourselves with jealous care. It was in some sense our participation in the reality of the universe, and therefore we should not to submerge it in a social unity, but rather nurture it even in its perversities and contradictions. Indeed, if there were to be true cohesion, it would need to be a unity of individual selves in their reality. Further, he taught what was already a commonplace of American radical Protestantism, especially among Quakers and Unitarians, that the ultimate moral arbiter for each person must be that person's own conscience, which is God or the Oversoul made manifest. It follows that the institutions by which we try to bring one another to heel, or to impose our own conscience on that of others, are violations of our nature and of Nature. And he also taught that as human individuality came to be cherished, institutions facilitating the power of persons over persons must dissolve, since ultimately they were violations of reality. "The less government we have the better,—the fewer laws, and the less confided power," wrote Emerson in his essay "Politics." "The antidote to this abuse of formal Government, is, the influence of private character, the growth of the Individual."[26]

Emerson developed these ideas with an incredibly compelling and passionate literary style aided by immense learning. Warren—as I say, without apparently any direct influence in either direction—sought to make these visions real. He had little interest in their religious origins or implications, but he asked whether it was possible to develop a society—economy, education, arts—that took the human individual as the fundamental fact, as the source, motive force, and purpose of social life. He wanted to show that an actual social system could be made that was based on respecting our differences rather than seeking to deny or expunge them. Even his experiments in printing and music were aimed at this result: he wanted to make it possible for every person to express and develop herself through publishing ideas and creating art.

The question of whether Emerson was an anarchist is a difficult matter; he was reticent to declare a straightforward political program. But Thoreau certainly was an anarchist, and his hymns to individual conscience and inviolable liberty would have been profoundly congenial to Warren, as would his experiment in rural economy at Walden. Here is a passage from *A Week on the Concord and Merrimack Rivers* that, but for excellence of the prose, could have been written by Warren:

> I love man-kind, but I hate the institutions of the dead un-kind. Men execute nothing so faithfully as the wills of the dead, to the last codicil and letter. . . . We bear about with us the mouldering relics of our ancestors on our shoulders. If, for instance, a man asserts the value of individual liberty over the merely political commonweal, his neighbor still tolerates him, that is he who is *living near* him, sometimes even sustains him, but never the State. Its officer, as a living man, may have human virtues and a thought in his brain, but as the tool of an institution, a jailer or constable it may be, he is not a whit superior to his prison key or his staff. Herein is the tragedy; that men doing outrage to their proper natures, even those called wise and good, lend themselves to perform the office of inferior and brutal ones. Hence come war and slavery in; and what else may not come in by this opening?[27]

For Thoreau, it is the attempt of human beings to escape from their ineradicable individuality—both their liberty and their responsibility—through laws, institutions, roles, and rules, that has led to the worst outrages in human history. And he believed that this is a traffic in delusions, that casting off one's freedom and one's responsibility was always impossible. On all these points Warren entirely agreed, including the idea that we were in thrall to the dead, specifically through their "letters and codicils," their texts and institutional arrangements. As Thoreau sought to realize his principles in his own life, Warren sought to realize them—with a slight touch of paradox—in larger social arrangements. The test of such arrangements was precisely whether they left the lines of liberty and responsibility clear.

Indeed, one might think of Thoreau's two years at Walden as a utopian experiment, along the lines of George Ripley's Brook Farm or Bronson Alcott's Fruitlands. But it more closely resembled Utopia, Ohio, than either of these: it was an experiment in individualism and basic economics of precisely the sort that Warren undertook with more than one person. And the simultaneous overweening idealism and pointed practicality of Thoreau's Walden was present in the same measures in Warren's communities.

Modern Times

Relatively little is known of the two communities (Equity and Utopia) Warren formed in Ohio, between his sojourn at New Harmony and the founding of Modern Times, though Warren does describe some aspects of them, including something about the educational and economic structures. This probably boded well for their success. Publicity was part of the difficulties faced at New Harmony and Modern Times; even revealing the precise location of the communities might attract speculators in land, which actually did wind up putting an end to a number of American ideal communities. Modern Times, on the other hand, became a sensation and a scandal, though we might point out that this had little to do with Warren and much to do with his partner, Stephen Pearl Andrews.

Andrews, though born in Massachusetts, had lived in New Orleans in his youth, where he became a radical abolitionist, and he had practiced as a lawyer in Texas, where he hatched an abortive scheme for the abolition of slavery. (This was an unusual arc but not unique; Bronson Alcott, for example, worked as a traveling peddler in the South as a young man.) He returned to the North an ardent abolitionist, and like many of the reformers of his era he derived his libertarian conclusions from his opposition to slavery. In the run-up to and aftermath of the Civil War, Pearl Andrews—again like many

American reformers—advocated a smorgasbord of radicalisms, including free love (in fact, his society, the Grand Order of Recreation, was busted by New York City's vice cops), spiritualism, and a merger of all human languages into his own Alwato, which would bring in its train the millennium of peace and brotherhood.

Josiah Warren met Stephen Pearl Andrews in Boston in 1848 or 1849, where Warren was giving a series of talks to reformers on equitable commerce. Though they seemed for a brief time to agree about everything (because Andrews loudly endorsed Warren's views, which never seemed to alter one iota), it would be hard to imagine two more different men. Whereas Warren was straitlaced (his son George said he never drank, smoked, or cursed)[28] and extremely direct, Andrews was something of a libertine and an obscurantist. Whereas Warren's ideas and their expression were characterized by simplicity and straightforwardness, Andrews eventually built an incredibly elaborate and more-or-less incomprehensible philosophical system called Universology, explaining absolutely everything from the ground up. Whereas Warren had a rudimentary education and a great deal of practical skill, Andrews supposedly read thirty-two languages and was drenched in French and German thought, especially that of Fourier and Comte, and his ideas and career were more wild and astonishing than practical. Whereas Warren was self-effacing, Andrews was spectacular.

On the other hand, the alliance was complementary. Andrews was a scholar (let me express some reservations on that), a writer (ditto), a speaker, and an organizer. These were all qualities Warren lacked. But Warren had a series of fundamental, comprehensible, and compelling ideas, elements that eluded Andrews throughout his career. Andrews called Warren "the Euclid of the social sciences," a nice tribute to the simplicity and scope of Warren's views.[29] He converted to Warren's position but always tried to mingle Warren's ideas with developments in European thought, even though a synthesis of Warren and Fourier is, as Warren saw, impossible. Andrews's *The Science of Society* (1851) elaborates Warren's principles and places them in relation to Comte's sociology and Fourier's socialism. But its statements of Warren's positions are, when the infelicities of Warren's prose are attenuated, both less clear and less systematic than Warren's original texts.

Madeleine Stern, in her biography of Andrews, describes the founding of Modern Times (now Brentwood) thus:

> The two reformers set out together to search for their new Eden— the short Yankee inventor and the tall, forceful discoverer. Early in 1851, when the frosty air nipped his long Roman nose, Andrews ferried to Brooklyn with the saint of equity and then, after a two-hour journey by railroad, arrived at Thompson's Station in Long Island.
>
> The Pine Barrens of Long Island, some forty miles east of New York City, had little to recommend it to the objective viewer. The area was filled with a heavy growth of scrub oaks which would have to be uprooted. Water would have to be carried in buckets from Dr. Peck's farm. The soil was impoverished. Sparks from the railroad might start forest fires, and there was not even a cow path in sight.
>
> Pearl Andrews dismissed such minor flaws with a wave of the hand. The air was pure; the ground was solid. Roses would bloom where the scrub oaks stood. Broad avenues could be marked out. . . . He would call it "Modern Times" and the era of its founding would be known as the "Utopian Era."[30]

Andrews wrestled *Equitable Commerce* (1852)—Warren's fundamental statement of his own philosophy—into some sort of shape; indeed, their respective roles in the final text are hard to sort out. But with regard Modern Times their roles were clearly defined. Warren would be on the ground overseeing the practical details of home building and keeping a Time Store to serve as a labor exchange. Andrews, a leading light on the reform circuit in New York City, would serve as agent, recruiting, raising money, and garnering publicity. In the matter of publicity, he succeeded well beyond expectations, and one suspects that Warren, then in his fifties and frustrated by his limited achievements in transforming society, overcame his misgivings in the hope that renown would lead to the widespread dissemination of his ideas.

Modern Times, in existence from 1851 to 1864 or so, eventually housed about a hundred residents. But initially, Warren, in a typical demonstration of self-reliance, moved alone to a shanty in the scrub oaks, where he surveyed a handsome hypothetical town and started manufacturing bricks with which he built a house, promptly sold. Lots were sold on the cost principle, so land was notably inexpensive, and New York City was accessible by rail. Moncure Daniel Conway, who visited Modern Times in 1858, said that he wasn't sure whether to travel to the town "by railway or by rainbow."[31] Warren stated the purpose of the community in a somewhat more down-to-earth manner: "If we do not secure homes to the homeless, we work to no purpose."[32]

The town managed to establish many institutions, such as a fire company, a theater, a gymnasium, a library, and a school, on the cost principle. Warren's Time Store, once again, was the hub of the labor exchange that drove the building. Charles Shiveley writes: "The character of Modern Times appeared in the dining hall, which was quite different from those of New Harmony or Brook Farm. Mr. Clarke Orvis, the inventor of a velocipede, established an 'eating saloon' which was set up like the modern cafeteria. Mr. Orvis cooked and prepared a wide variety of dishes for the members; he determined the price of his labor; to this he added the basic cost of the foods. When a settler came to eat, he paid for his food in the familiar time money, which Warren had printed."[33] Warren used his bricks to build a two-story "mechanical College" to inculcate skills both practical and philosophical. *Chambers' Edinburgh Journal* skeptically described the economy in terms Warren would have approved: "The most disagreeable work claims the highest remuneration. Washerwomen, shoe-blacks, and scavengers, constitute the aristocracy of Modern Times; while lawyers, clergymen, and *litterateurs* are at the foot of the scale."[34] The community marketed its fruits and vegetables in New York City, the primary source of income. Warren no doubt thought that Modern Times could build slowly and unobtrusively until it could be displayed as a success.

Andrews had other ideas and invited Thomas Low Nichols and Mary Gove Nichols to take up residence. The Nicholses were free love, plural marriage, and sex education activists, and this agenda— shared by Andrews though decidedly not by Warren—swamped every other aspect of the community in public consciousness and was the subject of sensational press coverage. It is worth noting that many of the American ideal communities—including the Shakers, the Rappites, the Mormons, and the Oneida settlement—experimented with various reconceptions of the marriage and family relation. Though Andrews was an activist in this cause, and later coedited *Woodhull and Claflin's Weekly*, in which the astonishing Victoria Woodhull (an occasional visitor to Modern Times) put forward her views on free love, Warren regarded free love as a terrible idea and a distraction. On the other hand, he was completely committed to letting anyone live however they liked, and he held that a few disastrous experiments would put an end to the whole program.

Andrews, Horace Greeley, and Henry James, Sr.—each a great reformer and a notable eccentric—debated the matter in Greeley's *New York Tribune* in 1852–53. The debate extended to Warren's basic principles, as Greeley identified self-sovereignty as license, an equation made all the easier by Andrews's direct advocacy of free love. He wrote, "Your sovereignty of the individual is in palpable collision with the purity of society and the sovereignty of God."[35] Meanwhile, Modern Times was associated with atheism and other heresies. But it should also be said that all the experiments in different family arrangements had a feminist edge, and this was explicitly so with Andrews and the Goves; the destruction of traditional marriage was seen to be a necessary condition of the liberation of women. They also advocated sex education and birth control as a way to make sure every child was wanted and that no woman was trapped.

The association of Modern Times with free love was enough to attract all sorts of eccentrics to the town, including anyone who felt oppressed because of their nonstandard marital arrangements. Edgar Allan Poe described Mary Gove Nichols in 1848 as "a Mesmerist, a Swedenborgian, a phrenologist, a homeopathist and a hydropathist," and she shared some or all of these enthusiasms, and a number of others, with the people who began to gather at Modern Times.[36] The town became for a time the center of American spiritualism and a haven for almost any variety of quackery. Warren cannot but have seen this as a replay of New Harmony, and the community again lacked practical skills and hardworking people. Further, Warren did not want to be associated with "free love," as he made clear when he circulated a petition that read, in part, "The Sovereignty of every Individual' is as valid a warrant for *retaining the present relations*, as for changing them."[37] Nevertheless, Modern Times persisted as a remarkable and notorious experiment into the 1860s, at which point it slowly disintegrated and became something like a standard town. William O. Reichert writes:

> The effect of this unwanted publicity, as Warren described it, was an influx of "crochets," each dragging with him his "particular hobby" by which he projected the total and immediate salvation of the world and all in it. One of the "imposters" assured the community that the liberation of mankind would follow at once if all its children were brought up without the burden of clothing. So reasonable did this proposition appear to another of the newcomers that she immediately put the theory into practice, forcing her child to go naked despite the severity of the bitter winds that blew from the Sound during the winter. One old man of German origin sought to cure the infliction of blindness from which he suffered by walking the street *sans* clothing, while some of the female residents took to the habit of dressing themselves in men's clothing as a sign of their emancipation. More serious in its consequences were the dietary notions of another female inhabitant who would eat nothing but beans on the theory that it was good for her health. "She tottered around a living skeleton for about a year," according to Warren, "and then sank down and died."[38]

This is comical of course, and tragic for the bean eater. But it is also a rather delightful portrayal of a Temporary Autonomous Zone, an actual bizarre anarchist community, and Warren even managed a crack about "the great sacred right of freedom to do silly things" (*Practical Applications*, p. 212).

And in a small way, Modern Times remained an inspiration to reformers all over the world, including John Stuart Mill, then developing his own theory of "self-sovereignty" on utilitarian grounds. In his autobiography, describing the works that influenced *On Liberty*, he wrote:

> [A] remarkable American, Mr. Warren . . . had obtained a number of followers [at Modern Times] (whether it now exists I know not) which, though bearing a superficial resemblance to some of the projects of the Socialists, is diametrically opposite to them in principle, since it recognises no authority whatever over the individual, except to enforce equal freedom of development for all individualities. As the book which bears my name claimed no originality for any of its doctrines, and was not intended to write their history, the only author who had preceded me in their assertion of whom I thought it appropriate to say anything, was Humboldt, who furnished the motto for the work; although in one passage I borrowed from the Warrenites their phrase, the sovereignty of the individual.[39]

Apparently the publicity had some effect after all. Many an idealist in the United States and in Europe projected on the community their fantasies of a new world. Auguste Comte—scientist and utopian—corresponded with Henry Edger at Modern Times, to whom he wrote: "Modern Times . . . constitutes the full development of Occidental anarchy. I am glad that you are not frightened by it. You have appreciated well the seed of reorganization in that bizarre mental *milieu*. . . . I share your hopes concerning the possibility of finding in Modern Times the nucleus of a true positivist Church."[40]

Warren and Anarchism

As politics, the principle of individuality is a direct attack on the whole of modern political thought: the Hobbes Leviathan, the Lockean contract, Rousseau's general will, and Hegel's state. And it also runs against more or less the entire stream of political reality since Warren's time, dominated by Marxist communism squaring off against welfare-state, bureaucratic capitalism. We must understand that Warren's thought gravitates no more toward modern capitalism than it does toward Marxism, nor the other way around: it is outside and prior to these categories, having been composed in the middle of nowhere (deepest Indiana, to be precise) in the early decades of the nineteenth century. It's worth saying that there is no evidence of his reading Locke, Hume, Smith, or (later in his life) Marx or Proudhon, or, for that matter, Emerson or Thoreau, though by the 1840s every literate American had heard of Emerson and had some idea of his teachings. In fact, between spasms of journal writing, Warren was not engaged in scholarship, but rather in developing novel processes for manufacturing bricks or printing up new varieties of currency.

Warren is also precisely prior to and outside the split between what I am going to call left- and right-wing anarchism. The left wing proceeds from Proudhon, and then develops as a movement against Marx in the late-nineteenth-century battles for leadership of the radical industrial labor movement. Mikhail Bakunin follows Proudhon as Marx's opponent, and Peter Kropotkin is easily the most able nineteenth-century theoretician of this view. Kropotkin was certainly aware of Warren and regarded him as an inspiration, despite all their differences. Kropotkin mentions Warren in his famous *Encyclopedia Britannica* article on "Anarchism" as a precursor of (and influence on?) Proudhon:

> It [mutualism] had also its precursor in America. Josiah Warren, who was born in 1798 . . . , and belonged to Owen's "New Harmony," considered that the failure of this enterprise was chiefly due to the suppression of individuality and the lack of initiative and responsibility. These defects, he taught, were inherent to every scheme based upon authority and community of goods. He advocated, therefore, complete individual liberty. In 1827 he opened in Cincinnati a little country store which was the first "Equity Store," and which people called "Time Store," because it was based on labor being exchanged hour for hour in all sorts of produce. "Cost—the limit of price," and consequently "no interest," was the motto of his store, and later on of his "Equity Village" near New York, which was still in existence in 1865.[41]

The Bakunin/Kropotkin strand came to be called "communist anarchism." It was marked by an attack on private ownership and called
for a true union of human beings: a spontaneous unanimity and
cooperation enshrined in Kropotkin's concept of "mutual aid" as
a factor in evolution: a profound refutation of social Darwinism.
Communist anarchism reached its American height under the aegis
of Emma Goldman and Alexander Berkman, Russian Kropotkinians
importing their ideas to Greenwich Village. This tendency came to be
despised between the time of the Haymarket riot and the anarchist
Leon Czolgosz's assassination of President William McKinley. The
prevailing image of the anarchist became a bomb-wielding, immigrant, nihilist, terrorist scourge of modernity.

"Right-wing" anarchism uses Warren as the Left uses Proudhon.
Lysander Spooner moves straight from Locke and Jefferson to a mili-
tant defense of deism and individual rights. If anarchism could have
a legal theory, Spooner in his capacities as a self-taught lawyer and
freakish polemical talent would have been its theoretician. Benjamin
Tucker—another provincial New England printer—used Warren and
Spooner as twin supports without fully exploring the tension between
them. But Tucker, as time goes on, adds an admixture of the egoism
of Max Stirner, of whom he was the first American publisher. Stirner's work, though striking in its diagnosis of modernity as the cult of
the state and in its continual paradoxes, would be an absurd guide
for social reform and is actually sort of pathetic: the assertion by a
tiny man of his unbelievable gigantism; the alleged fact that his self is
or commands the entire world. Despite Stirner's notion of a "union
of egoists," his philosophy is too solipsistic to serve as a political
guide.

Because they precede and transcend the schism between stateless
communism and Stirner-style egoism, between left- and right-wing
anarchism as it has played out ever since, it is particularly interesting to recover Warren and Proudhon's thought. Of course the communist anarchists rejected Marx's statist solution, but they accepted
to a large extent his analysis of history as class struggle. Indeed,
Bakunin's thought is little more than a pastiche of Marxism and

Proudhon. The communist anarchists held property to be at the root of capitalist exploitation, and hence proposed its outright elimination. This analysis was to some extent discredited by the development of capitalism into a modified socialism, bolstered by a huge state sector, regulation of the economy, and redistributive schemes, as well as by the success of the labor movement in increasing wages and benefits and decreasing hours. In addition, the communists organized internationally instead of trying to achieve local transformations, emphasizing world proletariat revolution rather than local community formation.

The egoists, on the other hand, came to celebrate exploitation itself as the result of voluntary contract, and to recommend self-seeking acquisitiveness. This point of view tried to manufacture the overman: the independent ego who needs no assistance and brooks no interference, who dares to do injustice, the blond beast or little gray chair of the Federal Reserve. The egoists refuse organization of attempts at societal transformation, and often think of activism, community construction, or even charity as little more than an expression of social slavishness, and dismiss justice and morality as a plot of the little people. Warren fits this picture no better—or perhaps considerably worse—than he does the communist ideal, despite his own brand of extreme individualism. The question for Warren is how decent folk can achieve a nonexploitative economy in which they contribute not only to their own material gain but also to social well-being, which he considers one of our natural impulses. It is one of the greatest errors in superficial readings of Warren to connect him to the later thought of Benjamin Tucker, Ayn Rand, and Murray Rothbard, even though the term "individualist" is used to describe them all.

A division in anarchist theory persists between those who wish to proceed by community formation—by carving out, within existing society, a zone of autonomy—and those who propose a global social revolution. To some extent this tracks the American/European and individualist/communist splits within anarchism. The Americans emerge from dissenting Protestant prophets and abolitionist saints. The Europeans emerge from the 1789 French Revolution and the works

of Rousseau. Each despises the other and thinks the other impractical
and defeatist. But each has also had some successes. The pre-immi-
grant American tradition takes the course of practical experiment (e.g.,
Lysander Spooner's postal service and challenges to licensing proce-
dures), along with an accompanying polemical publicity that serves as
a record of experiments and a recruiting brochure. Warren, at any rate,
belongs squarely in what is called by its opponents "lifestyle anarchism": that strain concerned with creating alternatives within the in-
terstices in the existing system rather than arming to overthrow it. In
any case, the opposition is tendentious; the approaches ought to be
complementary. Build a world, then take it public.

To consider yet another strain of anarchism, Warren was no primi-
tivist (à la the contemporary theorist John Zerzan), though his own
preference for small-scale, local economies might lend some comfort
to anarchists of this bent. His continuous activity as an inventor
shows his enthusiasm for technology. An article about Warren in the
journal *Printing History* is aptly titled "Every Man His Own Printer";
and, given his obsession with self-publishing, Warren would no
doubt at this point be a blogger.[42] He conceived his own economics
as practical, encouraging industry and trade. He is neither a technological optimist in the mode of so many thinkers of his time and af-
terward (such as the pragmatists), nor a pessimist of the back-to-the-
land movements of the 1960s. For Warren, technology cannot redeem
us, but it can contribute to a decent human life in many ways.

At any rate, to understand Warren it is crucial to grasp the political
spectrum of early-nineteenth-century American politics, in particular
radical politics. The most radical, progressive elements were by and
large religious fanatics. What we might think of as the far Left—the
feminist movement, abolitionism, the peace movement—attacked
the very idea of state power. Individualism was the political currency
of the American reform movement. The division of the Left and
Right, understood as statist socialism or communism versus libertarian, laissez-faire capitalism, just wasn't in play.

There is evidence that Warren sympathized with most of the major reform movements of the nineteenth century, especially feminism. He is among the few nineteenth-century authors you will find using gender-neutral locutions such "he or she": in the texts that follow, these expressions are not the result of my editing. Warren explicitly and at length decries the limitation of women to a certain set of professions, and frankly proposes equality of the sexes along with practical measures to make this possible (including day care).

Extreme religious forces in early-nineteenth-century America were on the far Left. What we would call "conservatives" were leftover Federalists or slavery enthusiasts, big-government Hamiltonians or bold pseudo-Cavaliers. Reform still meant freedom from "tyranny," meaning control by a foreign power. But the term "tyranny" soon came to mean simply any interruption of self-sovereignty—in short, slavery. That is why we need to return precisely to the moment of Warren: because this split between Left and Right as it developed under Marxism is invidious, extraneous, and arbitrary with regard to the subject matter. The Hegelian solution of the ever-growing state has in fact been adopted by nearly everyone on the political spectrum: the extreme Right and the extreme Left, as well as the moderate Right and the moderate Left. In a way, the history of American reform movements was co-opted by international statist socialism, which prevented the emergence of an indigenous radical understanding. After Warren, the apocalypse: the Civil War and the world wars, the genocides of colonialism and state terrorism.

Put simply, Warren was neither a communist nor a capitalist. True, the economy he imagined was regulated by the invisible hand of competition and the inexorable laws of supply and demand. He emphasized private property and free transactions. He never tried to out-nice his capitalist competitors, but rather to underprice them. Yet his entire program depended on the elimination of profit in all transactions, and he always proposed his "experiments" as a way to help the laboring classes as well as the destitute.

Note on the Texts

Warren's published texts are the result of multiple editings and reorderings, by Warren and others (in particular, Stephen Pearl Andrews). Most of the material no doubt originated in notebooks (now lost except for "D"). The two book-length works of political/economic philosophy published in his lifetime, and intermittently reissued in tiny editions since, are known as *Equitable Commerce* and *True Civilization*, the contents of which overlap. The first of these was presented explicitly as an attempt by Stephen Pearl Andrews to organize the mess of Warren's notebooks and periodicals. The second seems to have been Warren's attempt to do likewise, incorporating material emerging after about 1850. Both works are eccentric in their printing and organization. *Equitable Commerce* features Warren's marginal indexing. There is a numbered list of themes at the beginning, with numbers appearing in the margins opposite the paragraphs connected to the theme corresponding to that number. Warren appears to have entertained the idea that the work could be read in a number of different orders, allowing the reader to create a self-guided tour. *True Civilization* features (only) a nonlinear, thematic table of contents. These are typical Warren innovations—individualistic, ingenious, and premonitory (for their resemblance to hyperlink text structures)—but they tend to make the text even more off-putting, bristling with odd notations. I have not tried to reproduce these effects, except by including a conventional index to the book as a whole.

What I have attempted to produce, out of the welter of bewildering writings, is a reading text, and to accomplish that I have taken a number of steps, which could be summed up by saying that I retained textual order and performed no additions, but rather only deletions and corrections, as follows. I have severely curtailed Warren's penchant for emphasis, which could include several sizes of capitals, italics, underlining, and multiple exclamation points. I have liberally changed or corrected punctuation; Warren's is inconsistent and often infelicitous, and in the notebooks and letters, careless, as one would expect. I have also made many excisions, which are not specifically marked in the text; the plan is to present facsimiles of at least some works online. Producing a readable text of Warren's writings has presented a problem for his editors ever since his earliest publications. There could be other solutions, of course, especially an attempt to reproduce the various early typestyles and indexing systems. For the sake of clarity and simplicity, I decided to move emphatically in the other direction.

I want this volume to convey the practical value and continuing relevance of many of Warren's ideas. These ideas are fundamental to an important school of American political thought and deserve to be represented to a literate audience, so far as possible, in their originator's words. I wanted to produce something that, in short, people could or might actually read. To accomplish this, I typed my way through all the Warren material, trying to think both like the person who composed them and also as a writer.

I do regret having smoothed out some of Warren's eccentricities as a writer. But I think that as a consequence both his eccentricities and his universality as a personality and as a thinker stand out more clearly.

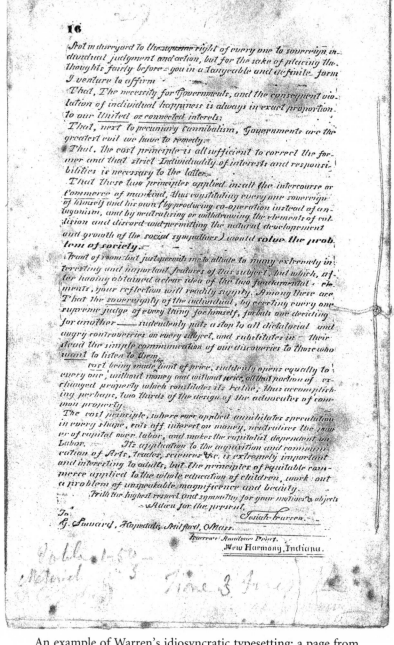

An example of Warren's idiosyncratic typesetting: a page from
the self-published *Letter on Equitable Commerce*, dated
"New Harmony, Ia. Feb 1844."

PLAN OF THIS WORK.

I have endeavored to reduce the great object of this work to the form of a definite problem, and to suggest the means of its solution in their most simple, practical form, and have associated each proposition with an initial or number, by which the reader can refer to their different illustrations or applications throughout the work. Thus, whenever I is placed either at the head of a chapter or in the margin of any page, there will be found some practical working out of the legitimate reward of labor. II refers to the security of person and property. I Points out the illustration of individuality, etc. There are many important subjects immediately connected with, though not constituting the social problem or its solution, which are referred to under the third class of figures 1, 2, 3, etc. Thus, suppose that the reader feels particular interest in the subject of *competition*. Let him turn to the contents, where he will find this marked 4. Now let him refer to any of the margins having the figure 4, and immediately opposite the figure he will find some illustration of the workings of competition.

If he wishes to see illustrations of the *sovereignty* of the individual, he will look in the margins for the letter S; and in a similar manner he will find the illustrations of any point of the subject, by referring to its corresponding figure or letter.

PROBLEM TO BE SOLVED.

I. The proper, legitimate, and just reward of labor.

II. Security of person and property.

III. The greatest practicable amount of freedom to each individual.

IV. Economy in the production and uses of wealth.

V. To open the way for each individual to the possession of and, and all other natural wealth.

VI. To make the interests of all to co-operate with and assist each other, instead of clashing with and counteracting each other.

VII. To withdraw the elements of discord, of war, of distrust and repulsion, and to establish a prevailing spirit of peace, order, and social sympathy.

MEANS OF THE SOLUTION.

I. INDIVIDUALITY.

S. SOVEREIGNTY OF EVERY INDIVIDUAL.

C. COST THE LIMIT OF PRICE.

M. CIRCULATING MEDIUM FOUNDED ON THE COST OF LABOR.

A. ADAPTATION OF THE SUPPLY TO THE DEMAND.

IMPORTANT POINTS ILLUSTRATED.

1. Disconnection, division, individuality the principle of order, harmony, and progress.

2. Different interpretations of the same language neutralize all institutions founded on words.

3. It is not each other, but our *commerce or intercourse with each other*, that we have to regulate.

4. Competition rendered harmless, and becomes a great adjusting and regulating power.

5. Use of capital on the equitable principle.

6. VALUE being made the basis of price, becomes the principal element of civilized cannibalism.

7. Power of circumstances over persons illustrated.

8. Sources of insecurity of person and property.

9. Illustrations of the origin or necessity for governments.

10. *Division* of labor the greatest source of gain to society.

11. Whatever operates against the division of labor, and exchange or commerce, makes against civilization.

12. Benefits of individual responsibilities illustrated.

13. Machinery, by the cost, or the equitable principle, made a benefit to all, an injury to none.

16. Report of demand or wants, the first step of practical operations.

17. To those who want employment.

18. Victims of the present social state—simple justice would do more for them than the highest stretch of benevolence ever contemplated.

19. CO-OPERATION WITHOUT COMBINATION produced by simple JUSTICE.

22. Subordination which does not violate the natural liberty of man.

25. Combinations, or "UNITY OF INTERESTS," the wrong movement.

27. Reasons for organizing society without government.

30. Natural government of consequences, in the place of man-made governments.

31. Where the consequences fall, there should rest the deciding power.

33. Simple justice, or Equitable Commerce, would naturally effect all the great objects aimed at by the best friends of the human race.

37. Value being made the limit of price, stagnates commerce, and retards the progress of civilization.

Education conducted upon equitable principles. (*See Appendix.*)

The customary apprenticeships an unnecessary cause of poverty, and a great obstacle to any improved state of society. (*See Appendix.*)

The thematic table of contents and marginal indexing system Warren developed for *Equitable Commerce.*

I cial harmony will avoid, by making every transaction an *ex-*
VII *dividual* one—settling each in the time of it, when all its peculiarities are fresh in the minds of both parties. Once being settled to the satisfaction of both, nothing is left to the memory or the indefinite guess-work of the future, which is almost sure to produce dissatisfaction to one or both parties.

A still more subtle, and more serious invasion of the rights of property, the natural liberty, and social harmony, is constantly at work in the form of *indefinite obligations*. If A lend B a hammer, it may be of great *value* to B, but no price is set upon it; this is considered a neighborly accommodation, and common morality says, "neighbors should accommodate each other." The next day A applies to B for the loan of his favorite horse. B wishes to train his horse in a particular manner, and knows that he cannot do this, if different people use him—besides, he wants to use him, or he wants him to rest, and no compensation is offered by A as an inducement. He evidently makes the request on the ground that "neighbors should accommodate each other;" and on this ground B loses all proper control over his horse; and, on the same principle, over every thing that he possesses which is not for sale; so that, by this means, his proper control over his own becomes almost annihilated. The cause is *indefiniteness* in our
I obligations. The remedy is definiteness in our obligations.
C Let every transaction be an individual one, resting on its own merits, and not mixed up or settled with another. If A lends B a hammer, and he thinks the cost of doing so is worthy of
25 notice, let B pay it at once, or give a representative of an equivalent; if it is unworthy of notice, it is best for entirely disregarded, and never be mixed up with its *value*, nor referred to in future transactions.
I It is only by thus *individualizing* of our transactions and their
VII elements, that each citizen can enjoy "the legitimate control over his own person, time, or property. It is only by this means that we can distinguish a disinterested present, or act of benevolence and sympathy, from one prompted by a mer-

cenary design. If we present a rose to a friend, it is understood to be an expression of sympathy—a simple act of moral commerce, and the receiver feels free from any obligation to make any other return than an expression of the natural feeling which immediately results therefrom; but if one should give half of his property to another, the receiver could not feel equally free from future indefinite obligations. Why? Perhaps, not that the property was any more *valuable* to the receiver than the rose, but, that it cost more.

A delicate regard to the rightful liberty of every one, and
VII the necessity of self-preservation, would seem to admonish us to make *cost* the limit of gratuitous favors, while those of im-
C mense *value*, which *cost* nothing, can be given and received without hesitation or reluctance, and will purify our moral commerce from any mixture with the mercenary or selfish taint, and carry it to the very highest state of perfection.

We will suppose our practical operations so far progressed upon our new premises, as to require the establishment of a
5 store. No one has money enough to stock one, and the sovereignty of each over his own at all times, seems to forbid borrowing of each other, or one becoming security for
VII another. The most harmonious mode will be found to be for the store-keeper to borrow money *outside* of these operations until borrowing is unnecessary. The next best resort, though not perfectly harmonious, but which may not be seriously disturbing, is for the store-keeper to borrow very small sums from the co-operators, giving them notes for the same, *payable*
on demand, so that if any one, for any cause, wishes to withdraw his investment, he can do so, at any time, without words. The store-keeper then proceeds, like ordinary store-keepers,
I to purchase on his own responsibility and risk, whatever he thinks is in demand, but he observes the time that he em-
A ploys in purchasing, and on his return opens an account against the store for his labor and contingent expenses—placing the labor in one column and the money in another. He then considers what per centage will probably pay these and all

Pages from Warren's *Equitable Commerce*, showing marginal indexing system at work.

EQUITABLE COMMERCE

On any account of Warren's writings, the material published under the title Equitable Commerce: A New Development of Principles as Substitutes for Laws and Governments, for the Harmonious Adjustment and Regulation of the Pecuniary, Intellectual, and Moral Intercourse of Mankind *must be considered central. Warren had published a version of the book in tiny, self-printed editions in 1846 and 1849. Stephen Pearl Andrews edited the 1852 edition. (Pearl Andrews was by then acting as publicist and agent of Warren's ideas with regard to the establishment of the town of Modern Times.) In his "Editor's Preface" to the 1852 edition, Andrews writes, "I gladly accept the pleasing task which my friend Josiah Warren, has consented that I shall assume, of editing and presenting to the world, in my own way, his works on 'Equitable Commerce.'"[1] The basic ideas and structure were all fully developed by 1842, when Warren published the* Gazette of Equitable Commerce *in New Harmony, Indiana. James J. Martin in* Men Against the State *describes the genesis of the book: "The final product of two years of collation and revision of a mass of notes taken sporadically over twenty years, all its imperfections considered, was a document of undeniable simplicity. . . . Warren's* Equitable Commerce *became the first important publication of anarchist doctrine in America, and with minor deletions, additions, and revisions, went into more editions within the next thirty years than any other product of native anarchist thought to this time" (48). Essentially, what follows is an anthology of Warren's thought and writing from the late 1820s to the late 1840s, the most productive years of his career. It contains by far the most elaborate development of Warren's individualist metaphysics, among other contributions to our understanding of his thought. It is filled with good ideas and extreme enthusing; only the former have been retained in this version.*

Introduction

The public are here presented with the results of about twenty-five years of investigation and experiments, with a view to a great and radical, yet peaceful change in the character of society, by one who felt a deep and absorbing interest, and took an active part in the experiments of communities at New Harmony, during the two years of 1825 and 1826, and who, after the total defeat of every modification of those plans which the purest philanthropy and the greatest stretch of ingenuity could devise, was on the point of abandoning all such enterprises, when a new train of thought seemed to throw a sudden flash of light upon our past errors, and show plainly the path to be pursued. But this led directly in the opposite direction to that which we had just traveled. It led to new principles, new views, and new modes of action. I have come to the resolution to place [this matter before the public] (as far as is practicable) in a manner that it may be studied in detail, in times of undisturbed leisure, where the attention can be fixed upon that alone, individually; for nothing short of this can do it justice.

I have many times sat down to perform the task now before me; but when I contemplated the overwhelming magnitude of the subject—the bewildering complication of its different parts—the liability to err, to make wrong impressions through the inherent ambiguity of language, and the impossibility of conveying new ideas in old words, I have shrunk in fear and trembling at the task, have lain down my pen in despair, and returned to the silent, but safe, though tardy, language of experimental action. This speaks unequivocally to those who see and study it; but this mode of introduction has its limits, depending on the locality of the experiments, and the intellectual capacities and pecuniary resources of those within its immediate sphere, neither of which may prove sufficient for the establishing of one complete example.

I deem it unnecessary to add any thing to what has been so well said of late, to show the imperious necessity of a total change in society's institutions. Almost every one now admits—what the few

far-seeing and deep-thinking have perceived in all ages of human institutions—that something is radically wrong somewhere. There has
always been a striving after a purer state of existence—a panting after
an atmosphere never yet breathed in the social state—a clashing between the theories and practices of men—a yearning after practical
justice and humanity. Society has been in a state of violence, of revolution and suffering, ever since its first formation; and at this hour
the greater number are about to array themselves against the smaller,
who have, by some subtle and hidden means, lived luxuriously upon
their labor without rendering an equivalent. Governments have lost
their power of governing. Laws have become powerless from their
inherent defectiveness, and irresistible by ordinary means; the right
of the strongest begins to be openly admitted to a frightful extent,
and many of the best minds look forward to an age of confusion and
violence, with the confidence of despair. We have contemplated suffering in different forms till the heart is sick; and, unless a speedy and
effectual remedy be applied, would fly from the scenes or shut our
eyes upon them forever. We are not alone in this feeling—the same
spirit is abroad, calling for aid, for sympathy, for remedy; and in response to this call, I come at once to our subject—social reformation.

Part II: Means for the Attainment of Our Proposed Ends

The first element of Equitable Commerce, or rather, the foundation
of the whole subject, is the study of individuality, or the practice of
mentally discriminating, dividing, separating, disconnecting persons,
things, and events, according to their individual peculiarities.

Do not be alarmed at the word "study," or at the dry and abstract
form of the heading of this chapter. I shall deal as little as possible in
the abstract, but subjects of illimitable magnitude admit of no other
form. The American Declaration of Independence is an abstraction,
and those who are incapable of examining subjects of this character
may as well lay down the book here and save further trouble; while I
invite the few more fortunately constituted to an examination of
mind upon which the success of our whole object depends, but which

constitutes no part of our education, nor scarcely of surrounding example.

The individualities of which I speak are so deep-seated, so subtle, and hidden, that they pass undetected by common observation, and almost defy scrutiny itself; and yet, as electricity seems to be the life-principle of the individual, so this individuality seems equally to pervade every thing, and to be the life-principle of society.

The word "individuality" furnishes an illustration of itself. It assumes different significations in different cases. We sometimes use it as a substantive, sometimes as an adjective, sometimes as a verb. Different persons understand it differently in either form; and the same person will understand and appreciate it differently at different times, according to different degrees of development and different states of mind, under different circumstances. Such is the indefinite diversity that will spring up out of the peculiarities or individualities of persons, times, and circumstances when the word is used; and this diversity is inevitable. We can scarcely write a phrase that will not be subject to similar diversity of interpretation, growing out of the subtle individualities of different minds and different states of the same mind.

The subject of Equitable Commerce has drawn forth many remarks and comments very different from each other. One says, "he sees nothing in particular in it"; another said he "perceived that it had all the features that a great redeeming revolution ought to possess." P "could see nothing in it but indications of insanity." The Rev. Mr. C pronounced it "the result of more wisdom than commonly falls to the lot of man." F saw in it "a design to make a little money"; while C, G, and E censure its author for spending his time and wasting his resources in attempts to introduce principles which require "more virtue and intelligence to carry out than mankind possess."

To contend against this diversity is to contend against our nature's constant production. Such is the subtle and inherent nature of this individuality, that it accompanies every one in every thing he does, and any attempt to conquer it is like undertaking to walk away from his mode of walking, or to run away from his breath—the very effort calls it more decidedly into play.

Out of the indestructibility or inalienability of this individuality grows the absolute right of its exercise, or the absolute sovereignty of every individual.

Words are the principal means of our intellectual intercourse, and they form the basis of all our institutions; but here again this subtle individuality sets at nought the profoundest thoughts and the most careful phraseology. There is no certainty of any written laws, or rules, or institutions, or verbal precepts being understood in the same manner by any number of persons. To require conformity in the appreciation of sentiments, or in the interpretation of language, or uniformity of thought, feeling, or action where there is no natural coincidence, is a fundamental error in human legislation—a madness that would be only equaled by requiring all to possess the same countenance or the same stature.

Individuality thus rising above all prescriptions—all authority—every one, by the very necessities of nature, is raised above, instead of being under, institutions based on language. Institutions thus become subordinate to our judgment and subject to our convenience; and the hitherto inverted pyramid of human affairs assumes its true position.

We will endeavor to justify the apparent extravagance of our announcements by a few familiar illustrations, although the complete elucidation of individuality must be the work of time and more extended opportunities.

When one finds his different papers, bills, receipts, orders, letters, etc. all in one confused heap, and wishes to restore them to order, what does he do but separate, disconnect, divide, and disunite them—putting each individual kind in an individual place, until all are individualized? If a mechanic goes to his tool-chest, and finds all in confusion, what does he do to restore them to order, but disconnect, divide, separate, individualize them?

It is within everyone's experience, that when many things of any kind are heterogeneously mixed together, separation, disconnection, division, individuality restore them to order. No other process will do it.

If a multitude of ideas crowd at once upon the mind of a speaker or writer, what can he do to prevent confusion, but divide his subject, disconnect, disunite its parts, giving to each an individual time and place?

It is this which constitutes the principal element of the very highest grade of criticism.

When two persons are talking at once there is not sufficient individuality in either voice to separate it from the other. Both uniting together, they make nothing but confusion. The efforts of both them and their auditors are thrown away.

The more the letters of the alphabet differ from each other, i.e., the more individuality each possesses, the more efficient and perfect they are for the purposes intended.

Musical harmony is produced by those sounds only which differ from each other. A continuous reiteration of one note, in all respects the same, has no charms for any one. The beats of a drum, although the same as to tune, are not so as to stress or accent; in this respect they differ, and this difference occurring at regular intervals, the strong contrasted with the weak, enables the attention to dwell upon them, with more or less satisfaction; but the unremitted repetition of one dull, unvarying sound would either not command attention or make us run mad.

It is when the voice or an instrument sounds different notes, one after the other, that we obtain melody; and it is only when different notes are sounded together that we produce harmony. The key note, its fifth, its octave, and its tenth, when sounded together, produce a delightful chord; but these are all different from each other, and retain their separate individualities, even while thus associated in the closest possible manner; so that, while they are all sounding together, the practiced ear can distinguish either from the others. They never become combined. They never unite into one sound, even in the most complicated nor in the most enchanting harmonious associations. If such were the result—if they were to lose their individualities in association, and unite into one sound, all musical harmony would be unknown, or be suddenly swept from the earth, as social harmony has been by the violations of the individualities of man. It is to the indestructible individuality of each note in music that we are indebted for this most humanizing art. And it is through a watchful regard to the equally indestructible individualities of man, that he is to be indebted for the harmony of society.

The commencement of constitutional governments was the first step of progress in politics, and it was disconnecting, dividing, disuniting the subjects of legislative action from those which were reserved sacred to the people.

The disconnection of church and state was a master-stroke for freedom and harmony. The great moving power—the very soul of the Protestant Reformation was, that it left every one free to interpret scriptures according to his own views.

Responsibility must be individual, or there is no responsibility at all.

The directing power, or the lead of every movement must be individual, or there is no lead, no order, nothing but confusion. The lead may be a person or thing—an idea or principle; but it must be an individuality, or it cannot lead; and those who are led must have an individual or similar impulse, and both that and the lead must coincide or harmonize, to insure order and progress.

The masses in a city, when meeting each other upon the side-walk, without any thing to lead to one individual understanding, may turn out in divers ways to avoid collision. One turns to the right, the other to the left, and they both counteract each other; and both stop, both change again, with the same result—no progress—nothing can result but uncertainty and confusion, until there is some definite understanding between them, which both co-operate to carry out. (Definiteness is attained only by an individuality of meaning in the proposition advanced.) Some one individual suggests through the papers that every one turn to the right on meeting another. As it is for the interest, and is the wish of every one to avoid collision and delay, their inclinations and their interests coincide with the idea thus thrown out, and the confusion is at an end. Here is individuality of purpose, individuality of understanding, individuality in the regulating or governing power, or lead, and yet the governing power is not a person, but an idea. Therefore, although the lead or governing power must be an individuality, it need not necessarily be a person. But if two suggestions were thrown out at the same time, the one proposing to turn to the right and the other to the left, and no one individual understanding were arrived at, and if each one had not an interest in avoiding collision, they would neutralize each other, and confusion would be the result. Can we not see, democrats as we are, that here may be an explanation of the defense of absolutism in governments, for the suppression of diversities of opinion, suppression of the freedom of the press, etc.?

Here is in miniature the grand issue between despotism and liberty. What is the answer? The right of supreme individuality must be accorded to every one; and though it is entirely impracticable to exercise this right in the present close connections and combinations of society, the true business of us all is to invent modes by which these connections and amalgamated interests can be individualized, so that each can exercise his right of individuality at his own cost, without involving or counteracting others; then, that his co-operation must not be required in any thing wherein his own inclinations do not concur or harmonize with the object in view. I admit that this makes it necessary that the interests of the individual should harmonize with the public interests. This is entirely impossible upon any principles now known to the public.

We propose to throw out such ideas or discoveries as, when they come to be examined, may, like any other definite or scientific truths, become like suggestions relative to the side-walk: the regulators of the movements of each individual, by the coincidence between these suggestions and his interests, or self-preservation.

Blackstone and other theorists, are fatally mistaken when they think they get one general will by a concurrence of vote. Many influences may decide a vote contrary to the feelings and views of the voters; and, more than this, perhaps no two in twenty will understand or appreciate a measure, or foresee its consequences alike, even while they are voting for it. There may be ten thousand hidden, unconscious diversities among the voters which cannot be made manifest till the measure comes to be put in practice; when, perhaps, nine out of ten of the voters will be more or less disappointed, because the result does not coincide with their particular expectations.

I admit that when we have once committed the mistake of getting into too close connections, it is impossible for each to exercise his right of individuality; that then, perhaps, to be governed by the wishes of the greatest number (if we could ascertain them) might be the best expedient. But it is only an expedient, a very imperfect one—dangerous when great interests are involved, and positively destructive to the security of person and property, from the uncertainty of the turning of the vote, or of the permanence of the institution arising from it. One man may turn the whole vote, and often for want of definiteness (individuality) in the meaning of the terms of the laws, their interpretation and administration are, of necessity, left to an individual; and this is despotism. The whole process is like traveling in a circle too large to be taken in at a glance, but yet, without being aware of it, we travel toward the point whence we set out, although we take the first steps in the opposite direction. Disconnecting all interests, and allowing each to be the absolute despot or sovereign over his own, at his own cost, is the only solution that is worthy of thought. Good thinkers never committed a more fatal mistake than in expecting harmony from an attempt to overcome individuality, and in trying to make a state or nation an individual. The individuality of each person is perfectly indestructible. A state or nation is a multitude of indestructible individualities and cannot, by any possibility, be converted into anything else. The horrid consequences of these monstrous and abortive attempts to overcome simple truth and nature are displayed on every page of the world's melancholy history.

Lamartine, in his admirable history of the first French Revolution, says, "Among the posthumous notes of Robespierre were found the following: 'There must be one will; and this will must be either

Republican or Royalist, . . . all diplomacy is impossible as long as we have not unity of power.' "[2]

We here see the very root of Robespierre's policy and the explanation of his sanguinary career. It was precisely the same root from which have sprung all the ancient as well as modern political fallacies. It was a demand for "unity," "oneness of mind," "oneness of action," where coincidence was impossible. The demand disregarded all nature's individualities, demanded the annihilation of all diversity, and made dissent a crime. All were criminal by necessity, for no two had the power to be alike. The true basis for society is exactly the opposite of this. It is freedom to differ in all things, or the sovereignty of every individual.

Having the liberty to differ does not make us differ, but, on the contrary, it is a common ground upon which all can meet, a particular in which the feelings of all coincide, and is the first true step in social harmony. Giving full latitude to every experiment (at the cost of the experimenters), brings every thing to a test, and insures a harmonious conclusion. Among a multitude of untried routes, only one of which is right, the more liberty there is to differ and take different routes, the sooner will all come to a harmonious conclusion as the right one; and this is the only possible mode by which the harmonious result aimed at can be attained. Compulsion, even upon the right road, will never be harmonious. The sovereignty of the individual will be found on trial to be indispensable to harmony in every step of social reorganization, and when this is violated or infringed, then that harmony will be sure to be disturbed.

Robespierre may have carried the old idea a little farther than some republicans, but he carried it no further than the Greeks, the Venetians, and even the ancient and modern advocates of community of property. In all of them, as well as in all forms of organized society, the first and great leading idea was and is to sink the individual in the state or body politic, when nothing short of the very opposite, which is, raising every individual above the state, above institutions, above systems, above man-made laws, will enable society to take the first successful step toward its harmonious adjustment.

Lamartine: "Couthon said, 'Citizens, Capet is accused of great crimes, and in my opinion he is guilty. Accused, he must be judged, for eternal justice demands that every guilty man shall be condemned. By whom shall he be condemned? By you, whom the Nation has constituted the great tribunal of the state.' "[3]

Here, by a jumble of sounding words, "great crimes," "eternal justice," "great tribunal of the state," all of which mean nothing whatever but the barbarian imagination of the speaker, a phantom is got up called the state, which is made to absolve the murderers from the responsibility of the murder. If this responsibility had rested individually upon Couthon, where, in truth, the whole of all that he was talking about existed, he would have shrunk back from taking the first step. But throwing all the responsibility upon the soulless phantom called the state, there was no longer any check to crime.

The state, or body politic, must result from individuality, instead of crushing it. If we would have a prosperous state, it must arise from the prosperity of the individuals who compose the state. Where every individual is rich, the state will be rich. Where every person is secure in his person and property, the nation, or state, is secure. Where every individual thrives, there will be a thriving state or nation. Where every individual should do justice, there justice would reign in the state or nation. Where every individual should be free, there would be a free state or nation.

Nothing is more common than the remark that "no two persons are alike," that "circumstances alter cases," that "we must agree to disagree," etc., and yet we are constantly forming institutions that require us to be alike, which make no allowance for individuality of persons or circumstances, and which render it necessary for us to agree, and leave us no liberty to differ from each other, nor to modify our conduct according to circumstances.

"To every thing there is a season, and a time to every purpose under heaven: A time to be born and a time to die; a time to plant and a time to pluck up what is planted; a time to kill and a time to heal; a time to break down and a time to build up; a time to weep and a time to laugh; a time to mourn and a time to dance; a time to embrace and a time to refrain from embracing; a time to get and a time to lose; a time to keep and a time to cast away; a time to rend and a time to sew; a time to keep silence and a time to speak; a time to love and a time to hate; a time a time of war and a time of peace."[4]

Such is the individuality of times.

There is an individuality of countenance, stature, gait, voice, which characterize every one, and each of these peculiarities is inseparable from the person; he has no power to divest himself of them—they constitute parts of his physical individuality; and were it not so, the most inconceivable confusion would derange all our social intercourse. Every one would be liable to the same name. One man would be mistaken for another. Our relations and friends would be strangers to us. No security of persons, of possessions; no justice between men; no distinction between friends or foes. All would be mere guess-work or chance, and universal confusion would reign triumphant. How much, then, are we indebted to individuality, even in these four particulars of physical conformation. The fact that these peculiarities of each are inseparable from each—not to be conquered—not to be divided or separated from each, is apparently the only part of social order that man, in his mad career of "policy" and expediency, has not overthrown or smothered. I have spoken of only four of the peculiarities of human character, and if these confer such benefits upon society, what may we not expect on a full development of all the capacities, physical, mental, and moral, with which every one is, to a greater or less extent, invested, but no two alike. And if the little intellectual development now extant results in an individuality that makes men and women restive and ungovernable under the existing institutions, what are we to expect from the future? Not only are no two minds alike now, but no one remains the same from one hour to another. Old impressions are becoming obliterated, new ones being made—new combinations of old thoughts constantly being formed, and old combinations exploded. The surrounding atmosphere, the contact of various persons and circumstances all contribute to make us more the mirrors of passing things than the possessors of any fixed character, and we have no power to be otherwise; therefore, to require us to be stationary blocks, all of one size, hewn out by laws, institutions, or customs, is a monstrous piece of injustice, and it is impossible in the very nature of things.

To what purpose, O legislators, do ye say "thou shalt not steal"? To what ends are all your horrid inventions of punishment? Stealing still goes on, and ye only repeat "thou shalt not steal," and still punish, even though you said at first that punishment was a remedy! Ye have no remedy, but only inflict tenfold more evils by your abortive attempts to overcome effects without consulting causes, or opening your eyes and ears to explanations. Our security against fire and gunpowder is in our knowledge of their natures and their incalculable modes of action, which knowledge raises us above their dangers, and renders them useful and comparatively harmless. Our remedies and securities against social evils are in our knowledge of our own natures, our inevitable modes of action, our true positions with regard to each other, and to our institutions. Even man-made laws, rules, precepts, dogmas, counsel, advice, may all be rendered comparatively harmless and useful by not allowing them to rise above the higher law, the highest utility, the sovereignty of the individual. We are liable to be deceived and disappointed in ourselves as well as others, until we are aware of this liability, which raises us above the danger; and we are subject, not only to constant changes, but to actions and temporary reactions, over which at the time we have no control whatever. The intrinsic philosophy of reactions may be beyond our reach, but the facts are notorious, that the reaction of fatigue of mind or body is rest; that the reaction of intense friendship is intense enmity; that the reaction of intense love is indifference, a temporary or intense hatred; the reaction of great benevolence is temporary malevolence; the reaction of philanthropy is misanthropy; the reaction of great hope or expectations is temporary or great despair; the reaction of great popularity is sudden unpopularity; and it is known that the greatest benefactors of the race, from high popularity, have often suddenly fallen victims to an unaccountable public hatred.

It is also notorious, that all of us are liable to strange inconsistencies of character, and that no effort on our part can prevent it; that the most reasonable are sometimes very unreasonable; the most accurate observers are very often under mistake; the most consistent are sometimes inconsistent; the most wise are sometimes foolish; the most rational sometimes insane. How unreasonable, then, how inconsistent, how unwise, how absurd, to promise for ourselves, or to demand of others, always to be reasonable, correct, consistent, and wise under all these changes, and actions, and reactions, and inconsistencies of character, over which at the time we have no control whatever. How difficult to regulate ourselves. How impossible to govern others.

The Proper, Legitimate, Just Reward of Labor

It is now evident to all eyes, that labor does not obtain its legitimate reward; but on the contrary, that those who work the hardest fare the worst. The most elegant and costly houses, coaches, clothing, food, and luxuries of all kinds are in the hands of those who never made any of them, nor ever did any useful thing for themselves or for society; while those who made all, and maintained themselves at the same time, are shivering in miserable homes, or pining in prisons or poorhouses, or starving in the streets.

Machinery has thrown workmen out of their tenth-paid employment, and this machinery is also owned by those who never made it, nor gave any equivalent in their own labor for it. These starving workers have no resource but upon the soil; but they find that this is also under the control of those who never made it, nor ever did any thing as an equivalent for it. At this point of starvation, we must have remedy, or confusion.

Society must attend to the rights of labor, and settle, once for all, the great problem of its just reward. This appears to demand a discrimination, a disconnection, a disunion between cost and value.

If a traveler, on a hot day, stop at a farm-house, and ask for a drink of water, he generally gets it without any thought of price. Why? Because it costs nothing, or its cost is immaterial. If the traveler was so thirsty that he would give a dollar for the water, rather than not have it, this would be the value of the water to him; and if the farmer were to charge this price, he would be acting upon the principle that the price of a thing should be what it will bring, which is the motto and spirit of all the principal commerce of the world; and if he were to stop up all the neighboring springs, and cut off all supplies of water from other sources, and compel travelers to depend solely on him for water, and then should charge them a hundred dollars for a drink, he would be acting precisely upon the principle upon which all the business of the world has been conducted from time immemorial. It is pricing a thing according to what it will bring, or according to its value to the receiver, instead of its cost to the producer. For an illustration in the mercantile line, consult any report of "prices current," or "state of the markets." The following is a sample, copied from a paper, the nearest at hand:

> No new arrivals of flour—demand increasing, prices rose since yesterday, at twelve o'clock, 25 cts. per barrel. No change in coffee since our last. Sugar raised on Thursday, half ct. per pound, in consequence of a report received of short crops; but later arrivals contradicted the report, and prices fell again. Molasses, in demand, and holders not anxious to sell. Pork, little in market and prices rising. Bacon, plenty and dull, fell since our last, from 15 to 13 cents. Cotton, all in few hands, bought up on speculation.

It will here be seen, that prices are raised in consequence of increased want, and are lowered with its decrease. The most successful speculator is he who can create the most want in the community, and extort the most from it. This is civilized cannibalism.

The value of a loaf of bread to a starving man, is equivalent to the value of his life, and if the price of a thing should be what it will bring, then one might properly demand of a starving man his whole future life in servitude as the price of the loaf. But any one who should make such a demand would be looked upon as insane, a cannibal, and one simultaneous voice would denounce the outrageous injustice, and cry aloud for retribution. If the producers and venders of the bread had bestowed one hour's labor upon its production and in passing it to the starving man, then some other articles which cost its producer and vender an hour's equivalent labor, would be a natural and just compensation for the loaf. I have placed emphasis on the idea of equivalent labor, because it appears we must discriminate between different kinds of labor, some being more disagreeable, more repugnant, requiring a more costly draft upon our ease or health than others. The idea of cost extends to and embraces this difference, the most repugnant labor considered the most costly. The idea of cost is also extended to all contingency expenses in production or vending.

A watch has a cost and a value. The cost consists of the amount of labor bestowed on the mineral or natural wealth, in converting it into metal, the labor bestowed by the workmen in constructing the watch, the wear of tools, the rent, firewood, insurance, taxes, clerkship and various other contingent expenses of its manufacturer, together with the labor expended in its transmission from him to its vender; and the labor and contingent expenses of the vender in passing it to the one who uses it. In some of these departments the labor is more disagreeable, or more deleterious to health than in others, but all these items, or more, constitute the costs of the watch. The value of a well-made watch depends upon the natural qualities of the metals or minerals employed, upon the natural qualities or principles of its mechanism, upon the uses to which it is applied, and upon the fancy or wants of the purchaser. It would be different with every different watch, with every purchaser, and would change every day in the hands of the same purchaser, and with every different use to which he applied it.

Now, among this multitude of values, which one should be selected to set a price upon? Or, should the price be made to vary and fluctuate according to these fluctuating values, and never be completely sold, but only from hour to hour? Common sense answers "neither," but, that these values, like those of sunshine and air, are of right the equal property of all; no one having a right to set any price whatever upon them. Cost, then, is the only rational ground of price, even in the most complicated transactions.

One may inform another that his house is on fire. The information may be of great value to him and his family, but as it costs nothing, there is no ground of price. Conversation, and all other intercourse of mind with mind, by which each may be infinitely benefited, may prove of inconceivable value to all; where the cost is nothing, or too trifling to notice, it constitutes what is here designated as purely intellectual commerce.

The performance of a piece of music for the gratification of oneself and others, in which the performer feels pleasure but no pain, and which is attended by no contingent cost, may be said to cost nothing; there is, therefore, no ground of price. It may, however, be of great value to all within hearing.

The intercourse of feelings, which is not addressed to the intellect, and has no pecuniary feature, is here distinguished as our moral commerce.

A word of sympathy to the distressed may be of great value to them; and to make this value the ground and limit of a price, would be but to follow out the principle that a thing should bring its value. Mercenary as we are, even now, this is no where done except by the priesthood.

A man has a lawsuit pending, upon which hangs his property, his security, his personal liberty, or his life. The lawyer who undertakes his case may ask ten twenty, fifty, five hundred, or five thousand dollars, for a few hours of attendance or labor in the case. This charge would be based chiefly on the value of his services to his client. Now, there is nothing in this statement that sounds wrong, but it is because our ears are familiarized with wrong. The cost to the lawyer might be, say, twenty hours' labor, and allowing a portion of his apprenticeship, twenty-one hours in all, with all contingent expenses, would constitute a legitimate, a just ground of price. The laborer, when he comes to dig the lawyer's cellar, never thinks of setting a price upon its future value to the owner; he only considers how long it will take him, how hard the ground, what will be the weather to which he will be exposed, what will be the wear and tear of teams, tools, clothes, etc.;

and in all these items, he considers nothing but the different items' cost to himself.

The doctor demands of the wood-cutter the proceeds of five, ten, or twenty days' labor for a visit of an hour, and asks, in excuse, if the sick man would not prefer this rather than continuous disease or death. This, again, is basing price on an assumed value of his attendance instead of its cost. It is common to plead the difference of talents required: without waiting to prove this idea false, it is, perhaps, sufficient to show that the talents required, either in cutting wood, or in cutting off a leg or an arm, so far as they cost the possessor, are a legitimate ground of estimate and price; but talents which cost nothing, are natural wealth, and, like the water, land, and sunshine, should be accessible to all without price.

If a priest is required to get a soul out of purgatory, he sets his price according to the value which the relatives set upon his prayers, instead of their cost to the priest. The same amount of labor equally disagreeable, with equal wear and tear, performed by his customers, would be a just remuneration.

All patents give to the inventor or discoverer the power to command a price based upon the value of the thing patented; instead of which, his legitimate compensation would be an equivalent for the cost of the physical and mental labor, added to that of his materials, and the contingent expenses of experiments.

A speculator buys a piece of land of government, for $1.25 per acre, and holds it till surrounding improvements, made by others, increase its value, and it is then sold accordingly, for five, ten, twenty, a hundred, or ten thousand dollars per acre. From this operation of civilized cannibalism whole families live from generation to generation, in idleness and luxury, upon the surrounding population, who must have the land at any price. Instead of this, the prime cost of land, the taxes, and other contingent expenses of surveying, etc., added to the labor of making contracts, would constitute the equitable price of land purchased for sale.

If A purchases a lot for his own use, and B wants it more than A, then A may properly consider what his labor upon it has cost him, and what would compensate him for the inconvenience of parting with it; but this is a very different thing from purchasing it on purpose to part with it, which costs A no inconvenience. We here discriminate between these two cases, but in neither do we go beyond cost as the limit of price.

A loans to B ten thousand dollars at six percent interest, for one year, and at the end of that year receives back the whole amount loaned and six hundred dollars more. Why? Because it was of that value to the borrower. For the same reason, why not demand of the starving man ten thousand dollars for a loaf of bread because it saves his life? The legitimate, the equitable compensation for the loan of money, is the cost of labor in lending it and receiving it back again.

Rents of land, buildings, etc., especially in cities, are based chiefly on their value to the occupants, and this depends on the degree of want or distress felt by the landless and houseless: the greater the distress, the higher the value and the price. The equitable rent of either would be the wear, insurance, etc., and the labor of making contracts and receiving the rents, all of which are different items of cost.

The products of machinery are now sold for what they will bring, and therefore its advantages go exclusively into the pockets of its owners. If these products were priced at the cost of the machinery, its wear, attendance, etc., then capitalists would not be interested in its introduction any more than those who attended it; they would not be interested in reducing the wages of its attendants.

One of the most common, most disgusting features of this iniquitous spirit of the present pecuniary commerce, is seen and felt by every one, in all the operations of buying and selling. The cheating, higgling, huckstering, and falsehoods, so degrading to both purchaser and vender, and the injustice done to one party or the other, in almost every transaction in trade, all originate in the chaotic union of cost, value, and the reward of labor of the vender all into one price. A store-keeper selling a needle, cannot get paid for his labor within the price of the needle; to do this he must disconnect the two, and make the needle one item of his charge, and his labor another. If he sell the needle for its prime cost, and its portion of contingent expenses, and charge an equal amount of labor for that which he bestows in purchasing and vending, he is equitably remunerated for his labor, and his customer's equal right is not invaded. If he add three cents upon each yard of calico, as his compensation, his customers may take one yard, and he does not get equivalent for his labor. If the customer take thirty yards, he becomes overpaid, and his customer is wronged. Disconnection of the two elements of price, and making cost the limit of each, works equitably for both parties in all cases, and at once puts an end to the disgusting and degrading feature of our pecuniary commerce.

Security of Person and Property

Theorists have told us that laws and governments are made for the security of person and property; but it must be evident to most minds, that they never have, never will accomplish this professed object; although they have had the world at their control for thousands of years, they have brought it to a worse condition than that in which they found it, in spite of immense improvements in mechanism, division of labor, and other elements of civilization to aid them. On the contrary, under the plausible pretext of securing person and property, they have spread wholesale destruction, famine, and wretchedness in every frightful form over all parts of the earth, where peace and security might otherwise have prevailed. They have shed more blood, committed more murders, tortures, and other frightful crimes in the struggles against each other for the privilege of governing, than society ever would or could have suffered in the total absence of all governments whatever. It is impossible for any one who can read the history of governments, and the operations of laws, to feel secure in person and property under any form of government or any code of laws whatever. They invade the private household, they impertinently meddle with, and in their blind and besotted wantonness, presume to regulate the most sacred individual feelings. No feelings of security, no happiness can exist under such circumstances. They set up rules or laws to which they require conformity, while conformity is impossible, and while neither rulers nor ruled can tell how the laws will be interpreted or administered. Under such circumstances, no security for the governed can exist.

A citizen may be suddenly hurried away from his home, shut up in a horrid prison, charged with a crime of which he is totally innocent; he may die in prison or on the gallows, and his family may die of mortification and broken hearts. No security can exist where this can happen; yet, all these are operations of laws and governments, which are professedly instituted for "the security of person and property."

A young girl is knocked down and violated in the country where law "secures person and property." She applies to law for redress, and is put in prison and kept there for six months as a witness, to appear against her violator, who is running at large, forfeits his bonds, and disappears before his victim is restored to liberty.

A woman is abandoned by a worthless husband, and reduced to the necessity of permitting a villian to board with her a year without remuneration. He has consumed her last loaf; she appeals to the law for redress; the villian brings the drunken husband to court. The law (for the protection of person and property) forbids the woman to apply for redress while her husband is alive (though drunk). Her appeal is suppressed—she is nonsuited, and put in prison to pay the cost of her protection.

Governments involve the citizen in national and state responsibilities from which he would choose to be exempt. They compel him to desert his family, and risk or lay down his life in wars in which he feels no wish to engage. Great crimes are committed by the government of one nation against another, to gratify the ambition or lust of rulers; the people of both nations are thus set to destroy the persons and property of each other, and would be martyred as traitors if they refused.

Some of our best citizens are torn from their families and friends and thrust into loathsome prisons, for not believing in a point of religion prescribed by law; another, for working in the field on a day set aside by the law for idleness. One case of this kind is enough to show that no security exists for the governed. But the greatest chance for it is with those who can get possession of the governing power; hence arises the universal scramble for the possession of power, as the preferable of the two conditions. These struggles and intrigues for power increase a thousandfold the insecurity of all parties. Rulers kill the members of society as punishment for offenses, instead of tracing these offenses to their own operations; and their pernicious example and prescriptions becoming authority for the uniformed, prompt them to kill their neighbors for an offense—to become their brother's judge or their neighbor's keeper; and crimination and recrimination, and slander, wrangling, discord, and murder are the natural fruits of these laws "for the security of person and property."

If B has done what the law forbids (although it be the preservation of a fellow creature), he is insecure while there are witnesses who may appear against him; and all these are insecure as long as B feels insecure. A large portion of all the murders since the invention of laws have been perpetrated to silence witnesses.

Again, words are the tenure by which every thing is held by law, and words are subject to different interpretations, according to the views, wills, or interests of the judges, lawyers, juries, and other functionaries appointed to execute these laws. In this uncertainty of interpretation lies the great fundamental element of insecurity which is inseparable from any system of laws, any constitution, articles of compact, and every thing of this description. No language is fit for any such purposes that admits of more than one individual interpretation, and none can be made to possess this necessary individuality; therefore no language is fit for the basis of positive institutions. To possess the interpreting power of verbal institutions, is to possess unlimited power.

It is not generally known, or practically admitted, that each individual is liable, and, therefore, has a right, to interpret language according to his peculiar individuality. A creed, a constitution, laws, articles of association, are all liable to as many different interpretations as there are parties to it; each one reads it through his own mental spectacles, and that which is blue to one is yellow to another, and green to a third; although all give their assent to the words, each one gives assent to his peculiar interpretation of them, which is only known to himself, so that the difference between them can be made to appear only in action; which, as soon as it commences, explodes the discordant elements in every direction, always disappointing the expectations of all who had calculated on uniformity or conformity. Every attempt at amendment only produces new disappointments, and increases the necessity for other amendments and additions without end, all to end in disappointment and the greater insecurity of everyone engaged in or trusting to them. To be harmonious and successful we must begin anew; we must disconnect, disunite ourselves from all institutions or rise above them.

But how, you ask, can this be, where each is a member of the body politic—where obedience to some law or other is indispensable to the working of the political machine? If every one was the law unto himself, all would be perfect anarchy and confusion. No doubt of this. The error lies further back than you have contemplated. We should be no such thing as a body politic. Each man and woman must be an individual, no member of any body but that of the human family. Blackstone says, "It is the wants and the fears of individuals which make them come together,"[5] and form society.

In other words, it is for interchange of mutual assistance, and for security of person or property, that society is originally formed. Now, if neither of these objects has ever been attained in society, we have no reason for keeping up a body politic. With regard to economy in the supply of our wants, this will be treated of in its proper place. With regard to security, we see that in the wide range of the world's bloody history, there is not any one horrid feature so frightful, so appalling as the recklessness, the cold-blooded indifference with which laws and governments have sacrificed person or property in their wanton, their criminal, or ignorant pursuit of some blind passion or unsubstantial phantom of the imagination. We have not the space, nor is it necessary, to enter into details. Let the reader refer to any page of history; let him remember that laws and governments are professedly instituted for the security of person and property, and let him consider each page an illustration of their success. Then he will be able to appreciate a proposal to secure them by some other means.

The security of person and property requires exemption from the fear of encroachments from any quarter. And, although governments have always been the greatest depredators upon the rights of persons and property, yet, there are other sources of insecurity which call for remedy, and which demand the operation of the cost principle. It will be seen, upon reflection, that value being iniquitously made the basis of price produces all the ruinous fluctuations in trade, the uncertainty of business, the uncertainty of the reward of industry, and the inadequacy of its reward. It produces poverty and the fear of poverty, avarice, and the all-absorbing pursuit of property, without regard for the rights or sympathy for the sufferings of others, and trains us, in the absence of all knowledge or rule of right, mutually to encroach upon and invade each other.

The Greatest Practicable Amount of Liberty to Each Individual

What is liberty? Who will allow me to define it for him, and agree beforehand to square his life by my definition? Who does not wish to see it first, and sit in judgment on it, and decide for himself as to its propriety? And who does not see that is his own interpretation of the word that he adopts? And who will agree to square his whole life by any rule which, though good at present, may not prove applicable in all cases? Who does not wish to preserve his liberty to act according to the peculiarities of future cases, and to sit in judgment on the merits of each, and to change or vary from time to time with new developments and increasing knowledge?

You and I may associate together as the best of friends, as long as our interests are not too closely connected; but let me become responsible for your debts, or let me, by joining a society of which you are a member, become responsible for your sentiments, and the discordant effects of too close connection will immediately appear. If my interest is united with yours, and we differ at any point in its management, as this difference is inevitable, one must yield, the other must decide, or we must leave the decision to a third party. This third party is government, and thus, in united interests, government originates. The more business there is thus committed to governmental management, the more must each of the governed surrender his liberty or control over his own, and the greater must be the amount of power delegated to the government. When this becomes unlimited or indefinite, the government is absolute, and the liberty and security of the governed are annihilated; when limited or definite, some liberty remains to the governed. Experience has proved, that power cannot be delegated to rulers of states and nations, in sufficient quantities for the management of business, without its becoming an indefinite quantity, and in this indefiniteness have mankind been cheated out of their legitimate liberty.

Let twenty persons combine their means to build a bridge, each contributing twenty dollars. At the first meeting for business it is found that the business of such combinations can be conducted only by electing some one individual deciding and acting power, before any practical steps can be taken. Here each subscriber must trust his twenty dollars to the management of some one, yet as the sum is definite and not serious, its loss may not disturb his security, and he prefers to risk it for the prospective advantages of himself and his neighborhood. In entering his twenty dollars into this combination he submits to the control of others, but he submits nothing more; and if he is aware beforehand that the business of all combinations must be conducted by delegated power, and if he is not compelled to submit to any condition not contemplated beforehand, and if he can withdraw his investment at pleasure, then there is no violation of his natural liberty or sovereignty over his own. Or, if he chooses to make a permanent investment and lay down all future control over it, for the sake of prospective advantage, it is a surrender of so much of his property (not his liberty) to the control of others. But, it being a definite quantity and the risks and conditions all being made known and voluntarily consented to beforehand, the consequences may not be serious to him. And although he may discover, in the course of the business, that the principle is wrong, yet he may derive ultimate advantage, under some circumstances, from so much combination— some may be willing to invest more and others less. If each one is the supreme judge at all times of the individual case in hand, and is free to act from his own estimate of the advantages to be derived to himself or others, as in the above instance, then the natural liberty of the individual is not invaded. It is when the decision or will of others is made the rule of action, contrary to his views or inclination, that his legitimate liberty is violated.

But now let us contemplate another degree of combination: combination as the basis for society, involving all the great interests of man: his liberty, his person, his mind, his time, his labor, his food, the soil he rests upon, his responsibilities to an indefinite extent, his security, the education and destinies of his children, the indefinite interests of his race. In such combinations, whether political or social, the different members can never be found always possessing the same views and feelings on all these subjects. Not even two persons can perform a piece of music in order, unless one of them commences or leads individually, or unless both agree to be governed by some third movement, which is an individuality. The same is true with regard to any combined movement. In political and social combination, men have sought to mitigate the horrid abuses of despotism by diffusing the delegated power, but they have always purchased the relief at the expense of confusion. The experience of all the world has shown, that the business of such combinations cannot be conducted by the whole of its members, but that one or a few must be set apart to lead and manage the business of the combination. To these, power must be delegated just in proportion to the amount of business committed to their charge. These constitute the government of the combination, and to this government all must yield their individual sovereignty, or the combination cannot move one step. If their persons, their responsibilities, and all their interests are involved in the combination, as in communities of common property, all these must be entirely under the control of the government, whose judgment or will is the rule for all the governed. The natural liberty or sovereignty of every member is entirely annihilated, and the government is as strong and absolute as government can be made, while the members are rendered as weak and dependent on the governing few as they can be rendered, and consequently, their liberty and security are reduced to the lowest practicable degree. If only half of the interests of the individual are invested in the combination, then only half the quantity of government is required, and only half of the natural liberty of the members need be surrendered; but as this definite quantity cannot be measured and set apart from the other half, and as government once erected, either through the indefiniteness of language in which the power is delegated or by other means, will steal the other half, there is no security, no liberty for mankind, but through the abandonment of combination as the basis of society.

When one's person, his labor, his responsibilities, the soil he rests on, his food, his property, and all his interests are so disconnected, disunited from others, that he can control or dispose of these at all times, according to his own views and feelings, without controlling or disturbing others; and when his premises are sacred to himself, and his person is not approached, nor his time and attention taken up against his inclination, then the individual may be said to be practically sovereign of himself and all that constitutes or pertains to his individuality.

Economy in the Production and Uses of Wealth

The first and greatest source of economy, the richest mine of wealth ever worked by man, is the division and exchange of labor. Where a man is so isolated from society as to be deprived of the advantages of the division and exchange of labor, and has to supply all his own wants, like Robinson Crusoe, there is nothing to distinguish him from the savage. It is only in proportion as he can apply himself to one or a few pursuits, and exchange his products for the supply of all his wants, that he begins to emerge from the crudest state of existence, to surround himself with conveniences and luxuries, and to reduce the burthen of his own labor.

Division and exchange are naturally carried to a greater extent in cities than in the open country. This, probably, in part explains the enigma of so many being sustained luxuriously in cities apparently almost without labor, while men in the country are always hard at work, but rarely have comfortable things around them. Being so remote from division and exchange, they are obliged to supply many of their own wants without the ordinary means of doing it: without tools, without instruction, without practice, they must mend a gate, repair their harness, make their own shoes, and expend, perhaps, three times the labor that a workman would require in the same operations, and it is badly done at last. They must also have as many kinds of tools as the different operations demand, which it requires care to preserve and keep in order, and between all their time and capital are frittered away to little purpose. Five hundred men thus scattered too remote from each other, or from other causes being unable to procure the advantages of decision and exchange, must have five hundred pairs of bench planes and other tools for working wood; five hundred sets of shoe-making tools; five hundred places and fixtures for working iron; and five hundred equipments in every other branch of business in which they are obliged to dabble. Now, if these five hundred men or families were within reach of each other, and each one were to apply himself to one business, and all should exchange with each other, each one would require only one set of tools, and one trade, instead of thirty or forty. His work would be well done instead of ill done. And if exchanges were equal, the wants of each would be well supplied, at perhaps the cost of one fourth the labor that is now required to supply one half their wants in an inferior manner.

If such are the enormous advantages of division and exchange, how can we account for the fact that so large portions of all countries are deprived, and that even in cities division is not carried out, excepting in a very few branches of manufacture? I attribute this barbarous condition of the economies chiefly to two causes. First, the practice of making value the standard of price—asking for a thing just what it will bring—balances the motives of the purchaser, so that a man wanting a pair of shoes, being asked as much as he would give for them, forms the habit of going without whenever he can, or of making them himself even at a disadvantage. Whereas, on the contrary, if he could always get them for that amount of his own labor which they cost the expert workman, he could have no motive for doing without them, nor to spend three times as much labor in making them himself. The same cause and the same reasons ramify into all our supplies.

In a society where even the first element of order had made its way into the intellects of men, there would be some point at which all would continually make known their wants, as far as they could anticipate them, and put them in a position to be supplied. All who wanted employment would know where to look for it, and the supply would be adapted to the demand. The adaptation of the supply to the demand, although it is continually governing the bodies of men, seems never to have made its way into their intellects, or they would have made it the governing principle of their arrangements. It is this which prompts almost every action of life, not only of men, but other animals: all animated nature. All man's pursuits originate in his effort to supply some of his wants, either physical, or mental, or moral. Even our intellectual commerce is unconsciously governed by this great principle, whenever it is harmonious and beneficial, and it is discordant and depreciating where it is not so regulated. An answer to a question is but a supply to a demand. Advice, when wanted, is acceptable, but never otherwise. Commands are never in this order, and produce nothing but disorder. The sovereignty of the individual must correct this.

Almost every movement of every animal is from nature's promptings toward the supply of some of its wants. Nay, more, if it is wounded, there is naturally an action toward the formation of new skin, or new parts to supply the deficiency created. The same principle runs even into the vegetable kingdom. The bark of a tree being torn away, nature goes to work to the demand thus produced with new bark, which otherwise never would have occupied that place. Even a pumkin-vine having run too far to draw nourishment from its original starting point, strikes down new roots, to draw a supply of nutrients necessary to its progress. Had "the combined wisdom" of any country equaled that of a pumkin-vine, that country would have had some arrangement for adapting the supply to the demand. But this will never be, while speculations are made by throwing the demand and supply out of their natural proportions, or while value, instead of cost, is made the limit of price. This false principle of price, in addition to all its direct iniquity, stagnates exchanges, interrupts or stops supplies, and involves every thing in uncertainty and confusion, discourages arrangements and order, and prevents division and exchange.

Another great obstacle to the development of this branch of economy, is the uncertainty, the insecurity of every business. Men dare not make investments for carrying on business to the best advantage while the markets for their products are unsteady—where prices "rise at eight o'clock" and "fall at twelve." If prices were equitably adjusted by the cost principle, we should know, from year to year, from age to age very nearly, the prices of every thing. All labor being equally rewarded according to its cost, there would be no destructive competition. Markets would be steady. Then we might subdivide the different parts of manufactures to any extent that the demand would justify at any time.

Another great obstacle to extensive division of labor and rapid and easy exchanges seems to be the want of the means of effecting exchanges. We cannot carry our property about us for the purpose of exchanging. If we could do this, and give one thing for another at once, and thus settle every transaction, such a thing as money, or a circulating medium, never would have been known; but, as we cannot carry flour, shoes, carpentering, brick-work, store-keeping, etc., about us to exchange for what we want, we require something which represents these, which representative we can always carry with us. This representative of property should be our circulating medium. Theorists have said that money was this circulating medium, but it is not. A dollar represents nothing whatever but itself; nor can it be made to. At no time is it any demand on any one for any quantity of property or labor whatever. At one time a dollar will procure two bushels of potatoes, at another time three, at another time four, and different quantities for different persons at the same time. It has no definite value at any time, nor if it had would its value qualify it for a circulating medium. On the contrary, its value and its cost being inseparably united with its use as a representative, disqualifies all money for acting the part of a circulating medium. It should have but one quality, one definite purpose: that of standing in the place of the thing represented, as a miniature represents a person.

Money represents robbery, banking, gambling, swindling, counterfeiting, etc., as much as much as it represents property; it has a value that varies with every individual that uses it, and changes as often as it is used. A picture that would represent at one time a man, at another a monkey, and then a gourd, would be just as legitimate and fit for a portrait, as common money is for a circulating medium.

We want a circulating medium that is a definite representative of a definite quantity of property and nothing but a representative, so that when we cannot make direct equivalent exchanges of property, we can supply its deficiency with its definite representative, which will stand in its place. And this should not have any reference to the value of property, but only its cost, so that if I get a bushel of wheat of you, I give you the representative of shoe-making, with which you should be able to obtain from the shoemaker as much labor as you bestowed on the wheat—cost for cost in equivalent quantities. And to effect these exchanges with facility, each one must always have plenty of this representative on hand, or be able to make it on the occasion, and so adapt the supply of the circulating medium to the demand for it. Where there is no circulating medium, there cannot be much exchange or division. On the other hand, where every one has a plenty of the circulating medium always at hand, exchanges and divisions of labor would not be limited for want of money. A note given by each individual for his own labor, estimated by its cost, is perfectly legitimate and competent for all the purposes of a circulating medium. It is based upon the bone and muscle, the manual powers, the talents and resources, the property and property-producing powers of the whole people: the soundest of all foundations. The only objection to it is, that it would immediately abolish all the great money transactions of the world—all stock-jobbing, money corporations, and money movements; all systems of finance, all systems of national policy and commercial corruption; all distinctions of rich and poor— and compel every one to live and enjoy at his own cost.

Everything being bought and sold for the greatest profit the holder can get, it becomes his interest to purchase every thing as cheap as possible; the cheaper he purchases the more profit he makes. This is the origin of the present horrid system of grinding and destructive competition among producers, who are thus prompted to under-work each other. Thus too it is that there is scarcely any article of food, clothing, tools, or medicines that is fit for use; we are always purchasing to throw away, to be cheated out of our money and time, and disappointed in our supplies. Responsibility rests nowhere. The vender does not make them, but imports them from those beyond the reach of responsibility. Why is every thing imported, even shoes, tools, woolen and cotton cloths? For profit.

Were cost made the limit of price, the vender of goods would have no particular motive to purchase them at the very lowest prices that he could grind out from manufacturers; and they would, therefore, have no motive to under-work and destroy each other. There would be no more of each than enough to supply the demand, no motive to import what could be made with equal advantage at home; and the manufacturer would be obliged to assume the individual responsibility of his work, because where profit-making did not stand in the way, the merchant would not otherwise purchase of him. And where land is bought and sold at cost, every man of business would own the premises where the work was done, and could not easily get away from the character of it. This must be kept good, or another would immediately take his place. Here, then, in the cost principle, is the means of rendering competition not only harmless, but a great regulating and adjusting power. Under its mighty influence should we not only escape national ruin from excessive importation of worthless articles, but should have good ones always insured, by their manufacturers being within reach of tangible responsibility. The scramble for unlimited profits in trade being annihilated by equitable exchanges between nations, the imports and exports would be naturally self-regulating and limited to such as were mutually beneficial. Each would have a co-operating interest in the prosperity of the other. When this takes place, the armies and navies now employed in consuming and destroying will be compelled to turn to producing, at least whatever they consume, and thus take off another crushing load from downtrodden labor.

Wars are, probably, the greatest of all destroyers of property, and they originate chiefly in two roots. First, for direct or indirect plunder; secondly, for privileges of governing. Direct plunder will cease when men can create property with less trouble than they can invade their fellow-creature's. Indirect plunder will cease with making cost the limit of price, thus cutting off all profits of trade. The privileges of governing will cease when men take all their business out of national or other combinations, manage it individually, deal equitably with each other, and leave no governing to be done.

Natural and Intellectual Wealth

Metals in the earth are natural wealth, and the cost principle would pass them to consumers at the cost of labor in digging, preparing, and delivering them.

The inventor of a machine may put wheels, weights, and levers together in a certain relation to each other, which may produce great and valuable results to the public, but this value is no measure for its compensation. The cost to him of putting them together is his legitimate ground of price. The qualities of a circle, the power of a lever, and the gravitating tendency of a weight are natural wealth, and are rightly the property of all.

Likewise, a teacher of music may communicate the principles of composition, which may be of great value to the receiver, but this value is derived chiefly from the inherent qualities and relations of sounds to each other, nor has man any right to make them the ground of price in communicating them to others. If a teacher of music be paid for his labor in an equivalent only, then the natural wealth inherent in musical elements, becomes accessible to all without price. The same may be said of all sciences, arts, trades, mysteries, and all other subjects of our commerce, whether pecuniary, intellectual, or moral. One may devote his time and labor upon an intellectual production, but who can measure its value? This depends chiefly upon the new truths developed or communicated. It is the cost only that can be equitably made the ground of price, and when this is refunded by an equal amount of labor, equally repugnant or disagreeable, and equally costly in its contingencies, the writer is legitimately compensated. The rest is natural wealth.

Part III: The Application

Elements of New Society

The first step to be taken by any number of persons in these practical movements appears to be that each individual or head of a family should consider his or her present wants, and what he can give in exchange, with a view to have them recorded in a book kept for that purpose. As soon as a movement is made by any one to this effect, a book will be wanted as a record of this report of wants and supplies. At this point, when this is evidently wanted enough to justify it in the estimation of any individual, he or she can furnish such a book upon his or her individual responsibility. If the cost of this is sufficient to justify a demand for remuneration, the keeper of this book can make this demand, according to the labor bestowed in each case, or otherwise, as he or she shall decide, the voice of the majority having nothing to do with it.

We will now suppose that the wants of twenty individuals are recorded in one column of a book, and what they can supply in another column; and in another the price per hour which each demands for his or her labor. These become the fundamental data for operations.

Every one wishing to take some part in practical operations now has before him, in this report of wants, the business to be done. It will immediately be seen that land is indispensable, and must be had before any other step can be taken to advantage. Some one seeing this want, after consulting the wishes or demands of the co-operators, proceeds on his own estimate of this demand, at his own risk, and at his own cost, to purchase or otherwise procure land to commence upon, lays it out in lots to suit the demand, and sells them to the co-operators at the ultimate cost (including contingent expenses of money and labor in buying and selling). The difference in the price of a house lot thus bought and sold, compared with its price when sold for its value, will be found sufficient to make the difference between every one having a home upon the earth, instead of one half of men and women being homeless.

We will now suppose the lots purchased and paid for by each one who is to occupy them. They will want to consult continually together, in order to co-operate with each other's movements. This will require a place for meetings. As soon as this want is apparent, then is the time for some one to estimate this want and take it on himself to provide a room, and see himself remunerated according to cost, which cannot fail to be satisfactory to all in proportion as they are convinced that cost is the limit of his demands, which he can always prove by keeping an account of expenses and receipts, open at all times to the most public inspection.

At this public room, provided each one is properly preserved from the ordinary fetters of organization, all can confer with each other relative to their intended movements. If one has a suggestion to make to the whole body, he can find listeners in proportion to the interest that each one feels, and a decent respect to the right of every one to listen if he chooses, will prevent disturbances from the indifferent, just in proportion as the right of sovereignty in each individual is made a familiar element of surrounding opinion.

When business commences, the estimates of prices must commence, and the circulating medium will be wanted. For instance, if the keeper of the room for meetings has expended a hundred hours of his labor in keeping it in order, etc., and if there are twenty who have regularly or substantially received the benefits of it, then five hours' equivalent labor is due from each.

This calls for the circulating medium, and he may receive from the carpenter, the blacksmith, the shoemaker, the tailoress, the washer-woman, etc., their labor notes, promising a certain number of hours of their definite kinds of labor. The keeper of the room is now equipped with a circulating medium with which he can procure the services of any of the persons at a price which is agreed and settled on beforehand, which will obviate all disturbance in relation to prices. He holds a currency whose product to him will not be less at the report of scarcity. From year to year, he can get a certain definite quantity of labor for the labor he performed, which cannot be said, nor made to be true, with regard to any money the world has ever known.

An extraordinary feature presents itself at this stage of the operations of equitable commerce. When the washerwoman comes to set her price according to the cost or hardness of the labor compared with others, it is found that its price exceeds that of the ordinary labor of men! Of course, the washerwoman must have more per hour than the vender of house-lots or the inventor of pills. We must admit the claims of the hardest labor to the highest reward.

The larger the purchases of lumber, provisions, etc., at once, the cheaper will the prices be to each receiver upon the cost principle, and these economies, together with the social sympathies, will offer the natural inducements to associated movement. But there is great danger that even these inducements will urge many into such movements prematurely. We cannot be too cautious not to run before the demand. Let no one move to an equity village, till he has thoroughly consulted the demand for his labor, and satisfied himself individually that he can maintain himself individually.

It will now be found necessary to ascertain the amount of labor required in the production of all those things which we expect to exchange. This naturally suggests itself to each one in his own business, and if all bring in their estimates, either at public meetings, or have them hung up in a public room, they become the necessary data for each to act upon. It is this open, daylight, free comparison of prices which naturally regulates them, while land, and all trades, arts, and sciences, will be thrown open to every one, so that he or she can immediately abandon unpaid labor, which will preserve them from being ground by competition below equivalents.

If A sets his estimate of the making of a certain kind of coat at 50 hours, and B sets his at 30 hours—the price per hour and the known qualities of workmanship being the same in both—it is evident that A could get no business while B could supply the demand. It is evident that A has not given an honest estimate, or that he is in the wrong position for the general economy. But he can immediately consult the report of the demand, and select some other business for which he may be better adapted. If he concludes to make shoes, his next step is to get instruction in this branch. He refers to the column of supplies, and ascertains the name and price per hour of the shoemakers. He goes to one of them, makes his arrangement for instruction, then provides himself with a room and tools, sends for his instructor, pays him according to the time employed, and becomes a shoemaker.

The new shoemaker, having paid his instructor for his labor, has the proceeds of it, together with his own, at his own disposal, and if these be sold for equivalents, he will find his new apprenticeship quite self-sustaining.

We have now progressed far into practical operations without any combination or unity of interests. Every interest and every responsibility being kept strictly individual, no legislation has been necessary. There has been no demand for artificial organization. There being no public business to manage, no government has been necessary, and therefore no surrender of the natural liberty has been required.

Now let us imagine one small item of united interests, and trace its consequences. We will suppose that A and B get a horse in partnership, to transport their baggage to the new location. The horse is taken sick. A proposes a medicine, which B thinks would be fatal; neither party has the power to lay down his own opinion, and take up that of the other. These are parts of the individualities of each, which are perfectly natural, and therefore uncontrollable. A brings arguments and facts to sustain his opinion; B does the same. Still they differ, and the horse is growing worse. One dislikes to proceed contrary to the views of the other, and both remain inactive for the same reason. What can they do but call a third party to act in behalf of both? To this third party they both commit the management of the horse, and surrender their right of decision. This third party is government. This government cannot possibly decide both ways, and either A or B, or both, remain fearful and dissatisfied. The disturbance now extends itself to the third party, producing a social disease in addition to that of the horse. We must take another course, retrace our steps, look into causes, and we shall find the wrong in the unity of interests. To be perfectly harmonious, all interests must be perfectly individual.

Those who are most averse to collision with others will find this an invaluable truth. Natural individualities admonish us not to be dogmatical on this or any other subject, but to be careful not to construct any institutions which require rigid adherence to any man-made rule, system, or dogma of any kind; to leave every one free to make any application, or no application, of any and all principles proposed, and to make any qualification or exception to them which he or she may incline to make, always deciding and acting at his or her own cost, but not at the cost of others. If the horse, in the above instance, should die under A's decision and treatment, while B held an interest in him, then A decides and acts partly at the cost of B, which is wrong and discordant. Let us now examine the motive for this partnership interest. Is it for economy? We have secured that in the operation of the cost principle, and therefore united interest is unnecessary. Under the partnership interest, A and B would each have half the labor of the horse, and would bear half of his expenses. If cost were made the limit of price, and A owned him individually, and should let him work for B half the time, the price would be half of his expenses: exactly the same result aimed at by united interests.

The difference is only, that the one mode paralyzes action, is embarrassing and discordant, and therefore wrong, while the other admits the freest action, works equitably toward both parties, is perfectly harmonious, and therefore right.

Again: let any laws, rules, regulations, constitutions, or any other articles of association be drawn out by the most acute minds, and be adopted by the whole. As soon as action commenced, it will be found that the compact entered into becomes differently interpreted. We have no power to interpret language alike, but we have agreed to agree. New circumstances now occur, different from those contemplated in the compact. New expedients are to be resorted to; two of more interpretations of the same language neutralize each other; an opinion expressed is misunderstood and requires correction; the correction contains words subject to a greater or less extent of meaning than the speaker intended; these require qualification. The qualification is variously understood, and requires explanation; the explanations require qualifications to infinity. Different estimates are formed of the best expedients, but there is no liberty to differ. All must conform to the articles of compact or organization, the meaning of which can never be determined. Opinions, arguments, expedients, interests, hopes, fears, persons and personalities, all mingle in one astounding confusion. What is the origin of all this? It is the different interpretations of the same language, and the difference in the occasions of its applications, where there is not liberty to differ.

Exactly the same reasons apply against one person being in debt to another, and it is only by settling every transaction in the time of it, either by equivalents or their representative (such as the labor note), that the liberty, peace, and security of all parties can be preserved. Running accounts between any two persons are liable to be erroneous, from omissions and mistakes which are entirely beyond the control of the best intentions; but errors from these causes cannot be distinguished from those of design.

It is only by individualizing our transactions and their elements that each citizen can enjoy the legitimate control over his own person, time, or property. If we present a rose to a friend, it is understood to be an expression of sympathy, a simple act of moral commerce, and the receiver feels free from any obligation to make any other return than the expression of the natural feeling which immediately results. But if one should give half of his property to another, the receiver could not feel equally free from future indefinite obligations. Not, perhaps, that the property was more valuable to the receiver than the rose, but it cost more.

A delicate regard to the rightful liberty of every one, and the necessity of self-preservation, would seem to admonish us to make cost the limit of gratuitous favors, while those of immense value which cost nothing, can be given and received without hesitation or reluctance, and will purify our moral commerce from any mercenary or selfish taint.

Working of Machinery

If one person have not sufficient surplus means to procure machinery for a certain business, all will have an equal interest in assisting in establishing it, provided that he will have its products at cost. But if there is no limit to their price, then they can have no such co-operating interest. The wear of the machinery and all contingent expenses, together with the labor of attendance, would constitute this cost. The owner of the machinery would receive nothing from the mere ownership of it. But as it wore away, he would receive in proportion, till at last, when it was worn out, he would have received back the whole of his original investment and an equivalent for his labor in lending his capital and receiving it back again. Upon this principle, the benefits of the labor-saving powers of the machinery are equally dispersed through the whole community. If one portion is thrown out of employment by it, the land and all arts and trades being open to them, so that they are easily and comfortably sustained during a new apprenticeship, they are not only not injured but benefited by the new inventions.

When any persons are thrown out of employment by the introduction of machinery, or when from any other cause there is no demand for their labor, it becomes necessary for their self-preservation that they turn to some other employment. At this point the apprenticeships established by custom stand directly in the way. During the nineteen years of the study and experiments of equitable commerce, it has been one principal object to test practically the necessity of these apprenticeships. The results of these tests are on record for publication, if necessary. No new proposition of equal importance is more susceptible of proof than this, that the period of apprenticeship can be far reduced. And at least one half of all the pursuits now monopolized by men, can be quite successfully performed by women, who are now confined by custom and craft to one or two pursuits, in which competition has ground them to beggary and starvation. Let women and all others whose labor is unpaid, abandon their pursuits and turn to others that will command an equivalent, which they can do when all kinds of instruction can be obtained on the cost principle, and where the prices of board, clothing, and every thing else are limited in the same manner. Under these circumstances, a few hours or days of instruction substitutes years of customary apprentice slavery, and be it more or less, the learner, besides paying his or her instructor equitably for his labor, can sustain himself or herself from the beginning to the end of it.

Child-Rearing

A proper regard to the individualities of person's tastes, etc., would suggest that residences be occupied by such persons as are most agreeable to each other. Therefore, children generally, as well as their parents, would be much more comfortable not to be so closely mixed up as they would be in a boarding-house with their parents. The connection is already, even in private families, too close for the comfort of either. Hotels for children, according to peculiarities of their wants and pursuits, would follow of course. I have seen infant schools, in which one woman attended twenty children not above two years old, and where the children entertained each other, taking more of their burthens on themselves than the best mothers could have carried.

Perhaps fifteen mothers were preserved from the most enslaving portion of their domestic labors. And if such institutions were opened and conducted by individuals upon individual responsibility and upon the cost principle, every mother and father, and every member of every family, would be deeply interested in promoting the convenience and reducing the cost of such establishments, and in taking advantage of them.

Instead of the offensive process of legislating upon the fitness of this or that person for those situations, any individual who thought that he or she could supply the demand might make proposals, and the patronage received would decide. Every mother would be free to send her child or not, according to her individual estimate of the proposed keeper, the arrangements, and the conditions, and it would, therefore, be a peaceful process. If every mother should be required by a government, or laws, or public opinion, to send her children, without the consent of her own approbation, we might expect resistance, discord, and defeat.

Education

With whom will we trust the fearful power of forming the character and determining the destinies of the future race? Every thing we come in contact with educates us. The educating power is in whatever surrounds us. If we would have education to qualify children for future life, then must education embrace those practices and principles which will be demanded in adult age. If we would have them practice equity toward each other in adult age, we must surround them with equitable practices, and treat them equitably. If we would have children respect the rights of property in others, we must respect their rights of property. If we would have them respect the individual peculiarities and the proper liberty of others, then we must respect their individual peculiarities and their personal liberty. If we would have them know, and claim for themselves, and award to others, the proper reward of labor, we must give them the proper reward of their labor in childhood. If we would qualify them to sustain and preserve themselves in after life, they must be permitted to sustain and preserve themselves in childhood and in youth. If we would have them capable of self-government in adult age, they should practice the right of self-government in childhood. If we would have them learn to govern themselves rationally, with a view to the consequences of their acts, they must be allowed to govern themselves by those consequences in childhood. Children are principally the creatures of example. Whatever surrounding adults will do, they will do.

If we strike them, they will strike each other. If they see us attempting to govern each other, they will imitate the same barbarism. If we habitually admit to the right of sovereignty in each other, and in them, then they will become equally respectful of our rights and of each other's. All of these propositions are probably self-evident, yet not one of them is practicable under the present mixture of the interests and responsibilities between adults, and between parents and children. To solve the problem of education, children must be surrounded with equity, and must be equitably treated, and each and every one, parent or child, must be understood to be an individual, and must have his or her rights equitably respected.

It will be seen, on a little trial, that children thus thrown upon themselves, begin to exercise all the self-preserving faculties; they are interested in looking at the consequences before they act and will ask the advice of parents, and listen with interest to their injunctions, which before they would have shunned as unmeaning, tedious inflictions.

Under these circumstances, if we call children in the morning, it is for them and not for us that we do it. If we advise them not to spend their money or time foolishly, it is for them and not for us. It is not our time or money they spend, and they can see that our advice is disinterested. Then they listen and thank us for that which otherwise they would have considered a selfish exercise of authority. I speak from seventeen years of experiments, of which more will be said in the proper place, but will add here, that these principles can only be partially applied under the present mixture of the interests and responsibilities of parents and children, that where parents are obliged to bear the consequences of the child's acts, the parent must have deciding power. But in things in which the child can alone assume the cost of his acts, he may safely be intrusted to the natural government of consequences.

Natural Organization of Society

It would, probably, not be advisable for less than thirty families to commence these operations, because less than about this number could scarcely commence the exchanges, so as to derive much economy from them. For instance, two families could not sustain a shoemaker, nor a carpenter, an iron worker, nor any other indispensable profession. Thirty families might sustain some of them, by which means each could have the benefits of all. Six families could not sustain a storekeeper; probably not less than thirty could. If fifty families commenced together, the economies would be greater, a hundred families greater still.

When they have commenced their operations, they will probably see what is wanted there or in the surrounding neighborhood. If the location is sufficiently near a city to afford a market for surplus labor, the co-operators can divide their time between the two places. Otherwise the greatest caution is necessary in the coming together, and the growth must be slow in proportion to the want of a sustaining demand. If some branches of business, such as stereotyping, publishing, etc., were commenced, the product of which will sell abroad, then any number within the demand can safely assemble at once after they have provided their first accommodations. When they arrive with their families, perhaps another carpenter can be sustained; when he and his family arrive, perhaps another mason can find sufficient employment. If each of these continually report their wants in the report of demands and supply, then any one wishing to know whether he can be sustained has only to get some one on the premises to consult this record, from which he can judge for himself.

In this manner, one after another can be added to the circle, till those living in its circumference are too remote from the boarding-house, the schools, and the public business of different kinds. Then another commencement has to be made, another nucleus has to be formed, and thus in a safe and natural manner may the new elements extend themselves toward the circumference of society. Commerce, on these principles, will be proposed with different individuals in foreign countries, which may give rise to similar beginnings in different parts of the world, each nucleus extending its growth outward till the circles meet, obliterating all national lines, national prejudices, and national interests, and in a safe, naturally and rapidly progressive manner reorganize society.

I decline all noisy, wordy, confused, and personal controversies. This subject is presented for calm study and honest inquiry. After having placed it fairly before the public, I shall leave it to be estimated by each individual according to the peculiar measure of his understanding, and shall offer no violence to his individuality, by any attempt to restrain or to urge him beyond it.

Josiah Warren
New Harmony, Indiana, U.S., 1846

THE PEACEFUL REVOLUTIONIST

*The claim that Josiah Warren was the first American anarchist (the sub-
title of William Bailie's 1906 biography) rests largely on the extremely
rare 1833 periodical* The Peaceful Revolutionist, *which Warren wrote
and printed himself. (He published at least one issue of a periodical
under the same title in 1848.) That date (1833) indeed places Warren's
expression of anarchism before Thoreau's or the radical abolitionist
Henry Wright's, though I daresay Warren's views specifically on the state
were fairly commonplace in radical Protestant religious movements from
two centuries before. (It should be noted that Warren never referred to
himself as an "anarchist.") But he was explicitly opposed to both the
political state and monopoly capital from the outset. We could say that*
The Peaceful Revolutionist *was a very early expression of secular anarchism, well after Godwin, for example, but preceding Proudhon. However we may adjudicate priority,* The Peaceful Revolutionist *is a clearly
anarchist text, contains some of Warren's liveliest writing (e.g., his comment that truly public-spirited officials "are not found even in the proportion of ten to the population of Sodom"), and demonstrates that his
anarchism and individualism were fully formed by that date. His economic theory was still nascent, and in place of the cost principle he de-
ployed Owen's principle of the equal exchange of labor; indeed, Warren's
economics were not formed fully until he had performed a variety of
practical experiments.*

*The PR was presented from the inner edge of the United States (deep-
est Ohio) and in a different context altogether than his better-known
work of the 1850s or 1870s. Warren's reaction to Owen was still his fundamental source of energy, and he had recently read Alexander Bryan
Johnson, who lends him a metaphysics of particulars. In addition, he's a*

bit bolder on some matters than he was later in his career: for example,
he rarely expressed his atheism post-PR. A piece on the nullification de-
bate from the issue dated February 5, 1833, expresses an early version of
a libertarian dilemma later faced by Lysander Spooner and others. As
advocates of radical decentralization of authority, Warren and Spooner
favored the idea of local bodies nullifying or overriding federal laws. As
advocates of human freedom above all, they could not but regard slavery
as a monstrously evil institution. Already in 1833, Warren summarized
his creed as "the sovereignty of every individual." The issue, or booklet,
published under the title The Peaceful Revolutionist *in 1848 is datelined*
"Utopia," and describes the formation of Utopia, Ohio, on the Ohio
River on equitable principles.

In this chapter I reproduce one entire issue (dated April 5, 1833, and
listed as vol. 1, no. 4),[1] which I think imparts a nice savor. I then give
extracts of two other issues. As far as I have been able to conclude, these
are the only issues extant, though there were at least five: four from 1833,
and one printed in 1848. The final bit reprinted here, "On Originality,"
is one of Warren's liveliest and most personal essays.

The Peaceful Revolutionist, *February 5, 1833 (vol. 1, no. 2)*

Surrounding Circumstances

A lone produce the differences between people of different nations: between a Hindoo who is painfully careful of the feelings
of the minutest insect, and a holy inquisitor of Christendom who sits
with perfect unconcern and hears the agonized shrieks and sees the
cracking skin and frying flesh of the burning unbeliever. It is the influence of surrounding circumstances that makes one man a king,
and another a beggar, which divides society into rich and poor, which
enables some to command and others unable to do otherwise than
obey. It is the influence of circumstances which produces different
classes in society, and that influence only, which divides men into

different political parties and ranges them under different banners of religion. By that influence alone some are made to observe with conscientious nicety the forms and ceremonies of the worship of a mass of hideously painted wood, and the same influence induces others to seek favor in the eyes of their god by murdering the former as idolatrous heathens.

If a child be placed at birth among cannibals and surrounded with them only, he will adopt their habits and manners, and will eat human flesh with as little compunction as he would eat the flesh of beasts and fowls, were he bred among us; and were he placed at birth among the Hindoos, he would respect and worship bulls with as conscientious a devotion as he would worship a mass of wood in India, or some form of his imagination among Jews or Christians.

If he be placed at birth exclusively among Presbyterians and their practices, he is likely to become a Presbyterian; if among Quakers, a Quaker; among Shakers, a Shaker. And upon the same principle he might be compelled to become a sincere believer in any religion in the world, or a disbeliever in all religions.

He may be rendered kind, hospitable, tender, and respectful of the feeling of others, or he may be made brutally careless of all but himself, and a demon of mischief to all around him.

It will be seen that this knowledge warrants us in a critical examination into our own condition and all the circumstances which have surrounded us from birth, to see whether they have been, or are, such as are most favourable to our happiness. And it teaches us not to reverence or perpetuate bad circumstances simply because we are born under them, for the same reason would justify cannibals in continuing the custom of eating each other.

This knowledge therefore lays a broad, rational, and consistent foundation for unlimited improvement. It furnishes us with the rational data by which to estimate ourselves and our customs, laws, habits, and opinions. And when we have so estimated them, we are enabled to respect our own judgment and persevere in the measures which it dictates and approves.

Of Our State Difficulties &c.

We daily and hourly hear our citizens ask each other, "What do you think of nullification?" "How will it terminate?" "How do matters stand now?" "What new states have come out in favor of nullification?" &c, all indicating an enquiring state of mind and that there have been no very good reasons offered to the public for taking a very decisive stand on either side, and evincing their good sense in waiting for reasons.

If I can form any clear idea of this subject, it is a quarrel between dignity and liberty—the one a shadow, the other a ghost.

Dignity insists upon it that the laws shall be obeyed, and that the union must be preserved. But these two words *must* and *shall* rouse the ghost of murdered liberty to resistance. Dignity abandons the real subject of dispute, and resolves the whole matter into a mystical reverence for the two words *union* and *laws*. I say for two words, because if we look for their meaning we find, as in all other words of a general and indefinite character, that there are very few if any who will agree in their manner of applying them. If the word *law* has ever meant one thing more than another, that thing has been the will of those in power.

By the word *union*, some refer to certain words on paper, which serve as an excuse for a great deal of speech making and disunion every year at the rate of eight dollars per day. Others by the word "union" understand a similarity of interests, feelings, and objects; co-operating action and mutual assistance in case of need. The question now occurs, which, or what union is it that is to be preserved? It can be the former only that can be preserved; the latter is to be attained. It never has existed since the revolution, and existed then only from the circumstances of the time. Mutual danger and similar interests at that time induced fellow feeling and union in sentiment and action. This union existed independent of words: it was the necessary and unavoidable effect of the circumstances of that time, and it as necessarily ceased as those circumstances ceased to exist. But our ancestors, under the influence of that excitement, were betrayed into a compact of union: a thing so extremely indefinite that perhaps there are no two individuals concerned who can construe or apply it alike, and they did not preserve the liberty to differ.

It might rationally be asked, what has that to do with us? yet this incomprehensible something now calls on us their posterity to feel and to act and talk alike, in cases where the reasons for it and the power to do so do not exist. If there is any one point upon which union of sentiment can be attained and to which every individual will consent, it is, perhaps, in their liberty to differ from others. And if we are ever to commence doing as we would be done by, now is the time to respect the liberty of others to differ from us.

"Language has no meaning when it does not refer to some taste, smell, sound, sight or feeling, or, to some combination of these sensations."[2] What does the word "union" refer to? Not a taste, not a smell, not a sound; it refers to nothing or, to sights or feelings. What sights? Co-operating actions? These will be seen only as force excludes co-operating feelings, or only when we have co-operating interests, as in the time of the revolution. What feeling does the word "union" refer to? Does it refer to such a sour clashing interests have excited during the last ten years? Are these to be "preserved"? Or, as artillery has been sent to enforce union, perhaps the word refers to those feelings which accompany a broken head.

Or, is the artillery sent there to compel our neighbors to bear expenses where they receive no benefits? Jefferson says, "A wise and frugal government which restrains men from injuring one another and shall leave them otherwise free to regulate their own pursuits of industry and improvements, and shall not take from the mouth of industry the bread it has earned; this is the sum of good government."[3]

Instead, therefore, of sending troops to compel our neighbors to appropriate a portion of their property contrary to their feeling or judgment, should we not have it sent to protect every individual in the "free management of their industry" and the disposal of their proceeds in any way they themselves may choose? If this is impracticable under present circumstances, then let us turn our attention to these circumstances. Let us direct our artillery against them rather than against persons. If the fault is in surrounding circumstances, we are as much to blame as our southern brethren.

If our southern neighbors cannot exercise their inalienable liberty without involving us in consequences contrary to our interests, it shows that connected responsibilities and clashing interests are the evils to be cured, and that disconnection or co-operating interests are the rational and proper remedies. Not a disconnection that would leave us liberty to act together where we might have similar interests, but an undoing of whatever was done by our ancestors in a moment of excitement. This makes us now think that we are bound to act together in all cases even though all parties would be most benefited and union be best preserved by encouraging the liberty to differ and to act individually. By preserving the liberty to differ, we do not necessarily bind ourselves not to agree in any cases, but let us preserve our liberty to agree or to differ as circumstances may govern. Liberty is a safe, and the only safe principle to which we can pledge ourselves. If it be objected that this liberty is unattainable, and that great national objects could not be attained where such latitude was encouraged, I reply that there can be no national object greater than national happiness, and that this, as I understand it, consists of the happiness of the individuals who compose the nation, and that individual happiness consists in nothing so much as the liberty of person and property. If this is unattainable in large masses, that shows us one circumstance with which we have to contend, and proves that society will have to dissolve its imaginary masses and resolve itself into individuals before liberty can be anything but a word.

The Peaceful Revolutionist, *April 5, 1833 (vol. 1, no. 4)*

Individuality

When Robert Owen promulgated the proposition that "we are effects of causes, and therefore cannot deserve praise of blame," a very few looked upon this as the proper basis of an entirely new state of society which alone could produce "peace on earth and good will among men"[4]; while others called Mr. Owen a madman, some charged him with being an agent of the king of England sent here to undermine our republic.

Some suspected he was a designing speculator; some thought he was the antichrist spoken of in the Christian bible; and some took him to be the preacher of some new religion.

Thus did this simple language of Mr. Owen produce almost as many different conclusions as there were individuals who heard it. The general observer referred it to all human thoughts, feelings, and actions, and attributed this difference to the different causes which had acted upon each individual, and therefore attached neither merit to themselves nor demerit to those who differed from them; and upon this knowledge individual liberty was so far established. But it was established only with a few, and with them, in the mind only. Our surrounding institutions, customs, and public opinion calls for conformity: they require us to act in masses like herds of cattle: they do not recognize the fact that we think and feel individually and ought to be at liberty to act individually. But this liberty cannot be enjoyed in combinations, masses, and connections in which one cannot move without affecting another.

Nothing is more common than such remarks as the following. "No two things are alike." "There can be no rules without exceptions" &c. Yet, we are constantly called upon to conform to rules that do not suit our case, to acquiesce in numerous different opinions all at the same moment, and no laws in the world preserve the liberty of the governed to make exceptions to the rules which they are required to obey. To give others the power to construe laws and make exceptions is equivalent to giving them the power to govern without laws.

A little observation will disclose an individuality in persons, times, and circumstances which has suggested the idea that one of our most fatal errors has been the laying down rules, laws, and principles without preserving the liberty of each person to apply them according to the individuality of his views, and the circumstances of different cases. In other words, our error, like that of all the world that has gone before us, has been the violation of individual liberty.

The first objection that is made to the above will illustrate the individuality of minds and show our error in depending on conformity.

The foregoing article was chiefly written soon after our experiment at New Harmony to suggest the cause of our failure. I had written much more to illustrate that individuality to which I have alluded and which may be considered the governing principle in every step which has been taken in the experiment now in progress.

But I suppress what I had written and refer readers to a much superior illustration of the same subject which came to hand last week in a pamphlet entitled "A Discourse on Language," by A. B. Johnson.[5]

This is a continuation of his invaluable labors on language. The perusal of it furnished another strong proof that there are great truths upon which men, even strangers to each other and in different parts of the world, will agree as soon as we begin to look through words to things. The singular coincidence of my own views with those of such a mind as Mr. Johnson's would amply compensate me for their being out of fashion with half the world beside.

I have already had, and shall often have, occasion to avail myself of Mr. Johnson's labors. I crave his forgiveness for detaching as it were an eye of the forehead of a fine portrait, but my apology will be found in utility.

The labors of this gentleman appear but little known. Whether it is because they are superior to the intellects of the critics, or whether because as he says "criticism like every other mercenary employment will conform to the market," or whether the veil of individuality precludes our investigation of motives, I shall not wait for critics, but act individually and without hesitation acknowledge the benefit I have derived from Mr. J's "Lectures on Language."[6]

It is the first of all books which I ought to have read, and I shall take care that my children benefit by it. I recommend it to all of whatever age or profession, and especially to those with whom I am to hold any intercourse; and, let me here inform my readers that I use language with a constant regard for its principles as developed by Mr. Johnson. Enquirers will thus always have a key to my meaning, and opposers (should I have them) may save themselves much labor by studying his work, as I do not intend to enter into any argument where the language does not refer to some sensible "phenomena."

Mr. Johnson's elucidation of language is a bridge over which I have escaped from the bewildering labyrinths of verbal delusions called arguments and controversies, and I do not expect to recross it but as a free child of a peaceful village would approach the uproar and confusion of a noisy city on a holiday in pursuit of variety.[7]

Ed. P.R.

Cure for the Ague

Passing through the New York canal in 1831, I was seized for the first time with a fit of the ague. It was soon stopped with sulphate of quinine. It returned again in '32, on getting wet in a shower. Quinine would now keep it off only a day or two; a little exercise or exposure to the sun brought it back repeatedly till I lost all faith in quinine and resorted to a variety of other prescriptions with little success. A friend referred me to an article in the *New Harmony Gazette* (3rd vol.) on Piperine, or extract of black pepper, which it described as superior to quinine as a cure for the ague, that it was more effectual and left the patient less liable to dropsy and some other diseases. A medical friend also concurred in this, and added that he had for several months used no other remedy than common black pepper. His common practice was to advise patients to take their pepper box and mix up the pepper with flour and molasses or any thing that will make it into pills, and to take one or two every hour or two. He said he had scarcely ever known this to fail, nor had the disease ever returned as after taking quinine.

I tried this and have not had a fit of ague since. I have also recommended to four of my acquaintance, one of whom had had the ague six months; it succeeded in every case.

How far these facts justify a general rule I leave each individual to judge.

Ed.

A Brush at Old Cobwebs

Laws and governments are professedly instituted for the security of person and property, but they have never accomplished this object. Even to this day every newspaper shows that they commit more crimes upon persons and property and contribute more to their insecurity than all criminals put together. The greatest crime which can be committed against society and which causes poverty and lays the foundation of almost all other crimes is the monopoly of the soil. This has not only been permitted but protected or perpetrated by every government of modern times up to the last accounts from the congress of the United States. For this enormous crime, according to the spirit of all law, these legislators ought to be severely punished. But the principles of law are false. Every act of every legislator has been an effect over which he could have no control while the causes existed. This is the only ground upon which they can rationally be acquitted, and the same would protect all other criminals from being lawfully murdered and should teach legislators to remove causes rather than spend people's money in punishing effects.[8]

Beauchamp was hanged for killing Col. Sharp to revenge what public opinion called an unpardonable offence, thus showing that he would risk his life to stand fair in the public eye.[9] Surely the public safety could not require the death of one so blindly obedient to its voice. But the law required his death; he was a sacrifice therefore to law, but not to the public good. If any cases would justify murdering a criminal, they must be very different from this, and if the experiments of three thousand years have not produced laws better adapted to the individuality of cases, perhaps we had better give up such projects and try the effects of so arranging our affairs that we can act in each case according to its merits.

Laws cannot be adapted to the individuality of cases, and if they could, laws are language which is subject to different interpretations according to the individuals who are appointed to administer them. Therefore, it is individuals rather than laws that govern. Every election illustrates this: we are told that our destinies depend on the election of this or that man to office. Why? It is men not laws or principles that govern society. There is an individuality among judges and jurors as among all other persons, so that he whom one judge or jury would acquit, another would condemn. Judge Jeffreys acquired the popular epithet of "bloody Jeffreys" from the remarkable number of persons condemned under his administration of the same laws which in other hands would have acquitted them; there is no security in laws. We must seek it elsewhere.[10]

Citizens cannot know today what will be lawful tomorrow; laws made this year are unmade the next and their repeal is often our only intimation that they existed. All these uncertainties must exist even when laws are framed with greatest wisdom and administered with the purest devotedness to the public good without the least tinge of personal feeling or private interest, provided such phenomena are to be found, but every newspaper that comes to hand convinces that such are not found even in the proportion of ten to the population of Sodom; but that, notwithstanding all that revolutions have cost the world, laws and governments still are what they always have been, viz. public means for private ends.

To be continued

From an English Paper: Glorious Uncertainty of the Law

The late Charles Gardyne, of Middleton, had an interesting lawsuit some time previous to his death, with the taxman of the tolls and the road trustees there, on the doubtful question whether the vehicle in which he rode was a taxed cart or a chaise—a point which made an essential difference in the rate of toll. After the decision of the supreme court, Mr. Gardyne had the result painted in large legible characters on the back of the carriage as follows.

A Taxed Cart by act of Parliament.
A Taxed Cart, by decision of the sheriff of Forfairshire.
A Taxed Cart, by decision of the court of session.
A Chaise, by a second decision of the same court.
Eight wise Judges said it was a Chaise.
Six not less wise said it was a Cart.

It has been three years on its law journey and at last has been obliged to
stop for want of law grease.

Charles Gardyne Froick's Taxed Cart.

Mr. G. rode in this vehicle on all necessary occasions, during the
remainder of his life, and exhibited it at Perth once during the circuit,
at the George Inn door, to no small dismay of the judges, council,
and agents, and the amusement of the citizens.

The Utica Co-operator

invites discussion relative to the use of machinery. This is well; it is
surely time that this subject was understood. I therefore invite attention to the application of the equal exchange of labor to the use of
machinery as was stated in our first number, and as illustrated in our
report of practical progress which will be found below.

I submit this view of this important subject for the consideration
of all those who are honestly pursuing the solution of this riddle.

J. W.

Principles and Progress of an Experiment
of Rational Social Intercourse

There is now in operation a steam saw mill, probably the first machinery of importance ever got up and worked upon such principles.
It is intended to work upon the principle of equal exchange of labor,
by which nothing is allowed for capital invested, but all who act upon
this principle are to receive the lumber by giving as many hours of
their labor as has been the human labor bestowed on the lumber.
Upon this principle machine labor benefits all equally, the owner receiving no more of its advantages than any other citizen.

It will be perceived upon reflection that the use of machinery upon
this simple and just principle will enable society to preserve itself
from the dreadful reaction to which machinery is now driving the
working classes.

The principle upon which this machinery is to work makes it for the interest of every one to assist in getting it into operation, therefore several persons have been steadily co-operating together for two years past to attain this result, without entering into any verbal contract, combination, or partnership. Every one has acted upon his own individual responsibility and judgment. No one has been required in any particular to conform to any laws, rules, or votes of majorities, nor to surrender any portion of his individual liberty. Rather, in every step of the progress the sovereignty of every individual has been strictly preserved, and the most complete and harmonious co-operation have been attained.

There is an old dogma held in as much mysterious reverence as many others equally vague and mischievous that "when we enter into society we must necessarily surrender a portion of our individual liberty." Aesop saw the subtilty and mischief in this verbal delusion when he wrote the fable of a man modestly asking the forest for a bit of wood, just to make him an axe-handle. The good-natured, unsuspecting forest readily granted it, but no sooner did the man get the handle then he fell to work prostrating the whole forest, who began to repent giving the little bit of wood. But it was too late; it should not have granted the axe-handle.

Men have consented to give up a portion of their liberty of construing their own language and of determining how much liberty the word "portion" shall mean in different cases, but they have left it to the rulers, who have almost invariably decided that the word means the axe-handle.

In our little experiment we have never granted this axe-handle: we have at no time agreed to surrender any portion of our future liberty, nor have we pledged not to make small sacrifices for the greater benefit of others, but we have preserved our individual liberty to act according to the circumstances of individual cases.

Thus, in Feb. 1831 the writer of this was present when one of a company suggested that the first thing requisite upon our future location would be a saw mill. This was seen by all, but had it not been,

no law or vote of the majority could have convinced any one. Therefore neither would have been resorted to, but such persons would
have been left to the free exercise of their own judgment, while others
who felt more confident would have gone forward. They could have
involved no one but themselves.

Another of the company suggested that we meet that evening to
ascertain what could be done towards raising enough credit for the
accomplishment of our purpose. It was enough to suggest this, for, as
the machinery would work equally for the benefit of all, each felt an
interest in attending the meeting and in contributing what he could
do to forwarding the object. So everyone attended without any rule
or law on the subject. When there, we did not refer to any laws or
rules to tell us how to act, but some one, knowing the object which
brought every one there, perceived that anything calculated to promote that object would be acceptable to all present. On this knowledge he acted, and proposed that anyone disposed to invest capital in
this undertaking by making it known would enable us to judge
whether our object was attainable; but no rule, law, dogma, or pledge,
or vote of the majority was resorted to in order to induce any one to
make an investment. Every one was left free to act according to his
individual means, and to be the only judge what portion of his individual convenience he would "give up for the general good" in that
particular case. Nor did any law or vote of the majority appoint any
person to receive the investments and manage the machinery, but
every one was at liberty to invest his means where he had the most
confidence, &c. Notwithstanding all this individuality of action, not
the least clashing or jarring has occurred on any one point, but the
machinery is now in operation; it employs the capital of several persons who are at liberty to withdraw it at any time they may choose to
do so. But while the machinery is used upon the principle of equal
exchange, we cannot choose to embarrass its operations. Therefore
any pledge or contract to invest for any certain time is not only unnecessary, but it would produce a feeling of restraint which would
render us all uneasy until our capital was withdrawn, and thus might

the machinery be stopped by the injudicious means adopted to ensure its permanence: and thus would this violation of individual liberty perhaps defeat its own object as laws and governments defeat
their object. Their professed object is the security and good order of
society. But the moment that any such power is erected over one's
person or property, that moment he feels insecure and sees that his
greatest chance of security is in getting possession of the governing
power—in governing, rather than being governed—of being the
hammer rather than the anvil. The strife for the attainment of this
power has in all ages up to the present hour produced more confusion, destruction of life and property, and more crimes and intense
misery than all other causes put together.

I venture the assertion that the establishing of such powers has
been the greatest error of mankind, and that society never will enjoy
peace or security until it has done with these barbarisms and ac-
knowledges the inalienable right of every individual to the sovereignty of their own person, time, and property.

J. W.

To the Readers of the *Free Enquirer*

In No. 18, third Vol. of the *Free Enquirer*[11] I commenced a report of
our new social experiment founded upon individual liberty and equal
exchange of labor, and partly promised a continuation of it.[12] But the
circumstances explained in the first number caused the delay of this
report until the present time.

Will the editor of the *Free Enquirer* if he please insert this, and inform his readers that *The Peaceful Revolutionist* is established for the
purpose of continuing the subject.

The P.R. is published on, or near, the first day of each month. Each
number consists of four pages of the same size as the pages of the *Free
Enquirer*. The price, when paid in money, is thirty-seven cents for
the first six months. But, as circumstances may require changes, no
subscriptions are at present received for a longer term.

All subscriptions payable in advance, as the amount would not justify any expense in its collection.

Any person who will forward one dollar post paid, will be entitled to have four copies sent to any names they may furnish, and in the same proportion for a greater number.

A few copies from the first to the present (fourth) number are yet on hand.

Address the proprietor of *The Peaceful Revolutionist*, or Josiah Warren, Cincinnati, Ohio.

Previous subscribers will perceive a little difference between the above terms and those proposed in a former number but the difference will be placed to their credit.

Society as It Is

If one wishes to hire a house, the owner knows not what rent to ask, he considers the demand or want for houses and asks whatever he thinks he can get without any regard to the cost of the house, and the one who hires it seeks to get it as cheap as possible and is regardless of the cost as the owner. Each contends for the victory rather than for justice. It is for the interest of one to make the other feel as much want as possible, and for the interest of the other to conceal his wants. Whatever either may say, neither can be believed. Confidence cannot exist under such circumstances.

The owner of the house goes to purchase a pair of shoes, and he knows by experience that the seller will ask as much as he thinks he can get and is therefore prepared to commence a little war about the price. He puts his shoes on and the sole rips off the first day. He goes to the seller who tells him the maker lives in Boston or Lynn or some place so far off as to be beyond the reach of responsibility. The responsibility is divided between the maker and the seller and rests on neither.[13]

The shoe seller wants to purchase a coat, but he cannot tell where to apply to the best advantage till he has tried all over the city, because "new arrivals" may have changed the prices since yesterday at twelve o'clock. After having made enquiries from one store to another and striving with the sellers to get it as cheap as possible and they sell it as dear as possible, he purchases perhaps a blue coat after having spent as much time and labor as might have made the cloth—he puts it on and is caught in a shower and his blue coat turns red. But the manufacturer lives in another state, or another nation, is beyond the reach of responsibility, and may continue to manufacture and sell blue red coats as long as this species of fraud enables him to get more than he could by any honest, useful employment.

No wonder that Jefferson called cities the sores of society.[14]

The equal exchange of labor would give as great a reward for honest and useful employments as for useless and fraudulent ones, and individual and unequivocal responsibilities (if for no other reasons) would induce a preference for the honest. The necessity of paying for what we consume in equal amount of our own labor might induce a preference for the useful.

To be continued.

The Western Courier

I thank the editor of that paper for publishing my advertisement regarding the printing apparatus, but by transferring the article without explanation it reads as if the *Courier* was printed with the apparatus. I need not suggest the necessity of a correction.

J. Warren.

Moral Philosophy According to Paley

Morality has for its object the good of society and is founded upon three laws, as follows:

(1) The law of the land.
(2) The law of custom.
(3) The law of scriptures.

Therefore, whatever practice among men is agreeable to the law of land, to the law of custom, and the scriptures is moral and just because it promotes the good of society.[15]

Remarks. Nothing is easier than to construe the language of these laws to mean any thing which suits the interests, prejudices, or passions of those who construe and apply them. Consequently, nothing is more common than to see them prostituted to the basest purposes.

Moral Philosophy According to Truth

Morality is the practice of securing to man his just rights, or permitting him to enjoy them, and has for its object the happiness of man. Otherwise, it is but an idle word, and worse than useless.

Man's rights are as follows.

(1) All men, women, and children have an equal right to the free use of all elements existing in a state of nature.
(2) All men, women, and children have a right to enjoy or consume whatever is produced by his or her labor, or an equivalent when exchanged. Therefore, any law of the land, law of custom, or law of scripture which has any tendency to prevent any man, woman, or child from enjoying these rights is immoral.

J. P.[16]

It may be objected that our friend J. P.'s language is as equivocal as Mr. Paley's, and like his admits of being prostituted to the worst purposes: but neither these nor any other verbal forms would be subject to this objection provided every citizen was at liberty to construe and apply them for himself, and only for himself. But the exercise of this liberty as in most other cases, requires an organisation of society without close connections of persons or interests.

Ed. P.R.

Education by Legislation

I received a few days since a copy of a petition to Congress "praying" their aid in the establishment of schools throughout the Union for the education of all children at public expense.

I know this measure has been advocated by some of the best heads and hearts in the world, but they are not of this world.

However benevolent the motives of those who are active in this measure, I fear it is not calculated to produce the results which the enlightened friends of the rising generation aim at. At least, this is my individual opinion, therefore I cannot find a motive to co-operate in this measure. I could give many reasons for this opinion, but it may be sufficient to state a few of the most prominent.

I would prefer to ascertain and assist in establishing remedies rather than waste time in exposing the sickening corruption that every where surrounds us, and would speak of principles rather than of persons, where the liberty of choice is allowed me. But in this case, as legislators stand in the way, I must say that I have no confidence in them, nor in the ultimate benefit of any measure that might be entrusted to them. If there are any among them who would not sell their people for a mess of pottage, they cannot place themselves above suspicion.

Again, I think that the power of educating the rising generation is of too much importance to be trusted in a manageable shape in the hands of any small body of men, as society is now constituted.

The iron ore while diffused through the quarry is at least harmless, though useless. But, converted into a surgeon's knife it may preserve life or administer death, according to the manner of application.

Another objection to such a measure in my mind is that it would increase our connected interests and divided responsibilities, which I think are two of the roots of our social evils. The reverse of this is the very foundation of the education which I expect to give my children, and which I will now attempt to give in a few general terms, but in detail hereafter as we progress in practice.

First, I shall dissolve as far as practicable all connected interests and connected responsibilities between myself and my children, throw them upon their own resources, and enable them to learn by experience the responsibilities of life, assuming all the consequences of all their actions and inaction. Thus situated, they see and feel the utility and the necessity of the instruction and the habits which we desire to give them, and ask our assistance as a favor, which is commonly resisted as an arbitrary infliction of tasks which they cannot appreciate and consequently can feel no interest in acquiring. Thus placed they will experience the natural rewards and punishments of their conduct, which I consider the only form of government that does not produce more evil than good.

I shall see that they are in possession of their natural birthright, the soil, and all the products of their own exertions, or their equivalent, and shall act as their friend rather than as their master: or, as one member of society should act towards another, strictly respecting their individual rights and thus teaching them by example to respect those of other people.

I am convinced from all I have read or seen that law makers will be the last to learn and respect these rights: a proof of which is they are nowhere enjoyed. Nowhere is the soil inherited as an inalienable right, scarcely anywhere is labor rewarded with its equivalent, nowhere under any government is personal liberty enjoyed, nor (except for a few individuals) is it even understood. Instead, therefore, of praying law makers to take care of my children, I should consider it as praying the fox to take care of the chickens.

A man of old called great, offered his services to Diogenes, who replied that the greatest service he could render would be to stand from between him and the sun.[17] And all I ask of law makers is to stand aside and keep from between me and my individual rights.

J. W.

To Subscribers

It is probable that the next number will be delayed by the removal of the printing apparatus to our new location, but this interruption will not be unnecessarily prolonged. As the time of removal is uncertain, it would be well to address all letters and papers to Cincinnati till the removal is announced.

Perhaps there has been too much repetition of the same ideas in our paper for the taste of some. I regret the necessity for this, but it appears unavoidable in coming to the understanding of others.

Ed. P.R.

Peaceful Revolutionist, *Utopia, May 1848 (vol. 2, no. 1)*

Progress

Straws are often better to show which way the wind blows than the most labored invention. I cannot give a better sign of progress, than that the store-o-crat in the neighborhood says we "must be stopped." I suppose he has heard of calicoes being sold here on the cost principle for eleven cents a yard, similar in quality to those often sold for twenty cents. It seems that his public spirit has taken the alarm; he cannot allow the public to be so imposed upon; threatens us with law on account of issuing labor notes as a circulating medium. Why, bless you sir, this is nothing. The sun will still rise as usual.

I was prepared for hostility from the store-o-crats, but found none that was alarming. On the contrary, I met with two merchants whose hearts had not been destroyed by profit making, and who acknowledged that these were the only correct and equitable principles, that the sooner they prevailed, the better for every one, that they almost hated themselves for the manner in which they were now compelled to get their living out of their customers. Some of my best friends are now store keepers in New Harmony, and were so, during the two years and a half of the Time Store in that place. However, if we cannot get attention to the subject in a more pleasant way, I, for one, should be glad of a little persecution, particularly from a source so evidently self-interested.

Signs of Returning Reason

The "combined wisdom" of New York, it appears, has passed a law to unmake the laws heretofore preventing married women from exercising their right of individual property, beyond the control, and free from the liabilities of the husband.

The legislators of several other states have already done themselves the credit of doing this little item of justice. It is but an item of their just rights, and yet this one step toward individuality constitutes one of the most important features of modern legislation. How long are Ohio, Indiana, and the rest of the states and the world to linger behind this simple demand of self-evident equity and common sense?

Revolution

All the world is convulsed with revolution. Labor has at last suddenly recoiled from the degradation, the starvation allotted to it and claims its rights. Alas! What are they? This is the great problem which they aim to solve in the midst of contradictory theories, clashing interests, and the confusion of political revolution. The people govern the governments, and yet they demand of the governments what they cannot do for themselves. If all the philanthropy, all the capital, all the intellect, all the labor that have been bestowed upon community and Fourierist experiments, by chosen spirits, peacefully stepping aside from the confusion of the world and acting at their leisure; with the best of motives and feelings; backed by the most desperate resolution; all end in defeat and disappointment, what will be the end of the attempts to carry out these systems, or any other, in large, promiscuous, national masses, in a day, in a moment, in a passion! in the frenzy of starvation? I tremble for the result. The spirit is good, is holy; it is glorious. But here alone may ye exult. Exult now, for the future is not for exultation. Ye plant the worm with the tree: the future is for disappointment, for confusion, perhaps for despair.

A Word on Originality

To J. H. L.[18]

It seems almost necessary since what you mentioned yesterday, to say a word or two upon a subject which I intended never to dwell upon, nor to be the first to broach. I have always found that the idea of merit for originality, by exciting envy of rivals, stood directly in the way of progress, and through the whole course of twenty-one years labor I have found the greatest obstacle in myself. My personality stood directly in my way at every turn I could make. I have seen a man deny the very success that he himself had prophesied beforehand, which I could account for in no other way than that he feels jealous of the credit which would attach to the author, and I have seen more than this.

I have a thousand times felt that if the subject had originated with some one who was dead I could have done, perhaps, a thousand times more for it. I have suffered and I know that the subject has suffered much from this detracting spirit. A man by the name of John Pickering in Cincinnati has put forth what he denominates a "criticism on Warren's system of equitable exchange" and says it "professes to be a new development" &c.[19] Now, whence this word "professes"? Does he wish to intimate that I have put forth claims for originality which are not true? My reputation is my property, and I am not ready to surrender it at the demand of every one who chooses to attack it. He calls it "Warren's system." I never called it so. He calls it "Equitable Exchange," thereby confining the subject to merely pecuniary matters. The work is entitled Equitable Commerce and it is explained on the title page as extending to all intercourse of mankind.

In Cincinnati, in 1827 and '28, when, by placing my labor on equal terms with his as clock maker, he saved about one third of his previous expenditures for store goods, he and all others, I believe, pronounced the operation new. When his son, about 14 years old, learned shoe making by paying 12 hours labor for instruction, instead of serving the customary apprenticeship, and when he afterwards continued for months to make shoes, which I sold out of the Time Store at ordinary prices, these "developments" were termed new. And when, in 1828 Mr. Pickering and his two sons attended my school for instrumental music over the Time Store on the corner of Fifth and Elm streets in Cincinnati, while some paid me ten dollars per quarter, they paid for the same instruction fourteen hours of their own labor. If such developments as these and others peculiar to equitable commerce in 1828 were made before the eighteenth of May 1827, then I was not the first to develop them, and the principal obstacle to my freedom of speech and action on the subject will be removed.

I entitled my work "a new development of principles" because I wished to inform the despairing that there were grounds unknown to them, upon which they might rest a hope; but I did not consider any man the originator of principles or truths. We only discover and develop them. The idea of labor notes was suggested by Robert Owen in 1826 as a medium of exchange between communities at New Harmony. Whether the idea was ever applied before the Time Store of 1827, I know not.

A man must have a good memory and more than memory to be able to trace his general conclusions back to all the minute circumstances and reflections that have led to them; and in this view, originality amounts to very little, even if it were worth establishing. I think it high time that these trifles ceased to assume so much importance with those who are acting the part of pioneers in the great work of man's redemption from error and suffering. The principal reasons that I can see for making this a subject at all are the necessity of replying to others when they broach it and that, after having passed nearly a lifetime in something like martyrdom for doing and thinking strange things, it is but natural to wish to show our censors that we were all the time right and they themselves were insane, were visionary. Having done this, we may consider the account settled and we can begin anew, if it is not too late, or we can die free from the affliction of having attached odium upon truth.

I hope this is the only time that I shall feel called upon to say any thing upon the subject. I would prefer to spend my time in a peaceful and uninterrupted practical exhibition of the subject itself, which may qualify everyone to judge of it according to its own intrinsic value, independent of any merely personal considerations.

J. W.

I make no apologies for the size of the sheet, for the type or the printing. I think that those who would require them are not very desirable as pioneers in a reformation based on common sense. If I saw a house on fire it is most likely I should cry out to its inmates without hesitating to consider what tones would be prescribed in the schools of elocution. I love to contemplate the beautiful, but cannot afford to be whimsical. Nor am I disposed to acknowledge an authority set up by capital, the direct tendency of which is to smother the voice of poverty and suffering because it cannot speak with "new type," "fine paper," "large sheet," &c., &c., &c. I refuse to follow any such lead; but rather intend to show at how cheap a rate the voice of improvement can be heard. Particulars relative to this will be given in the next number.

"NOTEBOOK D"

It is evident that Warren kept a journal for many years. Entries rarely reveal details of his family or intimate life; rather, they meticulously document his social experiments. He drew on these notebooks in many of his published works, especially Practical Details *and* Practical Applications. Apparently he had an idiosyncratic journaling system, retaining notebooks over decades, possibly sorting material by theme as in his indexing systems. The one surviving document of this type is labeled "D" and contains entries from 1840, 1860, and 1873. It is in the collection of the Working Men's Institute in New Harmony, Indiana. My text follows that version and was edited by Ann Caldwell Butler.[1] At the end of "Notebook D," Warren indicates that it was one of a set of ten ("A" to "J"). Butler suggests that members of Warren's family destroyed the rest of the notebooks, though she doesn't say why. Much of the material is redundant with other work, but I reproduce substantial selections below, using Butler's work as a base but removing, for example, dozens of exclamation marks. The selections show that underneath the apparently stern inculcation of liberty and responsibility lay a remarkable tenderness.

The first chunk is from 1840, and it recounts and comments on Warren's attempts to educate his son, George, and another boy (both about thirteen years old) by equitable principles.

The second selection is from 1860 and largely concerns free love. It is in the form of a dialogue or "conversational development." I reproduce a portion that gives something of a pragmatist view about truth.

The final selection, from 1873, gives a crisp summary of Warren's views on money, and shows that his idealism was undiminished at the time of his passing.

With a view to illustrate the foregoing principles and to prove their correctness and to show the fundamental mistakes which society has made in the management of children and the organization of schools, I began, on the 21st of January 1840, a seminary at what we will call No. 1 in New Harmony, where I intend to establish a little world organized and governed according to what I conceive to be the only way in which society can be organized so as to secure individual rights, justice, security, peace, and the means of abundance and enjoyment to all, and to solve the problem of natural liberty coexistent with social order. I shall take notes of interesting illustrations as they occur but shall confine myself entirely to the facts as they take place.

January 21, 1840

This day, commenced labor for labor[2] at No. 1 with only two boys, with the view of increasing the number as fast as they can sustain themselves with such aid as I can furnish. These boys were told that they were now to act entirely at their own responsibility, each to have the whole proceeds of his labor, to do with it just as he chose, and that no power of parents or anyone else was to interfere to compel them either to work or study or anything else, but if that if they did not they would suffer the natural consequences, which a very few words served to explain. G. W. W. are the initials of one[3] and E. H. of the other.

In order to preserve individual interests and individual responsibilities it would have been necessary for each to have had distinct premises of his own, but they preferred being in one room together. As it was impracticable to have separate rooms at the present time, they were both in the same room, but they were told that they would probably have some disagreeable consequences from having even so much connected interests. But as these are the arrangements for experimental education, I had no objection to their trying it, and ascertaining by their own experiences some of the consequences.

As they were to act entirely for themselves in all respects, they were to pay rent for the room. We now come to the first application of the cost principle. I told them that if they chose they might appoint some third party to ascertain the real cost in wear and tear of the building, and that should be the rent they were to pay me. The proposal to appoint a third party was to convince them that I received no more than an equivalent for the use of the building—in other words that I did not get their property for nothing.

But they left it to me, and they engaged each to pay one dollar per month for the room, which is about eighteen by twenty feet. I now told them as I had before that if they wanted my assistance in any way, whether by advice or instruction, I would render it on the principle of labor for labor and if I wanted any of their assistance or labor that I would pay for it in the same manner and that it would be necessary for each of us to set the price per hour which he would expect to receive, and that it was necessary to fix this price before any debt was incurred, so that one could not get power over another's property by setting the price after the receiver had incurred the debt. And as a matter of great convenience too it was recommended not to change the fixed price of time for light and trivial causes, that some pursuits being more disagreeable (or costly) than others it would be reasonable to ask more for the same length of time. And as no one can judge for another how disagreeable any pursuit may be, each must decide the price of his own labor in different pursuits, and that competition would be likely to keep us all within reasonable bounds.

Each then proceeded to fix a price per hour upon his time, which it is understood is to remain until he chooses to change it, of which he is expected to give notice before any debt is incurred.

The boys then proceeded to fix up their benches and tools. They required some advice which I gave at their request. They told me I must charge for my time, but I replied that it was so small an amount that it was best to take no account of it, but that I had already fixed my price high enough to cover any little items like that. E. H. wanted some boards to fix up his bench. I had some to sell. What is the price? he asked.

One dollar per hundred feet original cost at the saw mill. 20 cents per hundred for hauling, 12 cents for stacking up, about two cents for rent of drying room; and 30 cents per hour for the time spent in getting them from the mill; which, altogether, will make them cost $1.50 per hundred, without any interest on money. This their present cost. If I spend time in selecting and measuring them to you this will be added at the rate I have fixed for my time.

After having received the boards the next thing was for him to credit me with them. Here was the first natural introduction to bookkeeping, which occasion I made us of to prompt both of the boys to learn as they could not proceed without it. They perceived it at once and that night, one of them went voluntarily with my advice to apply to the best bookkeeper within our knowledge to see if he would give them some lessons!

January 29, 1840

We were conversing on the subject of toasts or sentiments for a public celebration when G. W. W., aged 13, said if it would be in place or proper for such little ones as he to give a toast, it would be propose that all children should be situated as he was! I do not know how this may strike others but to me coming from a little boy speaking in reference to his school and mode of government under which he was placed, it spoke more than I can find words to express. It was a boy placed in school, voluntarily acknowledging that he was happy!

January 30, 1840

G. W. W. said to me, "Father, I wish for you first to measure this board to see how much I must credit you for." Yes, certainly, said I, but you know if you could measure it yourself you would save what you will have to pay me for my time. "I must study arithmetic," said he with great emphasis, lifting up his little hand and bringing it down in a most decisive and resolute manner. And at night without a word being spoken on the subject took a light from the table and was gone so long that, as it was very cold, I was curious to know what he was doing, when after about 15 minutes he came in. He had been hunting up his arithmetic, and it being a stormy night he said he would not go over work tonight but would study arithmetic. And he did, all evening.

In the morning, although it was very cold I called him and asked him if he did not want to get up and study arithmetic. He got up without another call, which is unusual for him, and studied the tables most intensely while breakfast was getting ready. He asked me to take the book and exercise him in the multiplication table and this was all done with a smile upon his countenance, and he would take the book over to his room, and he and E. would exercise when it was too cold for work.

The two boys had agreed on a place for the key of their room, but G. remarked to me that E. had gone away with the key in his pocket promising to be back a certain time but had not, and he had lost an hour at least in consequence of his failure to fulfill his promise; now, says he, E. ought to pay me that hour, shouldn't he? Truly in strict justice I think he should though he may have very good reason to delay, said I, but the best way is not to lay the foundation of such things in having connected interests. You will remember that I told you in the commencement that you would probably discover some objections to having one room in common.

February 3, 1840

G. W. W. ate no breakfast and was evidently unwell—went to work and remarked that he had done nothing of any consequence all the forenoon. I do not feel as if I could work, said he. Then don't attempt it said I, I would not go to work unless you feel more able.

Comment: Now how could a parent—how could I, with any propriety, risk advising the child not to work when he did not feel like it, if he had not motive for working? If he had been working in my interest, as all children usually do for their parents, I should not have dared to advise him not to work when he did not feel well for fear that he might make that a plea when it was not true. How cruel to feel obliged to be suspicious that his complaint might be a false plea to escape from work—to doubt his account of his own feelings. Perhaps such doubts might prove fatal: fatal at least to his character for truth; for if the child cannot inspire belief when he tells the truth, he will not long persevere in the practice.

In a conversation today with a friend, I related the fact that my own boy was sitting by the fire in the morning when it seemed best that he should employ that time in preparing wood for the day. When I said that I should like to have him cut some wood—now here was the point—where should his motive come from to get the wood? We know that the common reply is in his sense of duty. But suppose that this does not move him? What next? fear of the rod, or what?

Perhaps the most desirable motive would be a kind feeling. But suppose he did not feel kindly just then? and besides he might with equal reason say that kind feeling on my part might exempt him from doing what he did not like to do.

Here is the explosion of that subtle mistake which has laid the foundation of so many cruel disappointments in the experiments on communities and other institutions built upon self-denial. When we once subscribe to the doctrine it works as much against us as for us; what we gain one way we lose the other and it is nothing but a delusion. The rule of self-denial works as much against happiness as for it, and leaves everything just where it finds it, as in the case of the boy getting the wood. If he is required out of kindness to me to get it, by the same principle, kindness towards him would require me to get it myself. This is all delusory verbiage. The question is still unanswered, where is his motivation rationally to come from to do what I require? Does not the law of his nature which prompts him to pursue his own happiness answer the question? Does it not say that the child should feel that it would result in some benefit to himself? And in conforming our requests to this law, do we not extend the greatest practicable amount of kindness towards him?

Now in conformity to this law of nature I had laid down all the power given me by ignorant legislators over my child, had made him feel sovereign of himself and all the proceeds of his exertions, and he knew that if he got the wood ready I should pay him according to the amount of labor performed. Here was the natural and rational motive brought to bear upon him and he went cheerfully about it.

There was no necessity of violating the "law of love": no force, no violence, not even command was necessary. The impulse was given by the force of natural consequences, of things instead of persons. The child acted as sovereign of himself, taking on the natural consequences of his actions. The action of the law of love is impracticable under the common relative position of parent and child. The principle exhibited here holds good in all our social relations. Our interests must all be individualized and each must assume all the natural consequences of his acts before we can cease to govern each other, and peace and love be realized.

The greatest extent to which we can ever exercise kindness towards others is in assisting them in their pursuit of happiness, in that particular course or manner that he or she may choose. This exhibits the point where the spirit of accommodation can be exercised with advantage until the circumstances which compel us to clash can be removed or abolished.

The organization of society is artificial: an invention, a continuance. The most ingenious person would be likely to succeed best in the invention of any machine, combining a number of elements for the accomplishment of certain objects. But to succeed well he must know the objects to be accomplished and the principles involved, and he must be able to trace any defect to the proper cause, not alter a wheel when it is a lever that is at fault, nor apply more power to force it forward when the wheels are out of true.

Some parts may be allowed to be a little imperfect without materially affecting the general result, but the laws of nature will not allow some other imperfections. The wheels of a clock must all be present, and they must not vary much from their specified size. A little imperfection may be allowed in the cogs, but very little or the clock will not go. The addition of ten thousand wheels will not supply the place of the pendulum. They, like the multiplicity of laws in the social state, would only serve to complicate, to perplex and clog the machine. We must have the pendulum, and that pendulum must be in proportion to the other parts, or else although the machine would go, it would not be a clock. It would not measure time, and although a little variation in its length from the true proportion would be to surrender "only a portion" of right, yet at the end of the year the machine, for all purposes intended, would be worse than no clock.

Society is the clock; individual liberty is the pendulum.

It is but a hackneyed as well as short-sighted objection to unqualified individual liberty that "if each one sets his own limits or no limits to his liberty" what shall prevent his encroachments upon others? The answer is included in the first proposition that each and every individual has this natural right: not some or a few or many but every one. So that is A encroaches on B, how shall this be treated? This is for B to decide because he has a right to sovereignty over his own person and all his own interest. It is an impertinent interference for any one or any set of men to dictate to him how he shall proceed. Different people would act differently under the same circumstances, and they have a right to do so. But perhaps we are troubling ourselves too much about assumed difficulties, for if the personal liberty and the right of property were habitually respected from infancy we are all too much the creatures of habit, of public opinion, and of example to encroach upon the rights of others wantonly. The fears on this point are derived from the notion of natural depravity.

The past furnishes no fair criterion. Justice has never yet been done in the social state to the individual. We must begin anew, watch the progress, and build according to necessities.

March 20 [1840]

Several interruptions have occurred which took me away from home since last taking notes, but I felt at ease leaving the boys to their own self-government. Why?

Because they could do no harm to any but themselves. They had no access to any one's property, nor any connection with anyone's interests but their own, and they had the proper natural stimulus to promote their own advancement in having all the proceeds of their exertions. In shorter terms, each was placed in his own natural and proper sphere. On my return I found that they had done all they had to do and were anxious for my return to advise them further.

E. took his first lesson in shoe making from Mr. V. today. The lesson cost him 3/4 of one cent and his labor amounted to 12$\frac{1}{2}$! G. took his first lesson in shoe making this evening of the same person. This lesson cost G. about one cent; he mended a pair of pumps for me and earned 12$\frac{1}{2}$ cents. He went immediately after supper voluntarily to take his lesson and pay for it himself out of the proceeds of his own labor, and all with as much hilarity and cheerfulness and interest as boys under common circumstances generally rush into the street to play.

He came home after I was in bed, but was so desirous to show me the results of his first lesson that he came into my room and awoke me, holding up triumphantly the mended shoes.

Comments: It is often remarked, when discussing these subjects, that the pecuniary affairs seem to occupy too important a place, that they are too prominent. That they seem to claim so much attention that children under the influence of such circumstances or even adults would be likely to become mercenary in their habits and feelings.

The reply to this if it were full and ample would occupy volumes. For the present let it be considered that pecuniary affairs are all we have to regulate, that this is the proper and legitimate subject of reform, that all the institutions of society are governed by property relations.

If it were not for property considerations persons would neither be dangerous nor endangered. Personal crimes are not always committed to obtain property, but all violations of personal rights will be found upon analysis to proceed either from a desire to obtain property, or from ignorance which might have been and would long since have been dispelled but that it was perpetuated by interested rulers and law givers, and those who wield the press for profit.

From the writings of Lord Bolingbroke: "I dare not pretend to instruct mankind, and I am not humble enough to write to the public for any other purpose."[4]

". . . the abuse philosophers are guilty of when they suffer the mind to rise too fast from particulars, to remote and general axioms."[5]

"I say, that all science, if it be read, must rise from below and from our own level. It cannot descend from above nor from superior systems of being or knowledge."[6]

July 9, 1860

Truth—absolute, pure, unadulterated truth—when brought to bear upon social life, is so transcendently beautiful and beneficent that there is a danger of misapplying our time and means in pursuing any and all truths, because they are truths or because we may possibly find some new truth, although when found, not the least use can be made of it. In this way I think reformers have missed their aim generally. A very intelligent gentleman, one with a large stock of information on things important and unimportant, when I declined going into the pursuit of some unimportant theme: "Don't you think you ought to get all the information you can, on all subjects?" Why no, I do not. If I were to undertake that, I should never make any use of the truths I know already. I know some now that I want to put in practice. When I come to feel the demand for further information on some particular point I will then thankfully receive it, but even then I should want to go to the one that I might for many reasons prefer as a teacher.

I know of no way to preserve ourselves from this kind of intoxication but to follow the order of our wants, to attend first to things and pursue the supply till we have some good reason to stop.

I have spoken of unimportant truths. I mean those whose importance we do not perceive. It may, some time, be thought important to know how many mosquitoes can be generated in a given area of water; what exposure, what temperature, etc., are most favorable; how many legs they have and whether always a uniform number: but before I should want to employ my time in the pursuit of such truths I should want to have settled some practical reliable way of procuring food, clothing, shelter, fuel, and heart repose for myself at least if not for the suffering millions of the best men and women on earth.

Voluntary Subordination

Natural liberty or individual sovereignty calls for freedom of choice in all cases, under all circumstances, and at all times.[7] By freedom of choice I mean exemption from the control of other persons in distinction from the natural and irresistible control of circumstances.

All social arrangements should admit of this freedom of choice of every individual and all subordination should be voluntary. For instance, in the performance of a piece of music at a private party each one who takes a part subordinates himself voluntarily to the lead of one person. The necessity of this is so obvious that it controls choice, but it is not persons that compel this subordination. It is between the control or force of circumstances or necessity, each person being the judge of it, and the control or force of persons or authority that we must draw the great broad line which is to distinguish voluntary from involuntary subordination. The one is in perfect accordance with natural personal liberty which constitutes the chief element of the happiness of human beings and the other violates it and is the chief cause of the Bedlam-like confusion which pervades all ranks and conditions of mankind.

The false step is in laying down any verbal processes which embrace any conditions or applications not distinctly seen and understood beforehand by the entering parties.

Thus in the attempts to organize society men have laid down general rules and indefinite propositions in words as the basis of the social compact which the entering party construed according to his own views, and he is therefore said to exercise his free choice regarding the conditions. But no sooner has he passed the entrance than he has found these verbal rules and laws to contain conditions he knew not of and to be subject to different applications by almost every member of the body. The vote of the majority is the next resort which acts as a power to compel those who differ into involuntary subordination. This is a violation of liberty which appears inevitable under the circumstances. But the circumstances are wrong, are false. The false step is in laying down any verbal processes which embrace conditions or applications not distinctly seen and understood by the entering parties.

In this subtle and unseen mistake has originated those melancholy defeats which have, so far, prevented much improvement in the social condition. But may we not hope that when natural individualities shall be fairly developed, the incapacity of language to express these individualities shall be subject to investigation? Our object is happiness, and there is no one element so indispensable to this as conscious liberty, and there is no one source of tyranny in all shapes and degrees so prolific as that of verbal rules, laws, regulations, dogmas, creeds—religious, political, and moral—which embrace conditions not contemplated by the parties who subscribe to them.

When individual rights shall be clearly appreciated, all rules of social arrangement will be definite; they will express all their conditions and all their applications, or if unavoidably some new application becomes necessary, the subscribing party cannot rightly be bound to sanction or conform to it contrary to his own free choice.

The blind and brutal subordination obtained through fear of punishment in the army of a despot whose use of it is the extension of his power, is involuntary or coerced subordination and works nothing but degradation to the subordinates and an insane self-importance in those who command, and destruction, disorder, confusion wherever that army is employed. The corrective is voluntary subordination. Every soldier should claim and exercise his free choice in every case in which he was required to act and should refuse to move in every cause but that of the defense of person and property.

The people of Paris, in the "three glorious days of July," all impelled by one interest, by common suffering and common sympathy, rushed into the streets to put down their oppressors.[8] But it was immediately evident to all that while each was left to doubt or to pursue different courses, without any particular course being marked distinctly out by some individual mind and some particular direction, their power could not be brought to bear to any effect.

This was so self-evident that they all with one voice on the first suggestion threw themselves under the direction of the youths of the Polytechnic School, and this they did the more safely as they did not pledge themselves to obey any order which their own views and wishes did not sanction. For they were at liberty at any moment even to disobey any orders of the commanders or directors which they might perceive to clash with their objects. But what was the result? It was a straightforward attainment of their object as if by miracle. And they exhibited such an example of rigid self-government from all excesses, and such ready co-operation in the measures and movements announced by their leaders, that it must stand as an everlasting monument in refutation of the false and interested doctrine in favor of coercive subordination.

Words will not embrace the wide range of destruction, desolation, of terror and suffering brought about by rulers by the means of coercive subordination which they pretend is so necessary for the preservation of order. But it is the principal source of disorder throughout the world: from the annihilation of whole nations at once down to the petty little jars on the domestic hearth.

It has often been asked what would become of the great interests of society if they were not looked after by rulers or law makers. Let the answer be derived from the real condition of all these great interests at the present time, compared with the amount of blood and treasure and suffering which their management has cost the world, and let us ask whether any plan could possibly lead to more injustice, or more confusion, uncertainty and insecurity of person and property, than we, supervising all society. But there is nothing in voluntary subordination that violates the natural liberty of the individual, and the fear that natural liberty would uproot all order is as groundless and as futile as the idea that coercive subordination has benefited mankind.

August 1873

Money

I never know when I have said enough about money. It is the pivot upon which every thing turns, and cannot be too well understood.

I have many times been asked why gold and silver could not be made to answer the true propose of money if they were recognized as the embodiment of so much labor?

There are many objections to this. In the first place, we never can ascertain the labor cost of either of them. Not long ago, it was announced that a man stumbled over a lump of gold that would make three thousand dollars while others had been digging and scratching in the dirt six months and found nothing. What, then, is the labor cost of gold?

"But why not average the labor?" Well now, let us see how that would not work. Five thousand men abandon all useful pursuits here, spend their money and time in going two or three thousand miles to hunt gold.

They are to have a share in the findings whether they find anything or not. Now here is a partnership formed between all the gold hunters whether they hunt or lounge about. This communism would immediately lead to quarrels that could never be settled. But if they were settled and each got an equal share, some would get what they never earned and all the expenses, time, and quarreling would be worse than thrown away. Because a ten-dollar piece came to be presented for a barrel of flour on the ground of its having cost as much labor as the flour had, the speculator could say, "It is of no consequence how much either the flour or the gold cost"—a thing is worth what it will bring, and "Flour has gone up. I must have fifteen dollars a barrel for it." Now what use would it be to have found out how much labor there was in the gold? No, we must be able to present to the flour man a positive promise for a barrel of flour on demand, and this positive promise must be based on a positive and sufficient responsibility. Paper or parchment is the very best material for such promises, and the cost is next to nothing.

Then again, it must be possible for the flour producer himself to make these promises for his own products. If any others, even governments, are allowed to do it, they can continue the enslavement of the producers. All government issues of money are so many drafts upon labor akin to forgeries or burglary. They get the product of labor by trick, by stealth, or else by force of arms like highway robbery: extorting by bodily fear; such are all "legal tender" laws and all statutes forbidding individuals from issuing their own notes. They damn up the natural flow of the river, leaving only a narrow passage for the fish into the net set for them.

No power on earth, no device, should be allowed to intervene between the laborer and his or her products; they should be held sacredly at his or her sovereign control.

Gold, silver, greenbacks, and devices heretofore and now used to intervene and make such confusion that even public writers and veteran leaders do not understand, and even say that the philosophy of money is past finding out.

The difficulty is the simplicity of the solution. We cannot carry mason work, carpenter work, or farm products about the exchange for what we want, and therefore require something that represents these, which we can carry about us, and which, being circulated, will procure for the holder of them what they represent. This is all that is needed in money or a circulating medium.

Any combination or organization which distinguishes a party from the rest of mankind cuts off those sympathies which are the natural and legitimate bond of society and which ought to have no limits. The first step toward counteracting this error will be to constitute every individual its own interpreter of language.

TRUE CIVILIZATION

This is an edited and condensed version of True Civilization: An Imme- diate Necessity and the Last Ground of Hope for Mankind, Being the Results and Conclusion of Thirty-Nine Years' Laborious Study and Experiments in Civilization as It Is, and in Different Enterprises for Reconstruction. *Printed in 1863 by Warren in Boston, it reveals a num- ber of difficulties and tensions within an American libertarian tradition faced with slavery and a war for its destruction. As with many libertar- ian theorists (Lysander Spooner and William Lloyd Garrison are notable examples), Warren faced the dilemma of obviously sympathizing with the abolition of slavery, while just as obviously finding the idea of seces- sion to be legitimate and well within the American political tradition. Indeed, Garrison had preached secession from the South for decades, and Warren had actually seceded from the United States many times. At any rate, Warren here, even more than usual, bases his ideas on the Declara- tion of Independence and connects his anarchism to the mainstream of American political thought. There is much that is new here, including the endorsement of a set of quasi-state institutions, including a libertar- ian military (or perhaps citizen militias) and a proposal for arbitration panels. At this time Warren was offering his services as a "counselor in equity" on a for-labor basis. In addition, there is a trenchant critique both of what Warren calls "clanship" and of nationalism. There is also much that is not new, including a fourth chapter that is essentially a republication of the economic sections of* Equitable Commerce *(and for that reason is not included). At any rate, herein is revealed the not-so- subterranean connection of radical individualism with a cosmopolitan outlook on humanity: individualism as a way to reveal the connections of all persons across nations, cultures, religions, and regions. Of course,*

the basic Warren positions of nominalism, pragmatism, and equitable commerce remain intact, but the mood has shifted. Whereas once Warren anticipated redemption, he now feared that he was living in an apocalypse. Whereas he once hoped that many would hear his call and adopt his principles, he now spoke as a lone voice in the wilderness.

Chapter 1: Government and Its True Function

I implore my fellow-men not longer to commit themselves to indiscriminate subordination to any human authority or to the fatal delusions of logic and analogies, nor even to ideas or principles (so called), but to maintain, as far as possible, at all times, the freedom to act according to the apparent merits of each individual case as it may present itself to each individual understanding. There is no other safety for us—no other security for civilization.

If I should prove myself right in ninety-nine points in this work, do not, therefore, conclude that I am right in the hundredth without examination and your own sanction: that one point might be the one in which I was wrong or misunderstood.

With all due deference to other judgments I venture to assert that our present deplorable condition, like that of many other parts of the world, is in consequence of the people in general never having perceived, or else having lost sight of, the legitimate object of all governments as displayed or implied in the American Declaration of Independence.

Every individual of mankind has an "inalienable right to Life, Liberty, and the pursuit of Happiness"; "and it is solely to protect and secure the enjoyment of these rights unmolested that governments can properly be instituted among men." In other terms, self-sovereignty is an instinct of every living organism; and it being an instinct, cannot be alienated or separated from that organism. It is the instinct of self-preservation. The votes of ten thousand men cannot alienate it from a single individual, nor could the bayonets of twenty thousand men neutralize it in any one person any more than they could put a stop to the instinctive desire for food in a hungry man.

The action of this instinct being involuntary, every one has the same absolute right to its exercise that he has to his complexion or the forms of his features, to any extent, not disturbing another; and it is solely to prevent or restrain such disturbances or encroachments, that governments are properly instituted. In still shorter terms, the legitimate and appropriate mission of governments is the defence and protection of the inalienable right of sovereignty in every individual within his or her own sphere.

But what is it that constitutes encroachment?

Suppose my house to be on fire, and I seize a pail of water in the hands of a passer-by, without waiting to explain or ask leave—this would be one degree of encroachment, but perhaps the owner would excuse it on the ground of its necessity. Suppose a man walks into my house without waiting for leave—it may or may not disturb or offend me, or constitute a degree of encroachment. If I find that he has no excusable errand, and require him to retire and he refuses, this would be a degree of encroachment which I might meet with a few words, and might need no government to assist me. If he proceeds to rob the house, I may have reason to think that he is driven to desperation by having a starving family, and I may not resort to violence; or I may perceive that he is a wanton and reckless robber or fillibuster, and that this is an unnecessary encroachment, which, in defence of my own rights, as well as the same rights in others, I am justifiable in resisting; and if I have not sufficient power to do so without endangering myself or property, I will call for help. This help, whether in the form of police or an army, is government, and its function is to use force, to prevent him from using force against me and mine; it interferes, with my consent, to prevent interference with my sovereign right to control my own. Its mission is "intervention for the sake of non-intervention."

If he has already got possession of my purse, I should want him to be compelled, without any unnecessary violence, to give it up; and, perhaps, to compensate the police; and, till I had learned better, I might have approved of his being confined in prison till he had done this, and compensated me for being disturbed. But there are objections to proceeding to these complicated measures. There is no principle (generally) known, by which to determine what constitutes compensation. He could not get properly compensated for his work, which might be a greater injustice to him than he had done to me; and it would inflict on his innocent father, mother, brothers, and sisters, his wife and children, and all his friends, incalculable injustice and suffering, and this would be no compensation to me: besides, I (as a citizen of the same world) am a partner in the crime by not having prevented the temptation to it.

With all these considerations against pursuing him farther, I think it the best present expedient to put up with the restoration of my purse, as he gains nothing to tempt the continuance of the business. The word *expedient* may look loose and unsatisfactory. But among all the works of mankind there is nothing higher than expedients.

The instinct of self-preservation or self-sovereignty is not the work of man, but to keep it constantly in mind as a sacred right in all human intercourse is highly expedient.

Perceiving that we can invent nothing higher than expedients, we necessarily set aside all imperative or absolute authorities, all sanguinary and unbending codes, creeds, and theories, and leave every one free to choose among expedients: or, in other words, we place all action upon the voluntary basis. Do not be alarmed, we shall see this to be the highest expedient whenever it is possible.

It is only when the voluntary is wantonly encroached upon, that the employment of force is expedient or justifiable.

It appears, however, that no rule or law can be laid down to determine beforehand, what will constitute an offensive encroachment—what one will resist another will excuse, and the subtle diversities of different persons and cases, growing out of the inherent individualities of each, have defied all attempts at perfect formulizing excepting this of the sovereignty of every individual over his or her own; and even this must be violated in resisting its violation!

The legitimate sphere of every individual has never been publicly determined; but until it is clearly defined, we can never tell what constitutes encroachment—what may be safely excused, or what may be profitably resisted.

We will attempt then to define the sphere within which every individual may legitimately, rightly exercise supreme power or absolute authority. This sphere would include his or her person, time, property, and responsibilities.

By the word *right* is meant simply that which necessarily tends towards the end in view. The end in view here is permanent and universal peace, and security of person and property.

First, then, while admitting this right of sovereignty in every one, I shall not be guilty of the ill manners of attempting to offensively enforce any of my theoretical speculations, which has been the common error of all governments. This itself would be an attempted encroachment that would justify resistance.

If the Declaration of Independence, or this sacred right of individual sovereignty, had been commonly appreciated a year ago in the "United States," they would not now be disunited. None of the destruction of persons and property which has blackened the past year would have occurred, nor would twelve hundred thousand citizens now be bent on destroying each other and their families and homes in these States.

Every individual would have been free to entertain any theory of government whatever for himself or herself, and to test it by experiment within equitable limits; an issue would be raised only where this sacred right was denied, or against any who should have undertaken to enforce any theory of government whatever upon any individual against his or her consent. The frank and honest admission of this inalienable right would even now change the issue of this present war, and carry relief and protection to the invaded or oppressed, and war or resistance to the oppressor only, whether he were found on one side or the other of a geographical line. Mere theorists say that "the laws of nations decide that a state of war (between two nations) puts all the members of each, in hostility to each other": and that "the laws of nations justify us in doing all the harm we can to our enemies." We need no death-warrant from "authority" against these barbarian theories. The very statement of them becomes their execution.

The whole proper business of government is restraining offensive encroachments, or unnecessary violence to persons and property, or enforcing compensation therefor: but if, in the exercise of this power, we commit any unnecessary violence to any person whatever or to any property, we, ourselves, have become the aggressors, and should be resisted.

But who is to decide how much violence is necessary in any given case? We here arrive at the pivot upon which all power now turns for good or evil; this pivot, under formal, exacting, aggressive institutions or constitutions, is the person who decides as to their meaning. If one decides for all, then all but that one are, perhaps, enslaved. If each one's title to sovereignty is admitted, there will be different interpretations, and this freedom to differ will ensure emancipation, safety, repose, even in a political atmosphere. All the co-operation we ought to expect will come from the coincidence of motives according to the merits of each case as estimated by different minds. Where there is evidence of aggression palpable to all minds, all might co-operate to resist it: and where the case is not clearly made out, there will be more or less hesitation. Two great nations will not then be so very ready to jump at each other's throats when the most cunning lawyers are puzzled to decide which is wrong.

Theorize as we may about the interpretation of the Constitution, every individual does unavoidably measure it and all other words by his own peculiar understanding or conceits, whether he understands himself or not, and should, like General Jackson, recognize the fact, "take the responsibility of it," and qualify himself to meet its consequences.

It will be asked, what could be accomplished by a military organization, if every subordinate were allowed to judge of the propriety of an order before he obeyed it? I answer that nothing could be accomplished that did not commend itself to men educated to understand, and trained to respect, the rights of persons and property as set forth in the Declaration of Independence; and that here, and here only, will be found the long-needed check to the barbarian wantonness that lays towns in ashes and desolates homes and hearts for brutal revenge, or to get office or a little vulgar newspaper notoriety.

But what shall ensure propriety of judgment or uniformity or co-incidence between the subordinates and the officers? I answer, drill, discipline—of mind as well as of arms and legs—teaching all to realize their true mission. The true object of all their power being clearly defined and made familiar, there would at once be a coincidence unknown before, and but slight chance of dissent when there was good ground for co-operation.

No subordination can be more perfect than that of an orchestra, but it is all voluntary.

If it be true that the sole proper function of coercive force is to restrain or repair all unnecessary violence, then the conclusion is inevitable that all penal laws (for punishing a crime or an act after it is committed except so far as they work to compensate the injured party equitably) are themselves criminal. The excuse is that punishment is "a terror to evildoers"; but those who punish instead of preventing crime are themselves evildoers, and according to their own theory they should be punished and terrified. But the theory is false: consistently carried out, it would depopulate the world. Such are the fogs in which we get astray when we trust ourselves away from first premises and substitute speculative theories in their stead.

The barbarian habit of shedding blood for irreparable offences ("as a terror to evildoers") carried fully out, mutual slaughter will continue till there would not be a man, woman, or child, living upon the earth.

A man cannot alienate his inalienable right of self-preservation or sovereignty by joining the military or any other combination. The assumption that this is possible has produced all our political confusion and violence, and will continue to produce just such fruits to the end of time, if the childish blunder is not exposed and corrected.

Having one man as general over thousands, arises from the natural necessity for individuality in the directing mind when numbers wish to move together; but it does not necessarily imply any superiority of judgment or motive in the director of a movement beyond those of the subordinates, any more shall the driver of an omnibus be presumed to know the road better than the passengers. They may all know the road equally well, but if they all undertake to drive the horses, none of their purposes will be answered; and it would be equally ridiculous for the driver, under the plea of upholding subordination, to insist on carrying his passengers where they did not want to go, or refuse to let them get out when they wanted to "secede."

The most intelligent people always make the best subordinates in a good cause, and in our modern military it will require more true manhood to make a good subordinate than it will to be a leader. For the leader may very easily give orders, but they take the responsibility of that only, while the subordinate takes the responsibility of executing them, and it will require the greatest and highest degree of manhood, of self-government, presence of mind, and real heroism to discriminate on the instant and to stand up individually before all the corps and future criticisms, and assume, alone, the responsibility of dissent or disobedience. His only support and strength would be in his consciousness of being more true to his professed mission than the order was, and in the assurance that he would be sustained by public opinion and sympathy as far as that mission was understood.

Subordinates have many times refused to fire on their fellow-citizens in obedience to the mere wantonness of authority, or of the ferocity of a crude discipline, and have thus, like William Tell, entitled themselves to the lasting gratitude and affection of generations.

Even children, when drilled and trained with this idea (which is simply the true democratic idea), would become an ever-ready police to protect each other and the gardens, fruits, and other property around them, instead of being, as they often are, the imps of disturbance and destruction. The height of their ambition being to play "soger" [soldier], and fight somebody or destroy something.

This is our fault. The democratic idea, theoretically at the base of American institutions, has never been introduced into our military discipline, nor into our courts, nor into our laws, and only in a caricatured and distorted shape into our political system, our commerce, our education, and public opinion.

A "Union" not only on paper, but rooted in the heart, whose members, trained in the constant reverence for the inalienable right of sovereignty in every person, would be habituated to forbearance towards even wrong opinions and different educations and tastes, to patient endurance of irremediable injuries, and a self-governing deportment and gentleness of manner, and a prompt but careful resistance to wanton aggression wherever found, which would meet with a ready and an affectionate welcome in any part of the world.

No coercive system of taxation could be necessary to such a government. A government so simple that children will be first to comprehend it, and which even they can see it for their interests to assist: and then would as readily play "soger" to prevent mischief, as to do mischief.

With our mind's eye steadily fixed on this great democratic principle and object, let us immediately commence the agitation of the idea of forming companies of home-guards on this principle.

Let any one who feels so disposed, take the first steps and invite the co-operation of persons sufficiently intelligent to comprehend the object to form a nucleus. (The known habitual regard to the "inalienable rights" of persons and property would be the best title to membership.) Then, commence drill and discipline, keeping in mind all the time the kind of discipline required, which would be partly in the form of lectures taking as texts the details of the destruction of persons and property going on all around us, and showing with how much less violence the same or better objects could have been accomplished: and in the drill, giving some orders to do some unnecessary harm, on purpose to be disobeyed in order to accustom the subordinates to "look before they leap" or strike.

Such a military force would be within but not under discipline. In other words, its "sabbath would be made for man—not man for its sabbath."[1] To be under instead of within discipline is a mistake as fatal as that of getting under water instead of within water.

Companies thus formed would do well to communicate with each other, which would be all the general organization required for a world-wide co-operation.

The charms of music, of mutual sympathy, the beauties of order, and of unity of dress and of movement in military displays, now so seductive to purposes of destruction and degradation, would entice to the highest and noblest objects of human ambition, which would never need a field of activity as long as wanton oppression (even of a single individual) has footing on the earth.

Government, strictly and scientifically speaking, is a coercive force; a man, while governed with his own consent, is not governed at all.

Deliberative bodies, such as legislatures, congresses, conventions, courts, etc., scientifically speaking, are not government, which is simply coercive force. But, inasmuch as that force should never be employed without a deliberate reference to its legitimate object, and upon which all available wisdom should be brought to bear, a deliberative council, acting before or with the government, seems highly expedient if not indispensable.

Moreover there are subjects now before us, and continually arising, on which, by timely forethought, violent issues may be prevented from arising, and many most important subjects may be adjusted by counsel alone, without any appeal to force.

Such counselors should not be tempted by unearned salaries and honors, nor by compensation measured by the necessities or weakness and defencelessness of their clients; nor should they consist of those who, like editors of news, can make more money by wars and other calamities than they can by peace and general prosperity, but let the counselors be those who are willing to wait, like tillers of the soil, for compensation according to the quantity and quality of their work. Let compensation or honors come in the form of voluntary contributions after benefits have been realized.

It is therefore suggested that any person, of either sex, who may coincide with this proposition, and who feels competent to give counsel in any department of human affairs, publicly announce the fact, as lawyers and physicians now do, or permit their names and functions to be made accessible to the public in some manner, so that whoever may need honest counsel on any subject may know where to find it. If a meeting of such counselors is thought desirable by any interested party, he or she can invite such as are thought to be most competent for the occasion, according to the subject to be considered.

These counselors, while in session, would constitute a deliberative assembly, or advisory tribunal. It might consist of both sexes or either sex, according to the nature of the subject to be deliberated upon.

After deliberation, or whenever any interested party feels ready to make up an opinion, let him or her write it down with the reasons for it, and present it to the counselors and the audience, for their signatures, and let the document go forth to the public or to the interested parties. If there are several such documents, those having the signatures of counselors or persons most known to be reliable would have the most weight; but, in order to ensure any influence or benefit from either, let compensation come to the counselors like that to Rowland Hill, in voluntary contributions after the benefits of the opinions have, to some extent, been realized.[2]

After having thus brought the best experience and well-balanced counsels to bear upon any subject without satisfying all parties, every person has a sovereign right to differ from all the opinions of the tribunal while not invading or disturbing other persons or property.

To ensure the best order in such a deliberative assembly, no other subject than the one for which it is called should be introduced without unanimous consent; as each and every one has a sovereign right to appropriate his own time and to choose the subjects that shall occupy his attention: and a constant regard to the same right, fully appreciated by all, will suggest the careful avoidance of all unnecessary disturbance which might prevent any one from hearing whatever he or she prefers to listen to. This sentiment becoming familiar to all as a monitor, but little disturbance would occur—when it did occur, the principle itself would immediately prompt its appreciators to stop it with as little violence as possible.

A subject of great or universal interest may be laid before all such tribunals in the world, and their decisions brought to every city, village, and neighborhood, and to every door; and the relief from all disturbing controversies would be felt at every fireside.

The sanction of such tribunals, to any enterprise for public benefit, would place its author or inventor fairly before the public for their patronage, instead of being left to starve for want of attention; while the absence or want of such sanction would put a sudden stop to the swarms of impostures and fallacies that now wear out the attention to no purpose, and render valueless the announcements of even valuable things: while with such a sanction, the public might look at advertisements with some prospect of benefit therefrom.

We will ask them what constitutes legitimate property? We will ask them for the least violent mode of securing land to the homeless and starving. Also, what would constitute the just reward of labor? We shall invite them to consider what ought to be the circulating medium, or money. How it happens that the producers and makers of everything have comparatively nothing. And we shall ask them for some mode of adapting supplies to demands, for a better postal system, for a more equitable system of buying and selling, for a program of education in accordance with the democratic principle.

A conservatory and library will naturally spring up, where the records of the tribunal decisions and other contributions to public welfare will be preserved for reference and diffusion; and the world will begin to know its benefactors.

A modern military, as a government, will be necessary only in the transitionary stage of society from confusion and wanton violence to true order and mature civilization.

When the simply wise shall sit in calm deliberation, patiently tracing out the complicated and entangled causes of avarice, of robberies, of murders, of wars, of poverty, of desperation, of suicides, of slaveries and fraud, violence and suffering of all kinds, and shall have found appropriate and practical means of preventing instead of punishing them, then the military will be the fitting messengers of relief and harbingers of security and of peace, of order and unspeakable benefits wherever their footsteps are found; and, instead of being the desolators of the world, they will be hailed from far and near as the blessed benefactors of mankind.

If others see in this only the "inauguration of anarchy," let no attempt be made to urge them into conformity, but let them freely and securely await the results of demonstration.

Chapter 2: Self-Preservation

Words, though they are things themselves, are mainly the signs of things.

We see the sign of "Dry Goods." The sign is exceedingly well executed, but it gives us no adequate idea of the goods within; no one would order any quantity of them before going within to examine the things to which the sign referred.

My words here are intended to be the signs of ideas or facts; but even the best-chosen and best-arranged words are full of ambiguity and imperfections, and it is unsafe for a reader to take it for granted that the writer on a subject of vital interest can do everything for him. There is a part which the reader is obliged to act for himself; that is, to look beyond or within the mere words or signs for the idea intended to be conveyed. With this precaution kept vividly before the reader, the mere execution of the sign is of secondary importance. Delicious foreign fruits and spices are brought to us in very rough and crude envelopes; but they are the best the conditions of their producers afford, and we are content to get our figs, our dates and cinnamon without much regard to the mats in which they are conveyed to us.

Before we begin to probe the festering mass now called "civilization," let us prepare ourselves with all the spirit of forbearance which the case allows, that we need not add any unnecessary pangs to the already exhausted and dying patient.

"I know," says B., "that you do not admit analogies as proof, but is there not some indication of the divine law in the large fishes eating up the little ones, and in spiders spinning webs to entrap flies? Is not this the work of the Deity, who is all perfection, and can we hope to alter these things permanently for the better?"

Answer. Are we willing to admit from the first glance at analogies that the law for fishes and insects is also the law for cultivated, civilized man?

Cultivation is as much the law for man as primitive crudity is. But suppose we admit that the same law governs men, fishes, and insects. What is that law which is inherent and indestructible in all? It is the instinct of self-preservation. Fishes and insects would not perhaps eat each other raw and alive, if, like man, they had the means of preparation and cooking; nor would they run the risk, nor take the trouble of pursuing each other in continuous warfare, if, like men, they had more safe or expeditious modes of preserving their existence. It is our particular privilege to have an abundance of superior modes, and it is only for want of the appreciation of them, or when cut off from them by casualties that we are driven to the level of fishes and spiders. Although we cannot talk at all without resorting to analogies to illustrate our meaning, nothing is more likely to lead us astray when they are too readily accepted as parallels.

Every thing and person is invested with some peculiarities, which constitute its, his, or her individuality. And it is not safe for us to lose sight of this for a moment in our intercourse with each other. The fishes, the insects, and perhaps all animals, man included, act according to their external and internal conditions.

This is one divine law; self-preservation is another divine or primitive law. The modes of living and eating are not laws, but customs, or habits, or expedients, and are subject to modifications as conditions change. (The Divine, as I understand and use the word, means, simply, the not human. The sun, the winds, the tides, electricity, and whatever else exists without the aid of man are of divine origin—that is, not of human origin. I prefer however, in order to avoid ambiguity and misunderstanding, to distinguish all these as belonging to primitive nature, and the works of man as of the secondary nature. Hence may arise the phrases primitive sphere, and secondary sphere.)[3]

The carefully bred and cultivated man or woman who would take pains to extricate a fly from a spider's web, or who would sit up all night to keep the flies away from a sick infant, or to wet its lips occasionally, and who from pure humanitary feelings would almost sicken at the idea of eating the smallest morsel of nicely cooked veal, might, in the frenzy of starvation on a wrecked vessel, involuntarily seize and devour with frightful voracity a portion of a fellow-passenger, even a dear friend, from the sheer, uncontrollable instinct of self-preservation.

Such is the overwhelming power of conditions. The same instinct is at work in both opposite cases: in the most delicate attentions to the happiness of others, pleasure is derived in proportion to the pleasure conferred or the pain averted; which, for want of better phraseology, may be ranked as one of the modes of pursuing happiness, or of the promptings of the instinct of self-satisfaction or self-preservation: exactly the same instinct that leads to such opposite results under other conditions.

Self-preservation is the law of fish, of insects, and of men and women, but let us take care that we do not assume an accident to be a law, and so content ourselves to remain on a level with worms and bugs. Our immense resources are as natural, as much (the law) to us as the want of them is to insects; and it is by using them that we have thus far ameliorated our condition; and, by still greater and better uses of them, we may reach an infinitely higher plane, or modes of life, than any ever yet realized. It is the difference in our capacities for improvement, not in the fundamental or primitive laws, that lead to such different results.

Chapter 3: Probing Civilization

The primitive, uncultivated, undeveloped man finds himself abroad among lions, tigers, hyenas, orang-outangs, gorillas, reptiles, and insects, all making war—no, not making war (they have not sunk so low) but from the unregulated instinct of self-preservation, and the pressure of conditions, all preying upon each other.

The same instinct prompts them to herd together, for mutual protection against outside aggression. Having once formed a tribe or clan, clanship becomes looked upon as the warrant for safety, and all outside of any particular clan or tribe become, by degrees, ranked as enemies, aliens, or foreigners, to be weakened, conquered, or exterminated; and he who proves most expert in the work of murder or of plundering the outsiders, is considered the one most fit to secure and administer peace, justice, and true order within his own tribe, and is at once proclaimed as the great Matiambo, Moene, Chief, King, or President of the tribe or clan.

There being, as yet, no constitutions, no legislatures nor Courts to regulate the internal affairs of the clan, this great Matiambo is, they think, a necessity, and it is equally a necessity, that, having a Matiambo, every one should render unhesitating obedience to his will, or all would be "anarchy and confusion."

Thus these poor primitive creatures reason. There is no fault in the logic and therefore there is no fault seen in the results. The Matiambo becomes drunk with power of which he knows not the true use. He may become crazy with vanity or with embarrassing cares, and they see him in the streets with drawn sword in his hand, cutting off the heads of whomsoever he meets to test the "loyalty" of his subjects, loyalty even to a crazy savage being the highest virtue known, and disloyalty punished with the most wanton barbarity. Thus the Matiambo proves a more destructive enemy than all the foreigners put together could prove, if each one was left to defend himself. But horror-stricken as the poor barbarian subjects may be, and trembling in every limb (for no one knows whose turn may come next), as a kind of propitiatory offering they break out in chorus:

Hurrah, hurrah, hurrah!
Hurrah for Hug-ga-boo-jug!
Hurrah for Hug-ga-boo-joo!
The king of the world is the great Hug-ga-boo.
Hurrah for the son of the sun!
Hurrah for the son of the moon!
If he ever dies, he will die too soon.

Buffalo of Buffaloes, Bull of Bulls,
He sits on a throne of his enemies' skulls,
And if he wants more to play at foot-ball,
Ours are at his service—All, all, all.
Hug-ga-boo-jug—Hug-ga-boo-joo!
The king of the world is the great Hug-ga-boo.

We are still, at this moment, in the midst of barbarism. Civilization has made no advance in the political sphere beyond the most crude and savage tribes. It has made little progress except in mechanism. Take that away, and what should we exhibit as civilization? Even in mechanism the arts of destruction have gone beyond those of preservation, and the best military commander is announced, without blushing, to be he who can most adroitly mislead, deceive, entrap, and kill his fellow-men, who are at least his equals in every view of manhood and worth.

No people can ever rise above this barbarian level as long as they unhesitatingly follow any leaders without thinking where they are going. We want a Luther in the political sphere, and another in the financial sphere, another in the commercial, another in the educational sphere, to rouse the people to use their own experience.

Clanship is the worst feature of barbarism. As soon as different tribes are formed, each member prefers, or is compelled to profess to prefer, his own clan or tribe to all others, on pain of being murdered as a "traitor." His motto must be, like that of Daniel Webster, My tribe, my whole tribe, and nothing but my tribe! That of Daniel Webster was, "My country, my whole country, and nothing but my country!"

This spirit arrays all tribes, clans, and countries against each other; and hostilities once commenced between them, they are increased and perpetuated for retaliation or revenge, and excused as "terrors to evildoers." In this way it becomes equivalent to a death-warrant to belong to any clan or party; and yet, if one belongs to none, but wishes to discriminate and do justice by acknowledging the right that there may be among either party, then all parties are against him; for, say they, "whoever is not for us is against us."

Our present internal war is of barbarian origin. It grows directly out of clanship, or tribeism. One portion of the tribe (or nation) wanted to form a tribe or nation by itself, but the other portion undertook to prevent them. They said that the "fathers had said that the tribe should remain one and inseparable now and forever." That the fathers had spoken, and that it was the duty of all of us to obey.

Yes, replies the other party, "and the fathers have said another thing too—they said that whenever the government of a tribe was not satisfactory to the governed, they have a right to 'alter or abolish it.'"

But, replies the first party, "you must take the mode prescribed by the constitution." But, says the second, "we don't choose to be ruled by your constitution—it is no longer our constitution. It does not suit us—we propose to have one of our own." But, says the first party, "you must get a majority of the tribe to consent to that." But, says the second, "we do not consent to ask leave of your majority; and if you insist on that, you deny all right of political freedom, which is a direct return to barbaric government, or to the right of the strongest."

To this, the first party replies that to permit disintegration without the consent of the majority is to "inaugurate universal confusion."

Now, reader, just pause a moment. Had there been no clan or "Union" formed at all, or had it continued no longer than the occasion for it, this war would never have arisen. Other disturbances might have come from other causes, but never from this. But, to preserve this clanship unbroken, and retain all its members in peaceful repose, the advocates of "unbroken Union" abruptly refuse to negotiate with the receding party (who offer compensation for what they must take with them), thereby finally denying their right to become a separate parley, and pronouncing the final word that the Union recognizes no two parties who can negotiate with each other; which is equivalent to saying that the political Union (or clanship) is more sacred than persons, or property, or freedom, or any other inalienable human right. Thus completely destroying the last vestige of union between the parties, and forcing both into hostile attitudes, and both prepare to destroy each other.

Now are heard the wails of distress from all quarters. The papers are filled with accounts of brutal violence on both sides—villages burning—men hanging—ferocity let loose in every horrid shape and form. The heated passions on both sides become more and more ferocious. A curious way to promote union! A frenzy of rage sweeps over the land while I write. The last step of despotism has been taken by both governments. Freedom of action and speech are annihilated in "the land of the free and the home of the brave." Even these written words may prove the death-warrant of the writer. Nothing but the clamor of war and the fear of prisons and violent deaths, smother, for the moment, the low moan from desolated hearths and broken hearts from the depths of the hell we are in.

In the mean time, where is the "Union"?

If the clan or "Union" had never been formed, or had it continued no longer than was agreeable to the parties to it, this war would never have occurred.

I take up some of the papers nearest at hand, and I read that one man is nailed to a tree—absolutely crucified and left, gagged, starving to death for several days; not for any of his own acts, but for the acts or theories of his clan or party. Immediately the cry of "revenge" is heard, not against the particular perpetrators of the horrid deed, but against the party or clan to which he belongs, the innocent portions of whom are more likely to suffer for the crime than the perpetrators of it. Thus clanship, annihilating all individual responsibility, leaves rapacity and cruelty unrestrained.

Again I read, "Ten thousand men killed and wounded, but a much larger number on the enemy's side. The town of S— in ashes; N— is threatened; the village of B— in flames within sight, and old men, children, and women screaming frantically, and running in all directions."

The blood boils, the brain is on fire when the corpse of a dear son, a father, or husband is found on the field, or amid the ruins of once peaceful homes. Frenzy and despair take possession of some, and a desperate spirit of revenge inspires other women who will soon be mothers; of the children born in the midst of these horrors, many will be stillborn, others wholly or partly idiots, others with an uncontrollable hereditary disposition to shed blood—to destroy whatever or whoever comes in their way. Then come more wars, murders, and violence beyond computation. What then, is the prospect for the next generation and their descendants? Let it be observed that, before displaying such shocking prospects, the preventive has been already presented in the first chapter. Let us see if the preventive is really there.

When one party first proposed to disintegrate itself from the political "Union" (clan), if the other portion had said, according to the Declaration of Independence, "As the right of any people to alter or abolish any government is absolute and 'inalienable,' of course, you have the whole of the deciding power in your own hands. We can have no voice in the matter unless you desire it as counsel. We think it would be a dangerous and difficult expedient for both parties; but this opinion we submit only as advice. If you decide on leaving us, we have some forts, mints, and other communistic property to divide, but we anticipate no difficulty in regard to that. Each party, or both together, can call councils of the best-balanced minds to deliberate on the subject and suggest the best modes of adjustment, and we dare say that this will not be difficult." Would not this mode, or rather this great principle, having been applied in the right time, have prevented all these horrors and this destruction?

What is the reply to this? Is it what we see in the newspapers?—that it would "encourage disintegration and be the inauguration of universal confusion"? That the war is "to preserve the nation as a nation and the Union unbroken"? These statements, uniformly insisted on, even by the executive himself, prove decidedly and fully that the war has been inaugurated and prosecuted merely to preserve clanship, as I have stated, for nationality is no more or less than clanship, and clanship is the worst feature of barbarism. I do not accuse any one of intentional wickedness nor of wantonness or indifference to the horrors that surround and involve us; on the contrary, I see the whole to be a lamentable mistake, the unavoidable result of a blind reverence for precedents, for legal technicalities and formal institutions, instead of for the deep underlying principles which gave rise to the institutions. Now look at the results. If we are now in civilization, what is barbarism?

Let us, in imagination at least, have done with clanship, and converse as two individuals disintegrated from all party or partial trammels.

A says, "I can find no fault with the proposition you make with regard to the councils of deliberation or reference, and feel happy to think that the great idea underlying our institutions is not forgotten or ignored, but that it even instructs us what to do in the greatest and most difficult trial. But why do you think that an immediate separation would be a bad expedient for both of us?"

B replies, "First on account of the geographical interlockings of our interests which may be very difficult to disentangle suddenly. Then there is your slave system. The right of self-sovereignty in every human being, which gives you the supreme right to leave us without asking our leave gives to your slaves the same right to leave you, and also gives to every man, woman, and child the same supreme right to sympathize with and assist the distressed or oppressed wherever they are found as the greatest and holiest mission of life; and this might lead to new disasters for which we have no preventive or remedy provided. You have been born under the system, and your habits make you entirely dependent upon slaves. I do not blame you for the circumstances under which you were born; I hardly know which of the two classes is most enslaved, or most to be pitied, slaves or masters.

"The principle upon which you claim the right to secede from us is perfectly unassailable; it is the inalienable right of self-sovereignty but it extends farther than you may have contemplated it. It is a full and complete warrant for any one of your citizens to place himself above all your legislation, above the whole confederacy, and appeal to the world for protection, and having asserted the principle in your own favor, you cannot successfully deny it to others.

"I cannot say what others may do, and, as you know, I cannot dictate to others, without denying their right to think, and decide for themselves; but while I assert the right of freedom to all slaves, black and white, I will exert myself to foresee and prevent, as far as possible, all unnecessary violence to you from slaves or from any other source."

A asks, "Is this the philosophy of your party? If it is, I belong to it, in the Union or out of the Union."

B, "I cannot speak for a party, but only for myself positively, and of probabilities with regard to other individuals as far as I know them. No other person is in any way pledged to or responsible for anything I may say or promise."

A, "But what shall be done with the Constitution?"

B, "I do not know what others may do with it—my constitution is within me. The right of self-sovereignty in every individual is my constitution."

A, "Really, this is rather a new view to take of politics, but it is in perfect accordance with the spirit of all constitutions. I find myself in union with you at any rate; on that principle there never can be secession at all. There can be no secession from the freedom to secede!"

I would gladly turn now from the sickening, fainting patient before us, but must probe a little farther.

Clanship, by destroying individual responsibility, enables the crafty criminal to escape, and expose the innocent of his tribe to retribution. Six men are hung on one tree for daring to be of the other party, and those who hung them belonged to the party professing to be contending for freedom. Others are forced to expose their lives and die fighting against the party of their choice. They must do this or be shot by order of their rulers.

Reader, which party do you think it was that hung these men for a difference of political preferences? Which party is it that forces men, with "inalienable rights of life, liberty, and the pursuit of happiness," to fight against their own wills or be shot? Which party is it that murders men for taking down a flag, or preferring one flag to another? Which party is it that professes to be fighting for freedom?

He must reply, It is both parties, and that both profess to be contending for freedom.

Both claim to be contending for self-preservation. That is nothing new, but that all the powers of both parties should be bestowed in destroying instead of preserving life, property, and freedom can be accounted for only by the blind readiness with which the present imitates the past, without any reference to the inevitable consequences. Which party is it that does not suppress the freedom of action, of speech, and of the press and punish with imprisonment or death an honest avowal of an opinion in favour of the opposite party?

Which party is it that does not treat as treason, punishable with death, the admission of a single point wherein the opposite party may be right, as "giving aid and comfort to the enemy"? In other words, which party is it that does not threaten to punish with death that single item of justice? Who would ever think of introducing such monstrous rules if they were new? But they are found among the "precedents," the "usages of governments," "the laws of war," "the laws of nations," and are therefore blindly followed though they lead the very leaders into the ditch or over the precipice. This blind repetition of barbarism must be criticised and stopped, or one continuous round of mutual murder and destruction will continue to the end of time.

The hanging of these men and the desolating of their families was in strict logical accordance with the barbarian "laws of war," which are an ever-ready excuse for every wild and shocking atrocity that rapacity, revenge, or wantonness may prompt. The "laws of war," say these barbarians, put all the members of a tribe (nation) in hostility with each other. And when at war we may properly "do all the harm we can to our enemies." Both parties take their texts from the same authorities. The "laws of war," "military necessity," the laws of nations, are constantly in the mouths of both parties as excuses for all their barbarian acts, and yet, when one commits an atrocity in strict accordance with these admitted axioms, the other party forthwith talks of revenge.

If one party is more humane or more civilized than the other, it acts less in accordance with these "laws of war"; and if one individual is more civilized or humane than the rest of his party, or both parties, he is not at home in either; on the contrary, for his beautiful humanitary feelings, for his high sense of honor, justice, and discrimination, he has two chances of being murdered, where blind, headlong party ferocity has only one.

There are no "laws of war," "nor laws of nations," nor military necessities, nor laws of men, that ought to command a moment's respect or attention, unless they tend to diminish suffering instead of increasing it: and true civilization will discard everything that prompts or excuses any unnecessary violence to any person or property.

The fatal tendency of an unquestioning readiness to follow precedents may possibly have led to the shocking ease of crucifixion mentioned; perhaps it was prompted by the common blunder as a "terror to evildoers," perhaps the horrid thought was first suggested to the perpetrators by the precedent so painfully familiar to all Christendom.

A similar atrocity was perpetrated in the French Revolution. A young woman only for being of the other party, a fact over which she had no control, was also crucified. Her feet were spiked to the ground, wide apart, and she was made to stand by a tree, to which she was bound, and a slow fire was placed and kept under her till she died in the most excruciating torture.

Now that the race is so far sunken, either by hereditary propensities, or by a continuous, unhesitating copying of the past, what can we do better than to step up at once above these horrid precedents and authorities, and interfere to prevent all unnecessary and wanton violence? This was probably the original design of making laws, as it is called, and trial by jury, etc., but they have all failed; for barbarism and insane violence reign triumphant throughout the misnomer of civilization.

Did human beings ever commit any other blunder so great as that of forming themselves into clans or nations? When the passions or propensities have possession, the intellect sleeps, and responsibility being annihilated, there is nothing too horrible to expect. I venture the assertion that there is but one way to emerge from this otherwise endless chaos of misery and degradation; that is, directly to bestow all practicable energies in the direction indicated in the first chapter, and to solicit the cooperation of all persons, without regard to party, sect, theories, sex, or nation, to consider in leisure and in calmness the basis of true civilization.

Clanship can exist among fishes of one kind, among ants, bees, and other insects, and among the crude clans of men, who like ants, bees, or dried herrings on a stick, have no individual development, but who are all alike. When the mental eyes they had have been punched out by barbarian power in the process of stringing them on the stick of subordination or loyalty: and if no intellectual expansion were possible, clanship would continue to desolate the earth; but just in proportion to intellectual expansion, individuality makes its appearance, and begins to conflict with the dried-herring subordination, and naturally gives rise to the first steps in disintegration or the commencement of true civilization.

Fortunately for us, external force cannot limit nor suppress ideas. Take a hundred persons as completely "unitized," and as destitute of ideas as dried herrings, and place them within a building having iron walls three feet thick, and guarded by a thousand men. Ideas may find their way among them that can liberate them from that condition, or destroy them.

A savage who has for half a lifetime eaten with his fingers out of the same dish with twenty others, all obstructing each other's movements, conceives, perhaps, the idea of a wooden paddle or a pointed stick to use in the communistic dish. But it's not "the fashion." It is not "according to precedents." It is not what "the fathers intended." But he may say to himself, "I am not one of the fathers, I am another person. I don't see why I should not have my way as well as they, provided I do not put the fathers, nor anybody else, to any inconvenience."

The germ of true civilization is now fairly planted and perhaps it expands so far that he sees that a separate sleeping apartment would be more agreeable to all in a hot climate than sleeping in one nest with twenty or thirty others, like a litter of pigs; but then this would be "disintegration," and might not be permitted by the "majority,"

for it is "isolation" and "selfishness," and not according to the "precedents" and "best authorities"; "society has a right to the society of
all its members." "Well," says the savage, "I will not then be a member of any society. I will be an individual."

Now a piece of ground is wanted to stand his house upon. This
possession of a piece of land disintegrated, individualized from the
communistic domain, has been considered one of the greatest and
most indispensable features of civilization, and so it is. But beyond
this, society has attained little or nothing by the way of adjustment.

A barbarian strolling, upon the beach, perhaps in search of tortoises, accidentally picks up a little shell that is rather new to him,
and he shows it to another savage, who, for the sake of the novelty,
offers to give him for it the beaver which he has just caught, and the
exchange is made; and so the second owner of the shell, when his
curiosity its satisfied, gives it to a third person for a tortoise-shell. A
ship arrives on the coast in search of tortoise-shells, and gives this
savage beads, nails, and a hatchet for his shell. Immediately every savage abandons his hunting of beavers and every other pursuit for the
hunting of tortoises; in the course of which they find more of the little
shells, and give them the name of "cowries." One cowry once having
purchased a beaver, this "precedent" is accepted as "authority" for
the "market-price" of a beaver; so as many cowries as each finds, so
many beavers he considers himself "worth," and, by degrees, as this
"roast pig" progresses, these cowries are given and received for ivory,
fish, etc., and become a circulating medium, or money. But, in making these exchanges no reference whatever is had to the time or trouble in procuring either the cowries or the articles exchanged for them;
it being altogether a matter of accident, no calculations can be made.

There is no basis for calculation; but the cowries prove very convenient; for they enable each one to confine his attention and preparations to one particular pursuit, and to exchange its products for all
the things he needs, instead of being obliged to do everything for
himself to disadvantage. By only catching beavers and giving them for

cowries, he can procure fish, tortoise-shells, ivory, musk-rats, mocca-sins, mats, spears, etc., which is an immense saving of time and trou-ble to him. Others, seeing this, imitate his example, and as the accumulation of cowries affords a prospect of everything needed, the pursuit and accumulation of cowries becomes the rage of all; every savage abandons his beaver-hunting, or his fishing, his musk-rat traps, etc., and all rush to the hunt for cowries. They get a large sup-ply, but there is nothing to buy with them. There are no fish caught, no muskrats, no mats made, no ivory found, no mellons raised. The ship has carried away all the tortoise-shells, and the cowries are com-paratively worthless.

One old cunning savage, seeing the general thoughtless rush for cowries, had taken advantage of it and "bought up" all the fish, musk-rats, ivory, mats, spears, nails, etc., against their return. He now has all in his own power, for "whoever feeds can govern," and he demands the whole of their cowries for the few supplies that they are obliged to have to supply present necessities, and the population give him all the cowries they have gathered along the whole coast for months, in exchange for a few necessaries which they could have made for themselves in as many hours. They feel that they are wronged, but do not see where the wrong is.

The next day the cunning old savage's house and sheds are set on fire for revenge, and no one being disposed to help him, they and all their contents are consumed, cowries and all, and he is reduced to beggary; but no one relieves him. The cowries have all been collected for miles along the beach and he can get none: he is not qualified to make mats, nor spears, nor nails, nor to catch beavers, and he wan-ders about a miserable and despised savage, having made himself mis-erable by overreaching his fellow-savages.

There has been no improvement upon that crude and barbarous money to this day of the Christian era, 1862, unless it is in substituting little bits of copper, or other comparatively worthless metals with the semblance of a man's head or some animal upon them, instead of the cowries, as a circulating medium.

Bank-notes, promising to pay these bits of metal on demand, if they were not the means of defrauding as well as of deluding the public, would be an improvement upon metals, as being more convenient of carriage, and costing less trouble in many ways; but, being, as they are, the means of innumerable and constant frauds and delusion, they are barbarian money barbarized. All the crudity in principle remains, with intentional frauds added.

No reference whatever is had to the comparative trouble that anything costs the one who first obtains or produces it, but whoever stumbles in his rambles upon a lump of any of these metals, has, forthwith, according to the size of the lump, a demand upon every product and service under the sun.

There being no principle known for the regulation or adjustment of the quantity of these metals, which should be given in exchange for any service or commodity, the whole is left to accident, or else to some, like the cunning savage, to take advantage of the necessities of others, and a general scramble ensues to get the advantage or to escape being overreached. In this general strife, those with the longest purses, or the most cunning, or who are most unscrupulous and false, prevail. Those who have few or no cowries and the less crafty are trodden under foot, and ground to powder and what is called society has blundered on into a universal scramble for the largest possible accumulation of cowry metals, as offering the best among poor chances of security against the general rapacity. In this melee the instinct of self-preservation in each one is almost wholly bent on keeping uppermost, instead of being crushed below. Political power and money are the principal means of attaining ends, and these are therefore pursued with unscrupulous desperation.

A little money (by usury) "makes more," but it takes from those who have less, till those with less have none to take. Then woe to those who are found in such ranks. Nobody will be found there who can avoid it. Driven to work for whatever money-holders choose to give, they take the pittance rather shall starve, and starve when they cannot get the work or the pittance. Then who that can avoid it will belong to the ranks of starved, ragged, abused, insulted labor? Whoever can avoid it will do so, and the burdens fall upon the weak who have no means of escape.

This is the origin of all slaveries. They all grow out of the fact that civilization has not yet proceeded far enough to discover what would be a proper, legitimate, equitable compensation or price even for a barrel of flour.

When the masses are silenced by weakness, the conflict becomes intensified between the few who have monopolized money and the governing or political power. The mass become mere ciphers to be placed by the sides of these figures, only to increase their magnitude and power in their contests with each other. The right of might is the only umpire known or acknowledged, and conquest becomes the object of all.

Looking at causes, and understanding the instinct of self-preservation, who wonders at the miser? Who wonders at the borders of black or white slaves? Who wonders at burglary, highway robbery, thefts, frauds, bribery, and corruption in office? or at the general distrust of man in his kind? or at the extremes of waste and walls that are so often found face to face?

The two great elements of power are the governing (military) force and money.

The equilibrium of the governing power has already been suggested in the first chapter; but until a principle is found and accepted which can harmoniously regulate compensation for labor (or regulate prices), and establish an equilibrium of the money power, we can hardly assert that civilization has fairly commenced.

Chapter 5: Organization and Co-operation Without Sectism or Clanship, and Conflict Without Freedom

Organization and clanship are both prompted, in some respects, by similar motives: the universal desire for sympathy, the need of mutual assistance, and other expected benefits. But while clanship, with its usual concomitants, is more destructive to the very ends proposed than any external enemy could prove, organization without these concomitants, and in accordance with the great primitive laws, may enable us to realize more than utopians ever dreamed of.

Such is the instinctive yearning for sympathy with our kind, there is no cost too great to pay for it.

It is so pleasant to coincide with those around us, and we are so wretched when in continuous collision with the feelings, tastes, or opinions of others, that it is not surprising that we often fall in with customs and fashions without examination, and go with whatever current is running rather than array ourselves hopelessly against them.

A poor young woman stole a fashionable bonnet, for the sake of appearing at church in the mode. She was arrested and sent to prison, and her self-respect destroyed for life, because her desire for the sympathy of her kind was stronger or more directly present to her than the fear of the prison. The word *glory*: what does it mean but the public sympathy or notice that one gets by a public act? The incendiary who set on fire the Temple of Ephesus, in order, as he said, "to immortalize himself," was contented to get even that degree of glory which followed from giving the public an event to talk about.[4] His name was necessarily in many mouths, and that was enough to tempt him to the crime, as he could get glory in no other way.

The devotees of India, who will hold one hand straight up above their heads, and never change its position during life, or fold both across their breasts, and keep them so for years; or Simon Stylites who remained on the top of a high naked column for thirty years, day and night, exposed to all weathers; and the devotees who voluntarily suspend themselves on hooks stuck through the flesh of their sides, and allow themselves to be suspended high in the air and swung around for hours, exposed to public gaze, all, probably, are or were actuated by similar motives to the one under contemplation.

Perhaps this explains the subtle fascination there is in the news of calamities—the destruction of life and property. They make everybody talk with each other; they find themselves, for the moment, on the same plane. The starved sympathies are fed.

The uncultivated girl, in Bulwer's *Last Days of Pompeii*, is made to say, "Oh, pray the gods send us a criminal for the lions to tear, or the holidays will be good for nothing."

Even hostility and persecution for unavoidable differences of opinion probably arise from this same desire for unity, harmony, or sympathy. This may explain the involuntary repugnance to even needed innovations or improvements, the tardiness in adopting them, and even the persecution of them; the spirit is, perhaps, the same. Probably this is the explanation of the pertinacity with which it is insisted on that "the Union must and shall be preserved," though compulsion is directly against the great principle that gave rise to it. The same impulse prompts thousands to join any movement, or noise of any kind, without much conscious design, or to do anything which feeds this natural yearning for sympathy or companionship.

What else can explain the omnipotence of public opinion where there is no opinion? Yet it holds, as it were, all the governments in the world between its thumb and finger, and in its hand the destinies of the race.

When we find ourselves on the immovable plane for the preservation of life, property, and happiness, this sympathetic element, a thousandfold stronger, will work for instead of against true civilization.

It is not till after long and painful experience and study that we discover that the precedents, traditions, authorities, and fictions upon which society has been allowed to grow up, do not coincide with each other, nor with the great unconquerable primitive or divine laws.

Far be it from me to attempt to conquer this greatest of all sources of human happiness, or to place one unnecessary obstacle in its way. The great problem is, How can this great, universal divine desire for sympathy be harmlessly exercised to its full satisfaction, and continue undisturbed?

Pigs, bees, fishes, ants, etc., being probably nearly alike, intellectually, can live in comparative peace and sympathy, having but few subjects to dispute about; but just in proportion to culture or expansion of the feelings, tastes, and intellects is the necessity and the tendency to take more room; so that each person, like a planet, can move in his own orbit without disturbing others. This is disintegration.

In closely entangled interests, as in all "communism," there is a necessity of agreement and conformity, and some must be more or less pained by the collisions of opinions, tastes, wishes, etc., between them. Not, perhaps, any more at the sacrifices required of one's self than from perceiving that others make sacrifices for us. One or the other is inevitable, just in proportion to the number or magnitude of the interests held in common.

Let us illustrate: In a certain town in Indiana there was, in 1841, a schoolhouse built by neighborhood subscription. The subscribers, however, as might have been expected, soon began to differ about the choice of a teacher; but there was no room to differ within the combined interest. Only one party could possibly have its way. The very best of reasons and arguments were furnished on both sides, and "irresistible logic" showed how right and how wrong both parties were; but none of the arguments had any other effect than to make the breach between them wider and wider. For, whereas they differed about only one thing at first, they differed about twenty things in as many minutes of disputation.

Meeting after meeting was had, and dispute after dispute roused, by degrees, a hostile feeling on both sides, so that, although both parties were "professors of religion," one man rushed at his antagonist with a huge club, but was in his turn subdued by an overpowering force, "and the meeting broke up in anarchy." That night some one, seeing no better means of putting an end to the war, set the valuable house on fire, and it was burned to ashes. The root of the whole of the trouble was communism, or union of property in the schoolhouse.

Had there been no union of property in the schoolhouse, and had the teacher acted on his individual responsibility with his patrons, the difficulty and destruction would not have occurred, whatever diversity there might have been between the parties. But having taken the first erroneous step in communism of property, if it had been fashionable in the neighborhood to have referred the case to judicious tribunals (as proposed in the first chapter) who understood the philosophy of the difficulty, these tribunals might, perhaps, have given such advice as would have averted all the trouble.

Another case. In the house of a friend, where I was staying, I heard, in a room next to my own, two girls disputing and crying for a long time. Passing by their door I learned that they had some playthings in common. *Mary* said that Annie wouldn't let her handle the cups and saucers, though "their governess told them that they must be accommodating to each other."

"Yes," replied Annie, sobbing, "but she meant that you must be accommodating as well as me, and when I want to put up the things you ought to let me." Both were really distressed to find themselves quarrelling, and I said to them, "Don't blame yourselves nor each other, girls; the fault is not in either of you; it is in having your playthings in common. There should be only one owner to one thing. Whatever was given to you should have been given to one or the other, or divided between you. I advise you at once to divide your things between yourselves, and that each should sacredly respect the absolute right of the other to control her own in any manner whatever, and not to set up any demand on each other to be any more accommodating than she is at the time. Such a demand is a partial denial of her right of control over her own, which not only makes you disagreeable companions to each other, but raises disputes that never can be settled by words."

At a place called Brush Creek, in Michigan, there was a meeting-house built by subscription among the neighbors, who happened to agree in that one particular idea, that a house of worship was necessary. It was built of logs, in the loghouse fashion, and locked together at the corners. It was no sooner built than their coincidence was at an end, for there was immediately a difference among them with regard to the doctrine that should be advocated there. Here, as usual, diversity took them by surprise, and it being a disturbing element under the circumstances, it was looked upon as an enemy, and each strove to conquer it in himself and in his opponents. They did not know that diversity was any part of Divinity, but they looked upon it as a proof of perversity, or the workings of the old virus of original depravity, and supposed that in warring against each other they were vindicating unity; for to admit of schism and diversity unrebuked was to encourage disintegration, which would "inaugurate universal confusion." So the parties contended with each other till they had exhausted all their resources, and destroyed all their union, and one man was so exasperated at the crude attempts to put him down, that he went home and got a yoke of oxen, hitched a chain to one of the logs in the side of the house, tore it out, and dragged it home for firewood, as his share of the communistic property.

Having committed the blunder of getting into communism, had the case been referred to an intelligent and disinterested neighborhood-council before building the house, it probably never would have been built on the communistic principle; but having committed this first mistake, it had become too late to exercise the right of individual ownership over one log, because this could not be done without doing greater violence to the same right of the other owners, whose property was seriously injured thereby. Had there been a clear idea among them of what the absolute right is, they would all have seen that they were equally partners in a blunder in forming the union, and not a violent word would probably have been spoken, and they would have talked only of individualizing or disintegrating their claims to the property. Different expedients might have been suggested, such as one party buying the other out, or some individual buying the whole out.

In this case the "government," seeing that the exercise of right had been rendered impossible by the union of the property, would restrain the persisting in its exercise in the particular form adopted by the desperate man, and might have required him to take an equivalent for his log, over which he could exercise his right of ownership without damaging the other parties.

This makes the government, as a last resort, a final umpire to decide between expedients when the right has been rendered impossible, but it does not rise above absolute human rights, and it is rendered safe by being dependent on the voluntary action or sovereign will of those who are required to execute any decision.

Another case. Two men were left joint heirs of one house; one wanted to sell it, and the other was opposed to selling it. They argued and disputed till they grew hot, and then one carried the case to the courts, and kept it there till more than the price of the house had been consumed in litigation, but all without decision, for the "precedents" and statutes were silent on the subject, and nothing could be done outside of "precedents" and "statutes." Finally, desperation took the case in hand: one party sawed the house in two from top to bottom, and moved his part away! Not a dollar would have been spent in litigation, and no feeling of desperation or enmity would have arisen, if both parties had known at first that disintegration was the remedy required; or had they referred the case to a neighborhood council called for the purpose (not elected to judge the case before it occurred), who were not trammeled by unbending precedents, statutes, and wordy forms, and who were not biased by the prospect of votes for office, or a large fee for making trouble, they might have given advice founded on a knowledge of the root of such difficulties, and most likely the parties would have been saved their quarrels, their expenses, and the desperate remedy resorted to.

Communists, like moths flitting round a lamp, seem to learn nothing from their burnt, disabled, and prostrate companions, and never know that the flame can kill till it is too late to profit by the knowledge; and the opposers, while they can reason like philosophers against the principle of communism, will advocate exactly the communistic principle in their political unions, organizations, confederacies and other combined interests.

What is called conservatism has all the time been entirely right in its objections to communism, and in insisting on individual ownership and individual responsibilities both of which communism annihilates; conservatism has also shown wisdom in its aversion to sudden and great changes, for none have been devised that contained the elements of success.

Let us proceed to examine our germs of true or harmonic organization.

A man wants to raise a house; he cannot do it alone, and invites his neighbors to help him. They are willing to do so, either from sympathy, for the enjoyment of the companionship of the occasion, or for pecuniary compensation, or without any particular conscious motive. Whether they are moved by one motive or another, their movement is voluntary, and the raising of the house is the point of coincidence between them—the object which brings them together, and which gives rise to the co-operation between them.

Twenty men assemble on the ground, but they can do nothing, if the whole twenty undertake to give directions. Even two cannot do so, without leading directly to confusion and counteraction. Primitive or divine law does not tolerate anything more or less than individuality in any lead. Who should be the lead on this occasion but he who takes the risks and bears all costs? He may prefer to delegate his function, but may with propriety resume it at any moment.

Ten men are requested to lift a timber; they all get ready to do so, but they cannot lift together till some word or sign is given. Select three of the wisest or most experienced of the company to give that word or sign, and confusion would result, but let only one, though a mere child, give the word, and the timber moves.

This I understand to be the philosophy of leadership, and also of monarchy and despotism. But why have they proved so destructive of the ends proposed by them? It is because of the unconscious attempt to unite or combine the lead and the deciding power or sovereignty in one person.

The twenty men had each a mind and a motive of his own to help at the raising, and though the motives were different, this difference did not prevent their coinciding or co-operating action in that one individual thing to be done. The owner of the house did not undertake to decide that these men should help him. Each decided for himself that he would help, and these coinciding, individual sovereign decisions only wanted a lead, and all was well.

I repeat that the great error has been in the attempt to combine the lead and the deciding or sovereign power in one person, instead of recognizing the deciding power where divine law has irrevocably fixed it, in every individual of the race.

Coincidence must be had before anything requiring the co-operation of numbers can be properly done. As intellectual culture and expansion give rise to this dreaded diversity, culture is looked upon as dangerous, and the expression of opinions adverse to the governments are forbidden and punished with heavy penalties or cruel deaths.

These penalties inflicted for diversity are practical acknowledgments that the deciding power is inevitably fixed in, and inseparable from, each individual, who is therefore presented with an assortment of evils to choose from and decide upon. If he desires to disobey orders, he may calculate the value of his life to himself or others, his repugnance to pain and death, his chances of escape, and on these calculations he decides for himself at last.

Common soldiers suppose, when they enlist in the regular service, that they put themselves thenceforth, for a specified time, under the commands of their officers, with whom rest all deciding power as to their movements; and this power is supposed by officers and men to be absolute, unqualified, and final, and either would stare at calling the idea in question.

A company of regulars in Scotland were on the march towards the river Clyde. At the edge of the stream, the soldiers, rather than walk in and be drowned, halted without waiting for the order to halt, which was entirely contrary to the contract and the discipline. Officers and men were both taken by surprise with the fact that the deciding power was not with the officers—that it had suddenly made its appearance in an unexpected quarter; the instinct of self-preservation had suddenly assumed its sway, like an irresistible third party, and annulled the contract of "unqualified obedience to orders," contrary to discipline and to the previous understanding and intentions of both parties.

Thereupon a little storm cloud (no bigger than a man's hand) arose between men and master; but when they begin to debate, good-by to the dried-herring subordination. The instinct of self-preservation does not always wait to consult precedents nor interpretations of constitutions, the right of rebellion, nor authorities of any kind. It is its own authority, from which all others are derived.

In these states, the institutions are supposed to place all deciding power in the hands of certain men appointed to wield it; yet this same instinct is now at work in every breast in the nation, and every one is involuntarily debating or deciding in his own mind and feelings, according to his conditions, and there is no coincidence among any large portion of us. The deciding power is not in the men appointed to wield it.

It is worse than useless, it is calamitous, to legislate as if it were possible to divest ourselves of this involuntary instinct of self-preservation or self-sovereignty, and those who accept or act on such pledge commit as great an error as those who give it, and all contracts to this effect being impossible of fulfillment are null and void. We may delegate the leading function often with advantage, but it is folly, blindness, self-deception, and may be ruin, to commit ourselves unqualifiedly to implicit and unhesitating obedience to any personal lead for a single hour.

The most perfect lead would be that which was best adapted to the particular occasion for it; and as every occasion may be peculiar in itself, no one personal lead may be equally adapted to various occasions. A child might lead the lifting of the timbers of the house, but could not lead in the framing of it. The president of a railroad company may lead its affairs very satisfactorily, but might not be equally adapted to lead a child in the study of music.

A very common mistake is made in taking it for granted that, because a man has shown great capacity to lead in one direction or department, he is, therefore, most likely to prove a good lead in other directions. The contrary is most likely to be the fact, inasmuch as that the more time he has spent in qualifying himself for one function, the less he would have to bestow in others, as illustrated by the very profound conchologist who thought that the beans in his garden had come up "the wrong end first."

The most effectual lead is not necessarily always a person. It may be a thing, an idea, or a principle. A clock or a watch leads or governs the movements of many of us more than men do. But two clocks which should differ widely from each other would neutralize the lead, and make only confusion. If they harmonized with each other, one would be superfluous. But a plurality of men to lead any one movement, having more elements of diversity within them than unintellectual clocks, are more likely than they to differ, and lead to confusion.

A single man may lead the whole race, as is already demonstrated by the inventor of railroads, of steam power, etc.; but if he undertakes to decide that the public shall patronize or follow him, he will find himself at once in conflict with the third party—a divine law, from which, sooner or later, he will be obliged to retire.

The sphere of lead may harmlessly extend over the whole earth; but the sphere of sovereignty cannot harmlessly be extended beyond the person, time, property, and responsibilities of the one person who exercises that sovereignty.

What, then, is invasion? If you come into my house, against my will, this is an invasion of my property certainly; but if you have heard screams within, and calls for help, and you have come in to restrain me from invading the life of an inmate, though it be my own child, you have made a justifiable and legitimate choice of evils in violating my right of property to prevent me from violating greater rights. If I would have my absolute rights of property and person held inviolate, I must observe and hold sacred all the rights of others.

Though John Brown went into Virginia to relieve slaves from oppression, if he had compelled any slave, by fear or force, to join him against his will, this would have been oppression or invasion of the slave. This personal sovereignty should be above all other considerations.

A nation consists of all the individuals in it. An army which has entered a nation to protect even one individual from oppression, and has committed no unnecessary violence in doing so, has made a justifiable choice of evils.

When clanship or political systems are outgrown, and every individual is recognized as a sovereign member of the party of the whole, the same idea becomes only extended when the whole of the race should protect one member of the race from invasion.

We have seen that the lead and the deciding or sovereign power are two very distinct elements; that for true order, they must be disintegrated from each other, the one having unlimited scope, and the other confined to the person, time, property, and responsibilities of one individual. Beyond this individual sphere no one, no number of men, have a right of absolute sovereignty. We all have a right to sympathize with the distressed in any part of the world with but not against their consent or will.

I speak with decision, because, after forty years' study and experiments on these subjects, I have arrived at decisions for myself, and because I think the reader will prefer it as the most convenient language for him as well as for me, and because I think be will prefer the assurance which is afforded by placing myself under the responsibility of definite and positive assertions, rather than that I should give out vague hints and throw the responsibility of conclusions upon him. And after and in the midst of continuous reiteration of the sovereign right of every individual to decide for himself, he will not suspect me of attempting to decide for him against his consent.

While the deciding or sovereign power is understandingly left undisturbed where it really is (in the heart or head of every individual for himself), it matters but little who undertakes to lead. He who most addresses himself to the largest coincidence or most pressing wants of the time will have the most followers.

We see that primitive or divine law demands individuality in a lead. This lead is sometimes a man, sometimes a woman, a child, or a thing; it is also sometimes an idea. This latter has always been practically admitted by those who have attempted to generalize the experience of mankind into axioms, rules, written statutes, or so-called laws, constitutions, etc. They intended these ideas as points of coincidence to lead or force the people into certain modes of action.

But in all these there has been the same fatal error: defective generalization.

A rule (or law) which may be good for the case in which it originated may not apply to any other case as well. New cases give rise to other rules which conflict with the first; which conflict, like that of the two different clocks, destroys the power of either to lead.

Then, again, arises (from the inevitable individuality of different minds) the different interpretations of the same rules or generalisms. Witness the different interpretations of the Constitution of the United States and all other constitutions.

They are liable to so many different constructions, that this diversity not only neutralizes their power to lead, but they become positive elements of antagonism and violent dissensions and mutual destruction, because their latent faults are too subtle for ready detection. They would be harmless and might be beneficial if there was no attempt to combine in them the sovereign power. To remedy this fatal defect, the word "shall" should be expunged, and the word "may" substituted.

Conscious of this defect to some extent, the makers of some of these verbal institutions have provided that the ultimate or final interpretation of them shall rest in the supreme courts; the practical working of which is to concentrate a coercive power in one person over the destinies of millions (witness the Dred Scott decision) which is a return to despotism, and in the worst form, because it is disguised and hedged round with bewildering fictions and formulas.

The Constitution of the United States contains a great many formulas and generalizations, the whole being intended to lead to prosperity, security, and freedom. The unavoidable difference in the interpretations of the instrument, being provided for only in a form which gave the monopoly of the interpreting and enforcing power into a few hands, has led to the sudden check of all prosperity—has rendered all persons and property in the States as insecure as possible.

The Declaration of American Independence embraces a great universal fact, or primitive or divine law, intended to act as a point of coincidence for the co-operation and harmony of all mankind. But the same instrument also displays other features more prominent and more striking to common observation, while the germinal, central idea of the whole instrument lies hidden within its well-chosen phraseology, like the life-giving germ of the seed, beyond the external eye, and cognizable only by the penetrating mental vision.

Even there, in that sublime effort of virtue and genius, there is that plurality of elements, which, like the plurality of men, neutralize each other as a lead according to its noble design.

Struggling through centuries with such subtle difficulties and obstructions, the best minds have been bent on simplifying. Hence arose the formula, "Do unto others as ye would that they should do unto you"; and Christendom rejoiced in the apparent supply of their greatest ethical want. The men or women of mature culture and experience and of delicate sympathies, who take pleasure in the pleasure they confer, and share the pain they are obliged to inflict, will interpret and apply this formula in a harmless and even a beneficent manner. They are careful not to inflict unnecessary pain on others nor to require sacrifices of them without pecuniary or moral compensation, while those who are indifferent to the pain they inflict, or under the influence of an ill-digested theory (though well intended), and who are satisfied with mere logical consistency, might excuse themselves, by this formula, for insisting on sharing or distributing the property of others, on the ground that the owners would be glad to have the same done for them, if the cases were reversed.

The same rule which at first sight appears to promise the point of coincidence required, and which in some cases leads to very desirable results, furnishes, by a different application, the excuse or warrant for the denial of all rights of property, would stop all stimulus to industry, foresight, and economy, and, which followed out, would lead to universal confusion, poverty, starvation, and violence.

The ancients, centuries ago, saw this inherent defect in all verbal laws and formulas, and came to the conclusion that none could be constructed by man that could regulate human intercourse; and they abandoned the attempt to construct them, and vested all power in one person within each certain district of country called a nation, which was a return to primitive despotism. A person was thought to be the unit of coincidence as well as the individual lead required; which, being a living organism, could adapt itself to the peculiarities (or individualities) of persons and events as each case arose: but it was soon seen that this "unit" was one day one thing, and another thing another day—that the very possession of the delegated power so intoxicated or bewildered the despot (though before a very good person), as to procure for him the titles of "the monster," "the cruel," "the mad," "the scourge," etc.

To remedy these long-suffered evils, the originators of the Catholic Church, also seeing the hopelessness of constructing any successful formulas, laws, or constitutions, adopted the human "unit" not only as a lead, but as a final, deciding, sovereign power or "umpire of peace" over all persons within their organization, and beyond which umpire there was to be no appeal, no dispute; viewing him as a father, papa, or pope, and investing him with the power to rescue the smitten and abused subjects of the intoxicated despots from obedience and from the oath of loyalty, and to protect them from insane violence; and, to secure themselves from similar violence and oppression, they selected a man for the papa whom they considered more than man: one who was inspired by divine influx, and they seem to have supposed that this divine influx came from a personal existence which was all perfection, and who would always inspire the papa to do exactly right.

Here was the point of failure. There is no coincidence between men as to what constitutes perfection, and though it now appears that the idea of an influx or inspiration from intelligent beings, above or beyond or outside of the human organism, was a true one, it seems not to have been clearly understood.

It appears that the influx came from beings once human, but in a second stage of existence, analogous to that of the butterfly from the grub (now called spiritual existence). That in this state there is no sudden leap to perfection, and that many spiritual inspirations or communications to us are no nearer to coincidence than our own opinions and theories are. And, moreover, that the most humble, even children, are more likely to become recipients of this inspiration than a man or men set apart for the purpose, because, being less embarrassed by cares and anxieties, they are more in that state of repose required as a condition necessary for the influx or communications.

This was probably soon known to the intelligent portions of the priesthood and laity; but such were the exceeding difficulties of their undertaking, and the crudity of the people they desired to benefit, and the immense and incalculable good promised to the race by the abolition of wars and a universal point of unity or coincidence, their whole aim seems to have been to attain this end, even by means that shock us to think of, on the ground that such means were the least of evils presented to them from which to choose.

Humanity is today without an umpire, without a principle, without an idea, without a policy, without a lead that can command the assent of any considerable number of intelligent men or women, or even the general assent of the uncultivated and careless. But all society so-called is exposed, unprepared, unassisted, and undefended, to the mere spirit of reckless adventure, corruption, quackery, and desperation.

A point of universal coincidence and co-operation which would naturally lead the race out of its chaos, is now, more than ever before, the great consideration.

If it is the work of man, it can be overthrown by man, and would, therefore, be liable to disappoint or ruin all who might build upon it. It must be indestructible, or it would be destroyed. It must be an individuality, or it cannot lead, except into confusion. It must be an individual idea (not a plurality) that, notwithstanding the infinite diversity of minds, motives, and conditions, it will be sure to coincide with the instinctive action as well as with the natural understanding of all people. Is not the great fact of self-sovereignty such a unit?

Opposition to it is as harmless as would be the pelting a beggar with gold. Dissent itself not being antagonistic, but coinciding with it, who can avoid being in harmony with it practically, whatever he may be theoretically?

I may have a neighbor who is an old line Presbyterian, and who goes every Sunday to hear what I consider destructive theories; but, holding his sovereignty as sacred, I offer no obstacle other than acceptable counsel. If I have anything in his way, I will hasten to take it out of the way. My public duty towards the Catholic and every other persuasion is the same. I have no issue with either till an attempt is made to enforce assent or conformity from me or others. And my duty towards all political creeds and theories is precisely the same. They are all entitled to forbearance till some attempt is made to enforce them on the unwilling. This attempt is an encroachment upon the great sacred right of self-sovereignty—an attack upon the divine law of individuality, and will always beget resistance and war.

The Reformation was based upon this great idea, but the Reformation will not be complete till it is clearly understood that each and every person is necessarily invested with an individuality of his or her own, that, like the countenance of its possessor, is inalienable, and therefore that we cannot build theories requiring and depending on conformity or uniformity of reasoning, without constant liability to conflict, confusion, and disappointment.

No matter how perverse any one may be, he never can get outside of the propensity to have his own way. The foundation for universal co-operation is now theoretically laid. In order to preserve harmony in progress, there must be freedom to differ in all things where difference is possible.

Therefore let us avoid all commitments to anything like what are commonly called organizations leading to clanship. Our organization will not consist of subordinating rules or any other external formulas but will exist in the understanding, internally, in fact and in spirit, while the external will consist of simply correspondence or communication with each other, and that which naturally and spontaneously flows from it.

NARRATIVE OF PRACTICAL EXPERIMENTS

Together, passages from the Quarterly Letter *(1867), the* Free Enquirer *(1831), and* Practical Applications of the Elementary Positions of "True Civilization" *(1873) embody a project that Warren assayed many times: a record of his experiments in equitable commerce and self-sovereign community.*

The narrative begins with a passage from The Quarterly Letter: Devoted to Showing the Practical Applications and Progress of Equity, a Subject of Serious Concern to All Classes, but Most Immediately to the Men and Women of Labor and Sorrow!, *dated October 1867. The* Quarterly Letter, *like the* Periodical Letter *and* The Peaceful Revolutionist, *was a one-off or extremely occasional periodical, entirely written, set, and printed by Warren himself. The typesetting and printing is extremely elaborate and relatively free of errors; the aesthetic is clunky but somehow sweet, reflecting Warren's personality. The text presented immediately below, which I obtained from the Labadie Collection at the University of Michigan, is more or less the entirety of the* Quarterly Letter. *Oddly, it tells Warren's story of disillusionment with Owen and realization of his own principles in a semi-fictitious way; he calls himself "Werner." This may be the best mature statement of Warren's philosophy, or at least his anarchism, and it displays an awareness that the conflict between labor and capital was in some ways fundamental to the late nineteenth century and to the ideological configuration of the progressive movements of that era. This piece narrates the beginning of the Time Store idea and is certainly the clearest description of the operation.*

An article from the Free Enquirer *(published first at New Harmony and then in New York by Robert Dale Owen and Fanny Wright) then narrates Warren's educational experiments at Massillon, Ohio, in 1830.*

That is followed by passages from the 1872 booklet Practical Applications of the Elementary Principles of "True Civilization" to the Minute Details of Every Day Life, Being Part III of the "True Civilization" Series *(text obtained from the Houghton Library at Harvard University). The description of Modern Times is both intentionally and unintentionally comical: the spectacle of Warren, the amazingly straitlaced advocate of absolute freedom, dealing with a bunch of eccentrics and libertines. The backwoods projector is lobbed suddenly into the ambit of New York City, and the 1830s reformer into the decadent phase of American reform.*

New Harmony and the Time Store Idea (from the Quarterly Letter, *1867)*

I t has come to be admitted by the best students of human affairs, that something is wrong at the foundation. That the history of the past is mainly made up of the failures of mankind in their efforts to make themselves comfortable. That it devolves upon the present generation to solve the problem of successful society, or become the pivot upon which civilization shall take a sudden turn toward barbarism. Whoever undertakes this solution, assumes too grave a responsibility in putting forth any abstract theory, but we are safe in stating facts in detail, leaving each mind to theorize for itself. This course is preferred in this work: beginning with the practical and letting theory follow.

A complete history of the experiments in equity during the last forty years would be too voluminous—too expensive to publish or to be read by those who most need it. But selected parts will be given showing how justice has been done to labor, in store keeping, in exchanging all kinds of products, and services, renting of houses, buying and selling land, &c.; what kind of money has been used and how it has worked; how the interests of all classes are made to co-operate by a principle without entangling partnerships or partial, conflicting and short lived combinations or organizations; and showing how competition is converted into being a regulator rather than a destroyer; how destitute and despairing people have been relieved by justice instead of charity, enabling thinkers to see how distress can be relieved and the existing and threatened conflicts between the luxurious and the starving may be neutralized or averted: all without seriously disturbing any class or person.

Labor for Labor: Its Origin and the Way It Worked

One whom we will call Werner went to New Harmony, in Indiana in 1825, with the celebrated philanthropist Robert Owen, who assembled eight hundred people, mostly selected for their superior intelligence and moral excellence, with the view of solving the great problem by communism of property. Mr. Owen and one of his coadjutors (Mr. Maclure) had an abundance (millions) of money and all felt an enthusiastic devotion to the cause and unlimited confidence in Mr. Owen, but all ended in disappointment.[1] Two years' time and at least two hundred thousand dollars were spent in making and breaking up organizations, constitutions, laws, and governments of every conceivable kind, for no result except to show what will not work, and that it is dangerous to risk much in untried theories, how ever plausible they may appear.

In one of Mr. Owen's lectures, he spoke of an idea that had been broached in England. It was a proposal to exchange all labors or services equally, hour for hour, with labor notes for a circulating medium. But the idea did not seem to make much impression and it passed away without any attempt at its development.

At the very commencement of our experiments in communism we were taken all aback by phenomena altogether unexpected.

We had assured ourselves of our unanimous devotedness to the cause and expected unanimity of thought and action: but instead of this we met diversity of opinions, expedients, and counteraction entirely beyond any thing we had just left behind us in common society. And the more we desired and called for union, the more this diversity seemed to be developed: and instead of that harmonious co-operation we had expected, we found more antagonisms than we had been

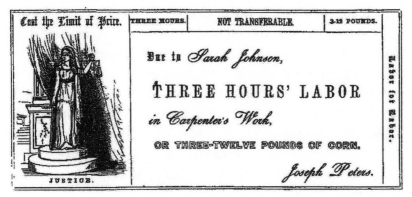

One of Warren's labor notes, date unknown.

accustomed to in common life. If we had demanded or even expected infinite diversity, disunion, and disintegration we should have found ourselves in harmony with the facts and with each other on one point at least. We differed, we contended and ran ourselves into confusion. Our legislative proceedings were just like all others, excepting that we did not come to blows or pistols; because Mr. Owen had shown us that all our thoughts, feelings, and actions were the inevitable effects of the causes that produce them; and that it would be just as rational to punish the fruit of a tree for being what it is, as to punish each other for being what we are: that our true issue is not with each other, but with causes.

Every few days we heard of the failure of some one of the many communities that had been started in different parts of this and other countries. Small groups of selected friends had moved out of the town upon the surrounding lands, each confident that they could succeed though all others failed; but a very few weeks or months found them returning to the town discouraged.

We had fairly worn each other out by incessant legislation about organizations, constitutions, laws, and regulations all to no purpose, and we could no longer talk with each other on the subject that brought us there. Many intelligent and far-seeing members had left— others were preparing to go, and an oppressive despondency hung heavily upon all. Werner shared the general feeling and nothing saved him from despair but that our business is with causes: and the question now was, what could be the causes of all this confusion and disappointment? What was the matter, when all were so willing to sacrifice so much for success? He dwelt upon this question till he could come to no other conclusion than that communism was the cause. What then was to be done? Must we give up all hope of a successful society? Or must we attempt to construct society without communism? for all societies, from a nation to the smallest partnership, are more or less communistic.

We had carried communism farther than usual and hence our greater confusion. Common society, then, had all the time been right in its individual ownership of property and its individual responsibilities and wrong in all its communistic entanglements. Even two children owning a jack knife together are liable to continual dissatisfaction and disturbance till somebody owns it individually. Had society, then, started wrong at the beginning? Had all its governments and other communistic institutions been formed on a wrong model? Was disintegration, then, not an enemy but a friend and a remedy? Was "individuality" to be the watch word of progress instead of "union"? Werner dwelt upon these thoughts day and night, for he could not dismiss them and was almost bewildered with the immense scope of the subject and the astounding conclusions that he could not avoid: but he had become so distrustful of his own judgment from his late disappointments, he resolved to dismiss these thoughts and leave these great problems to be solved and settled by the wise, the great, and the powerful. But he could not dismiss them; they haunted him; they haunted him, day and night. They presented to him society beginning anew. He found himself asking how it should begin. It could not be formed, for we had just proved that we could no more form a successful society than we could form the fruit upon the tree—it must be the natural growth of the interest that each one feels in it from the benefits of enjoyments derived from it. The greater these benefits. the stronger the bond of society. Where there is no interest felt, there is no bond of society, whatever its unions, its organizations, its constitutions, governments, or laws may be.

If the enjoyments derived from society are its true bond, what do we want of any other? "We want governments and laws to regulate the movements of the members of society, to prevent encroachments upon each other, and to manage the common interests for common benefit."

But the movements of society have never been regulated. Encroachments have never been prevented, but are increasing every day, and the common interests have never been managed to the satisfaction of the parties interested. It is precisely these problems that remain to be solved, which was our purpose in our late movement. It had been defeated by our attempt to govern each other, to regulate each other's movements for the common benefit, no two having the same view of the common benefit and no one retaining the same view from one week to another. Infinite diversity instead of unity is inevitable, especially in a progressive or transitory stage. Then why not leave each one to regulate his own movements within equitable limits, provided we can find out what equity is, and leave the rest to the universal instinct of self-preservation? But what constitutes equity is the greatest question of all. It is the unknown quantity that even algebra has failed to furnish. One thing is certain. If all our wants are supplied, that is all we want. Could we not supply each other's without entangling ourselves in communism and thereby involving ourselves in interminable conflicts and fruitless legislation? Could we not have a central point in each neighborhood where all wants might be made known, and where those wanting employment or who have anything to dispose of could also apply, and thus bring demand and supply together and adapt one to the other? Then, as to exchange —on what principle could it be equitably conducted? Here the idea of labor for labor presented itself: but hour for hour in all pursuits did not seem to promise the equilibrium required, because those who perform the most disagreeable kinds of labor make the greatest sacrifices for the general good, and should they not be compensated in proportion to the sacrifices made? If not, then (opportunities being equally open to all) starved, ragged, insulted labor would be shunned even more than it is now, by every one who can avoid it, and more respected and more agreeable pursuits would be overcrowded and conflict between all will continue and the demand and supply be thrown out of balance: but, as no pledges or compacts would be entered into, every one could make any exceptions to the hour for hour rule that suited him. This would be one application of equitable freedom.

Estimating the price of every thing by the labor there is in it promised to abolish all speculations on land, on clothing, food, fuel, knowledge, on every thing—to convert time into capital, thereby abolishing the distinctions of rich and poor—to reduce the amount of necessary labor to two or three hours a day, when no one should wish to shun his share of employment. The motive of some to force others to bear their burden would not exist, and slavery of all kinds would naturally become extinct. Every consumer becomes interested thereby in assisting in reducing the costs of his own supplies, and in doing this for himself, he is doing it for all consumers. Destructive competition would be changed into an immediate regulator of prices and property, and property might ultimately become so abundant that like water in a river or spontaneous fruits all prices would be voluntarily abandoned, and the high and noble aims of communists be reached without communism, without organisation, without constitutions or pledges, without any legislation in conflict with the natural and inalienable individualities of men and things.

Overwhelmed with astonishment and bewildered with the newness and immense magnitude of the subject, Werner began to doubt his own sanity, and to think that perhaps the late disappointments had deranged his thoughts. Day after day he retired into the woods outside of the town to ponder and to detect if possible some lurking error in his reasoning; but the closer he criticized, the more he was confirmed. He concluded to return to Cincinnati and place himself in some working position where he could bring these ideas to practical tests. If they failed under trial, he would give up all specific reforms and keep a common family store. For he would first apply these new ideas in store keeping. If they did not succeed, the transition would be easy, into a store of the common kind; but if successful, then the store must be wound up to commence new villages where the new ideas could be applied to the affairs of social life.

Werner thought he would try the experiment of presenting these strange ideas to one of his associates. What! he exclaimed with a sarcastic smile, no organization? no constitution? no laws? no rulers? Where is the bond of society and social order?

There has never been any bond to general society, said Werner; bonds have existed more or less strong within narrow limits of sects, parties, clans, tribes, classes, combinations, and corporations in proportion to the points of co-incidence between their members. But just in proportion to the strength of such bonds the different parties unavoidably became hostile to one another.

Society, even what there has been of it, has always been tumbling to pieces and thinkers and tinkers have always been employed in patching up some rent or leakage, but one has no sooner been stopped than two others have been opened; and now it is generally seen that patching is hopeless. We had come here with this conviction and with a view to remodel the whole structure.

The bond of society is the interest felt in the advantages (or enjoyments) derived from or expected from it, or there is no bond. The greatest advantages derived from civilization—all that distinguishes it from primitive or savage life—is derived from labor: but they have not been enjoyed by those who perform the labor. The workers are the foundation, soul, and substance of civilization, but they can scarcely be expected to feel much devotion to that which takes all from them and gives them little or nothing in return; and if a way is ever opened by which they can enjoy the benefits they are justly entitled to, no bond can keep them in their present condition. And when the foundation moves, the structure must move or fall.

The bond has been represented by a bundle of dry sticks and they are accepted as a symbol of union. But dry sticks never can be united; united sticks would be a log of wood. But the symbol is a good one to represent what some would have society to be: lifeless beings forced together by external bonds, retaining from age to age the same form, substance, and inertness. But human beings are not dead, dry sticks; they have a natural tendency to grow. A better symbol of what would now be called "society" would be the limbs of a tree all bent upwards, forced together at the top and bound round with iron hoops crushing all of them out of their legitimate shapes, stopping all their fruit-bearing power, chafing and bruising each other but still retaining life enough to grow larger if not beautiful, now bursting the bonds or else forcing their way into each other's vitals and becoming one united mass, a solid log, a barren, shapeless, hideous thing, an encumbrance to the ground.

Do justice to labor, and then we may see something of the bond of society and social order: not so much on paper as in every aspect of social life.

Werner returned to Cincinnati and began to talk with his friends about his intended enterprise, but they recoiled at once from any new movements. They said that nobody would listen now to anything of the kind while the failures at New Harmony were so fresh in their minds. But, said Werner, this is nothing like any of those experiments. Where there is no organization, it is only individuals that can fail. But, said the objectors, where is your bond of society? and where the capital to come from without organization? Werner replied that he was going to act as any common store keeper now conducts his business, excepting that he was going to set and regulate his prices by an equitable principle instead of having no principle; and that the benefits the customers would derive from this would constitute the bond.

After spending three weeks in this manner, going over the same ground, bond and all, with different persons, Werner perceived that scarcely a single one had got the least idea of what he intended: but that as old words will not explain new things, new things must explain themselves.

Although he had no capital he would not consent to any joint stock operation; knowing that he should have as many masters as there were stockholders, that no two of them could agree for a month in such a new undertaking and that mutual criticism and the friction of continuous legislation would be sure to wear out all parties and defeat the movement sooner or later.

He went to a wholesale grocer of his acquaintance and said to him, "I think I see the causes of our failures at New Harmony and I want to satisfy myself whether I am correct or not. If I am right, I shall sell a few goods rapidly. If I am deceived I shall keep a common store and let all reforms alone.

"There is to be no company formed, no organization, not offices to contend about. I shall act on my own responsibility and if I fail no one will suffer. If I succeed the public will get a new lesson."

After a little explanatory conversation, the merchant said, "I think I see something of your design and it may work well and perhaps revive the hopes of the reformers. You may come to my store and get whatever you want and pay when the goods are sold, and if you want what I have not got, I will pass my word where you can get them."

Werner took about three hundred dollars worth of groceries and a few staple dry goods and arranged them in his store; stuck up the bills of purchase so that all customers could see what every article cost; and a notice saying that seven per cent would be added to pay contingent expenses. But instead of mixing up the profit of the keeper along with the prices of the goods, the customers would pay the first costs and seven per cent; but from the labor of the keeper, they were to pay an equal amount of their own labor. A clock was in plain sight to measure the time of the tenders in delivering the goods, which was considered one half of the labor, and purchasing &c. the other half. An index resembling the face of a clock was fixed just below it; and when the tender commenced to deliver goods, he was to set the index to correspond with the clock. The index would stand still while the clock would run on, and a comparison of the two would show how much time had been employed. The labor in some of the most common necessaries had been ascertained, and a list of them hung up where all could see the labor price at which any of these articles would be taken in and given out, the customer paying for the labor of the tender and one twentieth of the price of the article for contingent expenses. These prices were permanent. The keeper of the store would give an hour of his labor in buying and selling goods for a pound of butter because there was an hour's labor in it; thirty hours for a barrel of flour because there was about that amount of labor in it. An hour of his merchandising for an hour of the drayman, the shoe maker, the needle woman, the wash woman, &c.

All being ready for operation, Werner went to a friend and invited him to come and try the experiment of buying some thing; and he promised to come at a certain hour but he did not come. Werner then went to another and he promised to come at a time fixed on, but he never came. Werner then went to a third one who promised to come at a certain hour, but he never made his appearance. In desperation Werner went to a fourth, one who could not refuse, and begged him as a favor to come and go through the process of buying something and if he did not wish to keep his articles, he could return them and receive his money. This man came and bought articles to the amount of a dollar and fifty cents and gave Werner his note for fifteen minutes of his labor and saved fifty cents.

He did not want to return the articles, but going home with them met C. P. who had been to New Harmony with us, and he came immediately to the store, exclaiming "My God! What fools we were at New Harmony. Why didn't we see such a simple and self-evident thing as this? Here, give me ten pounds of coffee, twenty of sugar" (&c.). He bought five dollars worth of the most common necessaries and saved a dollar and a half, or the wages of a day and a half of the hardest kind of labor. "Now," he said, "how shall I pay you for your twenty minutes?" Werner replied, "One great point is to show how we can emancipate our supplies as well as ourselves from the tyranny of common money. As I cannot make use of your labor, and as there will be many other cases of the same kind, I have set a labor price upon several articles such as tea, coffee, sugar, and spices, at which I am willing to receive them and run the risk of selling them again, not professing to have found out the exact amount of labor in them, for this is not of so much importance as it is to fix a price that shall remain the same when it is bought and when it is sold and which is satisfactory to the parties concerned. So, you may give me the price of a pound of coffee in money, I will weigh it out and put it among the labor articles and give you an hour of my labor for it. Deducting the twenty minutes already due me and the labor of weighing out the coffee I shall owe you about thirty five minutes, for which I will give you my note which you can use in future purchases. Or you can, at any time, take out the amount of coffee which it represents." This was entirely satisfactory and it was done.

C. P. went away and began to spread the news about the store. There was a department in the store for medicines, and the next articles sold were carbonate of soda and tartaric acid. They were bought by a lady who worked with her needle for about twenty-five or thirty cents a day. The medicines, bought in the common way would have cost her sixty eight cents; they now cost her seventeen cents and five minutes of her needle work, giving her note for the work. She saved the wages of about two days' labor in this little transaction of about five minutes.

The business now began to grow, but during the whole of the first week, only ten dollars worth of goods were sold, the next week thirty, and very soon a crowd of customers thronged to the store and many were obliged to go away unserved because they could not get where the goods were delivered. All this was natural growth without any stimulus from the news papers, for Werner could not hope to make the subject understood through them when he failed with friends in familiar conversation.

Werner now began to buy at auction. There he bought three barrels of excellent rice for a cent and a quarter a pound while the common retail price was eight cents a pound. The lady who bought the medicines bought thirty pounds of this for forty-five cents, and saved a dollar and ninety-five cents in five minutes, for which she gave Werner her note for five minutes more of her needle work. In other words she had saved the proceeds of about eight days of her labor in this equitable exchange of five minutes. Werner got her to make some cloth bags for the store, which employed her two hours. He now gave her back two notes of five minutes each, and gave his notes for an hour and fifty minutes in merchandising.

A store keeper came and wanted to buy the whole of the rice, but Werner declined selling it. "What? You keep goods to sell and don't want to sell them? The more you sell, the more money you make, don't you?"

No sir. In the first place I don't take money for my labor, and if I did I should not get any more for the same time spent in selling large quantities than small ones. But these are not my reasons for refusing to sell. I want to distribute it as a public educator and for the benefit of those who will be likely to reciprocate the same principle. If you had all along been selling goods on the labor for labor principle, I would sell you a part on it. But if I deal at all with you, I should deal as you deal.

"Do you mean to say that you should gain no more profit to yourself in buying and selling a hundred barrels of flour than in buying and selling five pounds, if it took no more time?"

Yes sir; certainly; which ever required the greatest sacrifice of my time or comfort I should charge the most for.

"Well, that is a strange idea!"

No doubt, said Werner, but does it not appear reasonable to charge the most for what costs us the most time and trouble?

"I cannot but say yes to that," said the other, "but it is so very strange, so new, I can hardly grasp the idea." Yes sir, said Werner, justice is a great stranger, but I will invite you to examine this labor for labor idea and see what you think it will lead to.

"Social Experiment," from Free Enquirer,
February 16, 1831 (vol. 2, no. 18)

I have never inserted a Communication in this paper, which I believe will be perused with more interest by many of its readers, than the following. As the facts come under our friend's observation, not mine, I shall add no opinions or deductions of my own, for each reader can make these for himself. I content myself with saying, that our friends may implicitly depend on the accuracy of

Josiah Warren's information: for he is a strictly attentive observer and an honest man. I need not tell him, that his letters will always be welcome.

R. D. O. [Robert Dale Owen],
Spring Hill [Ohio], Dec. 19, 1830.

My Dear Friend,

In accordance with our understanding when we parted, I sit down to give you, for the information of our friends at a distance, some of the practical results of our proceedings at this place; but I would have it distinctly premised, that this is not done with a view to obtrude me upon the notice of the public, but perceiving that the character is formed for us and not by ourselves, all aspirations after public applause, and all dread of censure are annihilated and leave us with no motive to attract or avoid the notice of others, but the promotion of their happiness or our own; and if in the course of this correspondence I speak often of myself, I offer my apology in the fact that we have a distinct understanding that whatever we do is done entirely in the individual character, each taking on himself all the responsibility of his own actions. There is no combination whatever among us; the personal liberty of each is considered sacred, and I shall therefore not use the term *we*, nor speak of others except in cases where the free choice of each individual concerned has been consulted.

The school at this place originated in the following circumstances.

About five years since, Mrs. Charity Rotch of the Society of Friends bequeathed at her decease the interest of twenty two thousand dollars to be appropriated to the establishment of a school for the benefit of poor children.

In January 1823, Hezekiah Camp of New York, William G. Macy of Nantucket, James Bayliss of New York, and Edward Dunn of Philadelphia, some of whom had experienced the failure of three communities to which they had belonged on the dissolution of the Kendal Community,[2] not discouraged by failures which they perceived were caused by want of knowledge, applied to and contracted with the trustees of said fund to take under their care twenty children; to feed and clothe them, to teach them the common rudiments of education, and to give to the females a knowledge of housewifery generally, and to the boys a knowledge of practical agriculture. They were to spend three hours per day in school in warm weather, and four in the cold season; they might be required to work eight hours per day, the proceeds of which the company were to receive, together with the school fund amounting to one thousand dollars per year.

The company began their operations with a capital of 1000 dollars, with which they stocked the farm, purchased farming utensils, furniture, bedding, &c.

I have been particular in stating these details, because it is a common impression that these arrangements require a large capital; and while this impression remains, the independence of the mass will depend on capitalists whose interest (as most of them view it) is to keep the mass in servitude.

At the expiration of the first year, on balancing accounts, the company perceived that these children who were between 10 and 15 years of age, aided by these four adults, had supported themselves within 200 dollars, leaving a surplus of 800 dollars of the fund so generously intended for their benefit. Let it be observed that this was done by agriculture alone, a business which is far more depressed than trades or manufactures; this shows that when legislators in this republic begin to learn the rights of citizens and secure to each the possession of the soil, that even children destitute of almost every thing else may render themselves independent by their labor; but while the soil of the country is chiefly monopolised and controlled by those who make no use of it, poor children destitute of friends will continue to be the victims of this legal barbarism.

It was in the fifth month of the second year that I visited this establishment, and beheld a demonstration of the influence of surrounding circumstances upon the characters of children, which, although I had reflected and observed much upon the subject, both surprised and delighted me. I saw children who a little more than a year before were destitute orphans, and who, had they been differently circumstanced might have been forced from every endearing object and shut up in a house of correction, a Bridewell, a house of refuge, or some other monument of human ignorance, now living as happy as they could well be; directed by intelligent friends who acted as benevolent guides, rather than mercenary masters, and who consulted the present and future happiness of these children equally with their own.[3]

I saw young females who, had they been in the cities, would have been compelled to waste away the bloom of life as unremitting toil at their needles for 12½ cents per day, or perhaps to be miserable dependents on the "societies for the encouragement of domestics," and to drag out a monotonous life of enervating servitude in the kitchens of the rich for a scanty pittance just sufficient to keep up the working power—I saw them here comparatively independent, and daily acquiring an education which would place them beyond the vain ambition of expensive show, which would enable them to supply their own wants and conduct their own affairs, and consequently place them beyond the humiliation and distress endured by poor but respectable females in our cities. As a proof of this, it has been a matter of complaint in the neighbourhood, that "since this school commenced no girls could be obtained to do kitchen work."

There I saw nothing of the studied effeminacy, the vacillating whims, or the tyrannical spirit of the oppressor; nor the cowering look, the hesitating speech, or the trembling deportment of the oppressed; but here were only "equals among equals," each exhibiting a fine, cheerful, unclouded countenance, which at once bespoke habitual health and peace of mind. Their deportment toward each other was kind and affable, but not timid; ready, but not obtrusive, and altogether delightfully pleasing.

Although about 17 months ago they were (with few exceptions) destitute of artificial learning, I now saw them go through their exercises in reading, writing, arithmetic, and grammar with accuracy and ease; their language in common conversation was more critically correct than that of adults in general, and their common remarks bespoke the habitual exercise of reason. The utmost confidence and good feeling between pupils and teachers was strikingly evident, although the latter assured me that they had labored as intensely to annihilate the feeling of fear in their pupils as teachers of the old

school generally do to excite it. The boys had acquired a practical
knowledge of agriculture generally, and the girls of housewifery and
domestic economy, and each went to his ploughing, planting, or
reaping, and to her cooking, spinning, &c., with a cheerful prompt-
ness and efficient energy which demonstrated what may be done
when the heart and hand work together.

It had been perceived that the new arrangements would require
us to turn our attention to business with which we have never been
acquainted, with an enquiry into the nature of apprenticeship resulting in the conviction that the common practice of serving seven years
to learn a simple art or trade is a relic of ancient barbarism, and is a
part of the same system of slavery to which belongs the present practice of monopolising land. Perceiving that all knowledge results from
the experience of the senses, we have a direct road to all knowledge
by bringing the senses to bear directly upon the objects we desire to
learn: this has in many cases reduced the customary apprenticeships
to a few weeks or days. I know that this position will be controverted
by established interests; and as I know of nothing but facts which can
sufficiently counteract the sophistry of words, I will give such facts as
have already occurred, and leave all else to the future.

Upon the principle of labor for labor there is no motive to with-
hold knowledge from others, but it is honestly given by the possessor
to any who desire it, he being paid for the time employed in conveying it; and under these circumstances, several adults here have, within
three months, learned to make good shoes who before had never
thought of it.

A boy between 11 and 12 years of age was placed in the shoe shop,
and his first effort was to make a pair of shoes, which have now been
in constant wear about six weeks, but no defect has yet appeared. Another boy about 14 years of age also began the same business with the
same success; they are now both constantly employed in that business, and the shoes of all the company are supplied from these
sources by those who have served no other apprenticeship than such
as above described. If any other proof be wanting that the customary
apprenticeships of seven years [are] unnecessary in this business

(where the interest of the instructor will permit him to be honest), abundance may be furnished.

Boarding is, under present circumstances, estimated at 20 hours per week, but is subject to some variation, according to the arrangements for cooking, the number accommodated, the kind of provisions in each boarding house, &c.

If we hire a saddle horse, we pay the owner an hour for every two hours we use him, his labor being estimated at half that of a man.

Wood upon this principle costs us 4 hours per cord for cutting, adding the labor of the man and team in hauling, this price remaining always the same. Upon this principle, we cannot feel the fraudulent fluctuations to which this article is subject, upon common principles.

Every article which is purchased with money is, upon this principle, sold again at prime cost, adding only the labor according to the time employed in buying and selling it. This strikes at the root of all speculation.

We have a ball every two weeks, and the music being paid for upon this principle, costs the company collectively about three hours labor: but upon the common principles it would cost three dollars, which would amount to a general prohibition of this healthy, graceful, and social amusement.

The average amount of labor bestowed by adults on any article constitutes its price, whether produced by them or by children.

The labor of females and children being rewarded upon this principle places them upon a footing of independence equal to that of men (where their power to produce is equal).

Each individual carries his own labor notes as his money, signed by himself, which he pledges for certain amounts of his labor when called for; these he issues when occasions require. Thus every one becomes his own banker, promises only his own labor, a capital always more at his own control than any other can be; and as there are no laws to recognize these debts of labor, we at once step aside from all laws for the collection of debts, as well as from that monstrous compound of fraud and cupidity, banking.

The Trial Villages (from Practical Applications, *1872)*

Tuscarawas, Ohio

The first village was attempted in Tuscarawas Co., Ohio, in 1835. Six families were on the ground—24 persons in all. 23 of them had the ague or some other billious complaint some portion of the first year! We became alarmed and dared not invite any friends to join us. We thought we would try one more year; but these complaints prevailed as before, and in addition to them, the influenza carried off twelve, mostly young, vigorous, healthy people within a circle of thirty families of the neighborhood, within two weeks. We now resolved to get away from the locality as soon as possible, and we did so, at the almost total sacrifice of buildings, furniture, and land, but with the view of concentrating again when our shattered finances had been recruited.

The time between 1837 and 1842 passed in repairing damages. In March 1842 another store (just like that in Cincinnati in 1827) was set in operation in New Harmony, the old seat of Mr. Owen's communistic experiments. This store worked with an immense power in revolutionizing the retail trade in that region. It consumed about three years. But these cheapening stores, however successful, and however revolutionizing, are chiefly valuable only as means of getting public attention to the principles upon which the great revolution required must be based. It is of only momentary consequence to cheapen the prices of supplies to those who live upon wages. If they could live on a cent a day, a cent or day would be their wages, while destructive competition rages between them. Nothing short of homes of their own and new elements to work with can bring the required relief.

Utopia, Ohio

In 1844 I was in Cincinnati when an association according to Fourier was being formed. I gave a discourse to a small audience, consisting mostly of those interested in that movement. My chief points were that joint stock necessarily involves joint management, and that joint management in such new and complicated movements is impossible, that we cannot construct any verbal organization that will not wear itself out by its own friction. And I said, "I know that a large portion of my hearers are engaged in an enterprise with the best possible motives and the highest hopes, but you cannot succeed; you will fail within three years. But when you come to fail, I beg you, for your own sakes, to remember what I have said tonight, and that there is a road to success."

In about two years and eight months I learned that they had broken up in the worst humor with each other, and in fact some had had a hand to hand scramble for some of the joint property.

In June 1847 I went up to their locality, thinking that they might be disposed to try "equity." I had not been landed from the steam boat thirty minutes when Mr. Daniel Prescott (a stranger to me) approached and said, "Well, we failed, just as you said we should—it worked just as you said it would. Now I am ready for your movement."

There were six families almost destitute, even of shelter. There was but little talking to do, no organization to get up, no constitution nor bylaws to make. The first step was to get land, but no one had the money to buy it. A proposition was made to the owner of a few acres, to lay them out into quarter acre lots and set a price upon each that would give him all he asked now for the land by the acre, adding all the costs of streets, alleys, surveying, and to pay for his own time and trouble in attending to it, and to bind himself and his heirs to keep that price, unaltered, for three years.

He consented, and the village was laid out at once and work commenced: though I doubt whether ten dollars in money could have been in the possession of the six families at that time. It was now about the middle of July 1847. On the first of December following, four of the six families had good houses and lots of their own, nearly or wholly paid for.

On moving into their new house in December (a brick house about thirty feet square and two stories high), Mrs. Prescott stood in her kitchen and casting a look of surprise round the room, exclaimed,

"Well! they say this is our house, but how in the world we came by it I cannot imagine!"

Mr. Prescott was a carpenter and exchanged more or less work with others. No common money passed between them.

Another of these pioneers, Mr. Cubberley, shall tell his own story. He wrote it out to be printed in 1848. Here it is:

"Mr. Editor, Here is a statement of the simple facts that may be of some value to the readers of your paper.

"Last July, when Mr. Jernegan had this town laid out, I thought I would buy a lot and get it fenced in last fall, and be gathering materials through the winter, for building on it in the spring. But the house that I then occupied was too bad to winter in, and as I could not get any other near, I came to the conclusion that I must build one. Well, I began to look round to see where the means should come from. I found I had about thirty dollars in money, and about nine or ten dollars worth of shoe materials (rather a small sum to think about building a house with!), but on enquiry of those who had the brick, lumber &c., I found that I could exchange my labor for theirs: that is, to give my labor for theirs in bricks, lumber, hauling &c. Well, I set to work with what means I had. The result is, I have got a brick house, one story and a half high, sixteen by eighteen feet, and a small wooden addition that serves as a kitchen. And all the money I paid out was eleven dollars and eighty five cents.

"All this is the result of equitable commerce.

"A word to the Fourierists, who contemplate such great advantages in a phalanx, combination, united interests &c.

"I was in the Clermont Phalanx for nearly three years, and paid two hundred and seven dollars, and worked harder all the time, with not the best of eatables either.[4] And at the end of that time I found myself rather badly situated: no money, no good clothes, no tools to commence work with, no anything.

"I borrowed twenty six dollars to commence my business with, and last July I paid all that, and had thirty dollars left. I now have a house and lot, and all I owe on it is two dollars and seventy nine cents in money, and about four days labor.

"I feel now that I am a whole individual—not a piece of a mass, or of somebody else, as I was in combination."

Mr. Cubberley is still living in that house and can be consulted if necessary: but it has been thought important from the beginning not to make the place notorious, as it would cause great inconvenience to the residents, there being no public house for the entertainment of visitors, and for other reasons that will appear as we proceed.

The way these lots were sold and the prices fixed, we believe to be a most peaceful, most satisfactory and efficient mode of stopping speculation on land. It makes no quarrel with present ownership. It satisfies the owners, not only giving them a price for their land which satisfies them, but tends to immediately surround them with the best of neighbors and growing better all the time, bringing the city conveniences to them upon equitable terms, and opens the way at once for the homeless to get homes of their own without legislation or any other vexation: all resulting from the simple application of the cost principle to land tenures as they now are, and I cannot see any other reliable solution to this great question.

In about two years after the commencement of this village, I was going down to Cincinnati, and anticipating enquiries as to our progress, and unwilling to give my own version of things, I went to the residents themselves to get their own words to report to our friends. I took my book and pencil and went to the first I met. "Well, Mr. Poor, what shall I say to our friends in Cincinnati about our progress?"

Mr. Poor. "Why, I hardly know. I am surprised that people are so slow to see and take hold. I expected that a great many would have come before this time. If they want homes, small homes, this is the place to get them. Tell them that when I landed here two years ago, I sent my last dollar to Cincinnati for a barrel of flour and hadn't enough left in my pocket to jingle, and now I have a comfortable house, with room enough, two acres of land, a yoke of oxen and a cow and a garden, and would not sell out for six hundred dollars."

Mrs. Poor. "Tell them if they want homes to come here and get them—that is the way we did and came five hundred miles for it: and

I would not now part with my home long enough to go on a visit to the East if they would pay my passage both ways."

Mr. H. B. Lyon. "Tell them the principles have benefited me and my affairs, and although I have been acting on them about two years, I see new beauties and have stronger confidence in them every day."

Mrs. V. "Well, I must say that I am discouraged. I cannot get any one to act with me on the principles. They will not give me employment and I give up."

Mr. Daniel Prescott. "I say now, what I have always said, that it works well, as far as we have anything to work it with, and the farther we work it, the better it works."

Mr. Geo. Prescott. "Why, it works well. We get on as well as we could expect with our means, and expect to do better as our means increase."

Mr. Wm. Long. "We want more numbers. Our advantages will increase with our numbers. I think people should understand that they will require means enough to set themselves going. There is plenty to do, but each must bring means to commence with, and then, all will go on finely."

Mrs. C. "I have not seen the workings of the principles long enough to express an opinion, but Mr. C. and myself have both been agreeably disappointed by the unexpected kindness and attention of the people here."

Mr. Francis. "I could talk half a day on the advantages of the principles. But I think talking almost useless. Action is what we want."

Little Amelia. "You may tell them it is just the place to come to learn music."

Mr. Cubberley. "You may tell them that I have all my life been wanting something, but didn't know what it was. Now I have found it."

Mrs. _____. "The principles embrace all that people will ever want, all they can ever enjoy. But I will not let you say this from me, because it might set down as effect of overwrought enthusiasm."

Mrs. Prescott. "You may say that I have always thought that the principles embrace all that is wanted. They are practicable too, just in proportion to numbers and means: with plenty of people and even a small amount of means in the hands of each, all would be worked handsomely out." (Observe, "in the hands of each," not in the hands of a committee of managers, or president and council.)

These persons mentioned were all adults who were on the ground at that time. The singular coincidence between them cannot be attributed to any pre-arranged understanding, for not one of them knew before hand that their opinion would be asked for.

Mr. W. "The reason why the village does not grow any faster is that the public know nothing of the subject. They judge it by what they know of common reforms which have so repeatedly failed. They have no idea that they have a whole new lesson to learn."

Mrs. Poor. "Why, do you think we grow slowly? Isn't there twenty six buildings put up here, out of nothing, as you may say? When we landed here not two years ago, we had but five dollars in the world, and now my husband says he would not sell out for six hundred dollars for his gains over and above the support of the family; and all this the result of our own labor. We have not gained it off other people—they have had all that belongs to them. And besides, the boys have got trades without the loss of a day in apprenticeships, instead of enslaving themselves seven years of the best part of their lives for nothing. There is a door our boy made; he has made sashes too. I speak of our own case. I have a right to do that, but others have done as well as we have. Look at H. That boy is, even now, a smooth workman, and his first attempt was upon our own house."

In less than three years there was a good saw and grist mill running, owned (not by a company) but by an individual who had not a dollar when the village commenced, but who was favored by a gentleman who sympathized in the movement, and who had a steam engine and boiler to dispose of. And he had the assistance and cooperation of all the residents, because they were to have the lumber at the cost price; the more assistance they could render, the less the price would be. But if the price of the lumber was to have been set by common practice (the owner of the mill demanding all he could have extorted from the necessities of the settlers) then no such motive to cooperation would have existed. As it was, the cooperation was as perfect as cooperation could be, yet everyone was entirely free from all trammels of organizations, constitutions, pledges, and every thing of the kind.

The owner of the mill issued his labor notes, payable in lumber.

H. B. Lyon paid for his lot with his labor notes. The mill needed his labor and the owner of the land needed lumber. Mr. Lyon issued his notes, promising his labor in the mill. The owner of the mill took them of the land owner for the lumber, and Mr. Lyon redeemed them in tending the mill. With all my hopes, I had not dared to expect to see land bought with labor notes so soon as this.

While the types are being set for these pages (October 1872) there comes an article written by Mr. Cubberley for publication. Alluding to the labor notes, he says, "These put us here into a reciprocating society. The result was, in two years, twelve families found themselves with homes, who never owned them before. Labor capital did it. I built a brick cottage one and a half stories high, and all the money I paid out was $9.81. All the rest was effected by exchanging labor for labor. Money prices, with no principle to guide, have always deceived us."

When it is stated that this village was started twenty five years ago, very natural questions are often asked: How large is it now? Why have the public not heard more about it? Why are not a hundred such in full operation? &c. No short, complete answer can be given to these very reasonable questions. This particular village consisted of only about eighty quarter acre lots (if I remember rightly). All the surrounding lands were controlled by speculators who demanded such high prices that after about four years the largest portion of the first settlers moved all together to Minnesota, where land was abundant and cheap.

The contract with the land owner to keep the prices of the lots unchanged for three years had expired before all the lots were taken up, and it is labor and trouble thrown away to bestow them when the prices of lots can be raised just in proportion as they become desirable.

"Well," asks Mr. Jones, "did those who went to Minnesota still act on the principles where they went?"

The only report I have heard from them is an incident between Mr. Poor and a speculator who applied to him for his crop of potatoes. Mr. Poor declined to sell them. "Why not?" asked the speculator. "I will give you thirty cents a bushel, while the highest price you can get from any one else is thirty cents."

Mr. Poor. "No I will not sell them for speculation at any price. Twenty-five cents a bushel will pay me for my labor and I shall supply my neighbors with them at that price."

As has been before stated, the public have learned but very little of the subject, because the common, mercenary newspapers could not do it any justice, and it has been kept out of them as much as possible.

The next resort was publishing in book form. But people will not buy books on a subject that they feel no interest in, and they cannot feel an interest in that which they know nothing about. The little progress that has been made has mostly been effected by giving away the works published to here and there to one who could be induced to look at them. It is easy to see that no ordinary private resources could make very rapid or extensive progress in that way. There are other reasons for slow growth that will appear as we proceed.

Modern Times, New York

The third village was commenced on Long Island, N.Y., in March 1851, on the Long Island R.R. 40 miles from New York.

One man went on the ground alone and built a little shanty, ten or twelve feet square.[5] There was not, at that time, even a cow path in sight, among the scrub oaks that were everywhere breast high. In a few days two others joined him: they built the first house with funds supplied by a sympathizing friend.

The soil was so poor that it was generally considered worthless. Many attempts of capitalists to turn it to account had failed. But a few persons were very anxious to try the new principles and thought that the soil might answer for gardens, while mechanism might furnish the principal employments.

There was nothing on the land to make lumber of, and even the winter fuel (coal) had to brought from the city. Even with these drawbacks, houses seemed to go up, as they did in the other village, without means, and those who never had homes of their own before suddenly had them.

We were going on very pleasantly without notoriety, but one of the most active pioneers published an article in the *Tribune* relative to the movement at Modern Times (as the village had been named). The effect was a rush of people ignorant of the principles upon which the enterprise was projected. Among these were some that were full of crotchets, each one seeming to think that the salvation of the world depended on his displaying his particular hobby. One regular impostor traveled over the Island announcing himself as the founder of the village, and he put forth such crude theories, especially with regard to marriage, that his audiences were disgusted, not only with him, but with what they supposed the village to be, and some very good neighbors who had kindly welcomed us to the neighborhood shut their doors in the face one who was offering them hand bills to counteract the blasting influence of this lying impostor.

Another favorite crotchet of his was, that children ought to be brought up without clothing! And he inflicted some crazy experiments on his children in the coldest weather. A woman, too, got this notion, and kept her infant naked in the midst of winter. With all his genius and noble efforts, Lord Bacon has not entirely secured us against the delusions of mere fancies, instead of building our theories on experience.

A German, who was wholly or partly blind, paraded himself naked in the streets, with the theory that it would help his sight. He was stopped by an appeal to the overseer of the insane asylum.

He could see well enough to take a neighbor's coat from a fence where the owner of it had been at work. This gave the neighbors an idea that we were a nest of thieves as well as fanatics. To counteract this, hand bills were printed and circulated describing the person, and advising the neighbors who might miss any thing to come to that village and look for it in his premises. This placed the responsibility upon him, individually, where it belonged, and put an end to his pilfering.

One woman took a notion to parade the streets in men's clothing, having a bad form, the clothes a bad fit and of the worst possible color and texture, she cut such a hideous figure that women shut down their windows and men averted their heads as she passed. Yet it was very easy for the sensation news paper reporters to say that "the women of Modern Times wore men's clothing and looked hideously enough!"

I can believe the woman dressed in this manner, for the purpose of breaking in upon the tyranny of fashions, and to vindicate the right to dress as she pleased. But there was no need of any vindication where her absolute sovereignty in all things (within her own sphere) was already admitted. It seemed not to have occurred to her that this same right of sovereignty in other people, should secure them against being unnecessarily disgusted and offended. But it is nothing new, especially with reformers, to "lose our manners in learning our philosophy."

It seemed not to have occurred to the woman in men's clothes, that the influence of woman is one of the greatest civilizing powers we have, and we need to know when we are in their presence.

It had gone abroad that "the women of Modern Times wear mens' clothes," and those who were disgusted at the imputation had no means of defending themselves against it. This communistic reputation is the most formidable obstacle to peace and progress that the world has to overcome. All the inhabitants of a village, or a nation, all the members of a party, a sect, or a family, are involved by it in the acts of every or any member, sane or insane, on the horrid principle of the old Japanese law that condemned a whole family to death when any member of it had offended. There is no escape from this monstrosity, till the public generally can be taught something about the great, preservative fact that we are individuals, and that no one should be made responsible for the act or word of another, without his or her known consent.

There must freedom to differ before there can be peace or progress, and this freedom can come only by placing responsibility where it belongs.

The world needs new experiences, and it is suicidal to set ourselves against experiments, however absurd they may appear, and we can afford to tolerate them if we are not too closely mixed up with them. Some people can learn nothing from the experience of others; they must have measles, the whooping cough, and small pox for themselves, before they can be secured against them. All we can demand of them is that they do not endanger the health of others.

A young woman of the village had the diet mania to such a degree that she was said to live almost wholly on beans without salt. She tottered about a living skeleton for about a year and then sank down and died (if we can say there was enough of her left to die). Though her brother also had the diet theory dangerously, he had the candor to acknowledge, at her funeral, that he believed the poor girl died in consequence of theoretical speculations about diet.

The next report was "those people there, are killing themselves with fanatical theories about their food."

Another trial. A man came there with three young women to live with as wives in the same house, and they started a paper to vindicate themselves, full of sickly, silly, maudlin sentimentality that perfectly disgusted the surrounding neighborhood so that even the name of the place was something like an emetic. But, the settlers, faithful to the great sacred right of freedom to do silly things, and knowing that opportunity to get experience would work the best cure, they were suffered to go on entirely undisturbed, though the effects of their conduct were disturbing every other settler in the village.

They seemed to be totally ignorant of the fact that no four people, nor even any two people can govern one house or drive one horse at the same time, that nature demands and will have an individual deciding in every sphere, whether that government is a person, an idea or anything else. It must be an individual or all will be confusion.

Three months trial taught them this inevitable lesson, but the effects were much more enduring.

These are a few of the trials to which such enterprises are always exposed, and that keep people of culture and sensibility from taking any part in them unless they are impelled by motives that are irresistible.

It is impossible and perhaps unnecessary to give an account of all the obstacles that beset the village. But I will give one more. There was a man (as I suppose we must call him) came there, planted himself in our midst, publicly slandered and abused the most active friends of the movement, apparently with a view to discourage them. He deliberately wrote the most unqualified falsehoods and sent them to England, where the subject was beginning to get respectful attention from men of influence. He actually made a particular point of saying and doing those very things that he afterwards caused to be published as a disgrace to the place, and which had the effect to disgust friends abroad and turn their eyes away from us, just as the enemies of liberty did in the French Revolution: they mixed in with the crowd and urged on and committed such monstrous crimes, that the world recoiled in disgust and horror at the idea of revolutions and even of liberty itself.

Another case. A man, a preacher of some influence, came there to investigate and returned to Cincinnati and delivered a public discourse from the pulpit, which was afterwards published in the *Cincinnati Gazette* under the heading of "Bohemianism." Of twenty-six statements made, twenty-five were wholly or partly false and one was equivocal. The citizens felt outraged. A letter was sent to him and he promised to rectify his stupid statements, but he never did.

With such infernal elements as those to contend with, is it not a wonder that there is any village left at all? Yet, there is a very pretty one, and it is improving faster than any other in the neighborhood. Where many capitalists have lost all their investments in attempting to turn the soil to account, a few industrious individuals with nothing but their hands and their good sense have made themselves homes and business. Where there was not even a cow path at the beginning, there is now an avenue straight as a line, a hundred feet wide and nearly a mile long, and other avenues and streets crossing each other at right angles. There is a railroad station and a post office there, and an excellent road six miles long, running out into the country in one direction and extending to the South Bay in the other, and running right through the town. The name of the place is changed [to Brentwood] and the annoyance from that source is at an end.

One of the most common remarks of the citizens was that the village was the greatest school they ever knew.

But it is not only what they have got but what they have not got that constitute the gains of the residents. They have no quarrels about what is called "religion." No demands for jails. No grog shops. No houses of prostitution. No fighting about politics. No man there has dashed his wife's brains out with an axe, nor cut her throat, nor murdered her in any other way. No wife there has poisoned her husband. No starving child has been torn from his home there and sent to prison for "unlawfully" taking "a penny's worth of potatoes." No poor, suffering girl or woman has been persecuted to death there for that misfortune which is, of itself, too grievous to be borne. No man or woman has murdered another for rivalry, jealousy, or any other cause.

The gardens and strawberry beds are mostly without fences, yet no one belonging to the village is seen in them without the owner's consent. Few if any doors are locked at night, and the fear of robbers and fire disturbs no one's sleep.

"We have heard," says an enquirer, "that the movement was a failure, and that the principles were abandoned by the inhabitants. I heard one of the most devoted friends of the movement propose to make a public announcement to that effect, to protect themselves against the annoyances of too much public notoriety." He was not afraid that the laws of nature would fail, whatever might be said of them.

Individuality is the great prevailing fact of all persons and things. This never fails. Any denial of this only illustrates it. Self-sovereignty is a form of expressing our natural promptings to have our own way.

This, also, is illustrated by all that is said, for or against it: it is a universal propensity, a natural, primitive, divine law. The cost principle is intended to express the fact that it is the sacrifices or trouble incurred in the performance of a piece of service that should measure its price. This is derived from our instinctive aversion to that which is painful: another natural law. Adapting supplies to our demands or wants is what we all aim at in every move we make, whether we succeed or not. No one ever abandons the desire to have what he wants. Equitable money is the only human contrivance in the five elementary principles of the movement. The four others are not the work of man, but natural phenomena: everywhere and at all times around and within us, whether recognised or not. Like the process of breathing, like the digestion of food or like the circulation of blood, they are constantly acting whether we will or no, either with or against our surroundings, and to talk of "abandoning" them is like the attempt to run away from one's legs: it is an effort to do as they want to, and it brings their right of self-sovereignty into more active operation.

No body talks of the principles of arithmetic having failed. If the results disappoint the operator, he attributes it to some mistake of his own, because he knows that arithmetical laws never fail. The blunder of our critic is in not knowing that our enterprise is not based in human inventions, but on natural laws that are as old as creation.

Q: Do the people in these villages use the equitable money now?

A: In the first stages, when they were building their houses, they used it extensively because they needed each others' labor, but they cannot use it any farther than they can supply each others' wants. Twenty families cannot do much in this way, till they commence domestic manufactures. But being obliged to draw most of their supplies of food, clothing, and fuel from abroad they must use the common money. And here is a reply to a very common remark, that "if every body was free to issue notes for their labor, there would be an inundation of them." Exactly the opposite is the fact. We found that people generally preferred to use the notes of others rather than to issue their own, and instead of there being a flood of notes afloat, they disappear in proportion as the necessity for them ceases.

Q: You have intimated that the odious doctrine of "free love" was fastened upon the village in order to set the public against the movement. Your assertion of the right of self-sovereignty certainly gives free scope to free love, or any ism or crotchet, however ridiculous or dangerous.

A: Yes, certainly it gives perfect freedom for anyone to do any thing that he can do at his own cost.

Every one is now free to wear a crown of thorns upon his head all the time, but no one does it. Whoever tries what is vulgarly called "free love" (if I understand what the words mean) will find it more troublesome than a crown of thorns. And there is not much danger of its becoming contagious where the results of experiments are made known. But forbid it and keep people ignorant of the effects of it, and there is danger of trouble inexpressible. Among about thirty persons in and near New York who tried the experiment, two men shot themselves, one hung himself, one died in the insane asylum, and another told me that he would sooner commit suicide than to live as he had (in that way) the last nine years, and although decidedly against the common marriage system, he went back under it, as the least of present evils.

In what I have said, I have not mentioned the worst effects of promiscuity. These are best made known by a visit to Dr. Jourdain's gallery of anatomical specimens at number 397 Washington St., Boston.[6]

For thirty-three years spent in the midst of controversies and experiments on the subject, I remained in doubt as to what form that relationship would assume in the reign of equitable freedom. But about thirteen years ago, with the help of an English publication I did come to conclusions that have, ever since, remained undisturbed. One of these conclusions was that this great subject is involved in the labor question, that justice to all labor of men, women, and children will settle it, as probably nothing else can, and without justice to labor, there is no escape from a return to barbarism.

In studying individuality as the great principle of order, and of security against confusion, you will see that it sanctions the most essential features of the common marriage systems, which are, one man to one woman for a definite, specified length of time, renewable by consent of both parties.

Q: Have you come to any conclusions as to the expediency of forming these villages?

A: Yes, I think it will be necessary to form them at any costs. If our efforts do not secure homes to the homeless, we work to no purpose, and these homes cannot be secured in the cities now built. But the hardships that pioneers encounter can be borne only by those of the hardiest constitutions. These hardships are incident to new lands and new principles, and to those who cannot bear them, I would recommend introducing the new elements into villages already partly formed, wherever land can be had on the proposed terms, and not far from where the movers had been accustomed to live, making no public proclamations, but letting the practical operations commend the principles to surrounding minds by natural degrees, so that fruits shall come by growth, not by any attempt at formation.

Q: You speak of getting land on the proposed terms. I don't know as I quite understand your idea.

A: It is to get the holders of land to bind themselves by legal contract to sell certain specified lots at certain specified prices for a certain term of years.

In laying out the first village, the term was three years, but this was not long enough. In our second (Modern Times) we had five years, but considering the obstacles, this was not long enough. At the expiration of this term, speculation grasps at the unsold lots, and then it is no longer worthwhile to do anything for further growth. While the principles are so little known, I would suggest ten years in which to fill up a settlement of, say, a thousand acres.

Points Suggested for Consideration in Laying Out Towns

1. While securing to every settler all the land that can be necessary to him or her (when labor is properly paid) to positively cut off the power to monopolize the soil.
2. Positive security against desolating fires.
3. Security against the spread of dangerous diseases.

4. To secure as far as possible, to every one, the choice, at all times, of their own immediate surroundings and companionship or neighbors.

5. To give every one, as nearly as possible, equal advantages of locality, in regard to public resorts and places of business.

6. The distances from dwellings to places of business to be short as practicable while preserving sufficient room to avoid mutual disturbance.

7. To give equal facilities for the use of the roads.

8. To be able to begin in a small way, yet complete in itself, so that growth will be only a repetition of what has already been done, and given satisfaction, and which can be continuously extended outwards, so that enlarging will not compel emigrations to remote regions, deprived of all the conveniences that habit has rendered necessary—perhaps to die of new peculiarities of climate, or hard work without help.

9. The world needs free play for experiments in life. Almost every thinker has some favorite ideas to try, but only one can be tried at one time by any body of people, and there is but little chance of getting the consent of all to any thing new or untried. If a new project can find half a dozen advocates, it is unusually fortunate. If a hundred experiments were going on at once, there might be fifty times the progress that there would be with only one. To attain this very desirable end, it should be practical for the few advocates of any new project to try it without involving any others in risks, expenses, or responsibilities or disturbances of any kind. And yet all might benefit by the results of such experiments, either positively, or negatively as warnings.

EPHEMERA AND MISCELLANEA

Early Writings

Articles in the Owenite New Harmony Gazette *and its successor, the* Free Enquirer—*under the editorship of Robert Dale Owen and Fanny Wright—and in* Mechanics Free Press, *represent Warren's earliest known writings. Shawn Wilbur—who runs the website "In the Libertarian Labyrinth" and is a preeminent researcher of nineteenth-century American radicalism—unearthed these texts in various collections. The first item below, from the* New Harmony Gazette *in 1828, shows the direct influence of Owen on Warren, and gives a basic statement of the derivation of political freedom from metaphysical determinism. The second piece, from the* Free Enquirer *in 1830, displays a rather remarkable satirical edge. He suggests that politicians' words are uttered so mechanically that machines, specifically random phrase generators, could replace them. Warren is no doubt aware of the picture of the law as a dispassionate and neutral machine; he points out that legal institutions in practice are in fact infested with randomness and subjectivity. Then he suggests that it would be more rational and far more economical simply to spin a wheel to assign penalties for crimes.*

There is evidence that the material published in the Mechanics Free Press, *which reprinted a number of Warren's early writings, had an effect. In 1828 an organization was formed in Philadelphia called the Producers' Exchange of Labour for Labour Association, distributing goods on equity principles. A flier of the group (in the collection of the Indiana Historical Society in Indianapolis) advertises such goods as lemon acid, oil of wormseed, fine black ink, and tartar emetic (accompanied by "directions for taking the vomit").*

"From the March of Mind"
(*New Harmony Gazette*, September 10, 1828, vol. 2, no. 46)

T he acquisition of any new fact always produces in my mind a feeling of pleasure, especially when I perceive that it will in any manner promote my future happiness; and the more does it increase my happiness if I can make it subservient to the happiness of others. This will be sufficient apology to the reader for my observations, when it is considered that they are not obtruded upon him as rules for his own conduct, but that they are here placed for his consideration, to be accepted or rejected as his own judgment shall determine.

It is now about three years, since a gentleman by the name of Robert Owen, promulgated in the most unequivocal and in the most public manner, the proposition that "man is the creature of the circumstances that surround him," and he also stated, that "this is a fact over which man has no control." Although I perceive that my happiness as well as that of all others is deeply involved in the truth or utility of this principle or proposition, I have never seen nor heard any serious or candid attempt to prove it false, either from any one of the governments of the old or new continent, or from any of the teachers of the people, whether speakers or writers, or from any other individual, although Mr. Owen offered five thousand dollars as a reward for any effectual refutation of those statements.

Now, therefore, having examined the statement made by Mr. Owen as far as my own power of comparison will permit, and not being able to discover in it any thing contrary to, or disagreeing with any facts within my knowledge; and having for three years looked in the public prints, and to public teachers, who as guardians of the public good should protect us against imposition, and having seen from them no attempt to prove this proposition untrue, I as one individual am induced to conclude, that Mr. Owen has developed to us a great and important truth.

I shall therefore in future make this fact, the basis of my judgment and my conduct, as far as my previous erroneous instruction and other circumstances will permit. Being subject to the influence of the circumstances around me, and being liable to be moulded by them, whether true or false, right or wrong, and having nothing to protect me from error and misery, but the knowledge which I may require of these circumstances, and the use I may make of this knowledge, I shall begin to analyze the circumstances around me and learn to distinguish the good from the evil; and as I have heretofore been misled by false instruction and by bad example, I shall claim the free exercise of my own judgment with regard to my own opinions and my own conduct.

I shall do that which I perceive will produce the greatest amount of happiness to myself and others, without any more regard to the examples or habits of others than this rule will point out.

In selecting my companions I shall choose those that are most agreeable to myself. Those who make no attempt to deceive or mislead me, who make no attempt to take advantage of my ignorance, for their own aggrandizement; but if they deal me fair and equal justice—if they be ready to treat me with kindness and my errors with forbearance, if they exhibit no disposition to inflict pain upon me or others but I may feel secure and happy in their company, them will I choose for my companions, whether they be born in the eastern or western states; whether their dresses be made of fine or coarse cloth; whether in opinion, they be Infidel, Jew, Christian, or Mahometan; or whatever peculiarities they may have which produce no pain to me or others. But those who are induced, whether by false instruction, or from other circumstances, to take from me more than fair and equal justice will allow, or to take advantage of my weakness or my ignorance, or to deceive me by my false instruction, whereby I may be led into error, or who are disposed to abridge my freedom in the pursuit of happiness, or who are disposed to inflict pain of mind or body upon me or others: them will I avoid, and will not dare to trust myself in their company; but will remove if possible out of their reach, whether their dresses be made of fine or coarse cloth; whether they be born in the eastern or western states; or upon the new or old continent; or whether in opinion, they be Infidel Jew, Christian or Mahometan; or whatever names, parentage, manners, or customs, may be peculiar to them. And this choice will I exercise, without regard to any public or private prejudices, as they are produced by surrounding circumstances and will disappear as real knowledge increases.

In choosing my dress, I shall analyze the various circumstances connected with it, and shall choose that which will give me more pleasure than pain. If I wish for a dress which costs much pain and labor to obtain, and if I perceive that I can apply my time to more advantage than to the obtaining of such a dress, I shall wear a less costly dress, without any other regard to the examples around me, than regret that I can not please their tastes consistently with my own happiness. And I shall endeavor to examine into, and reason upon, all things with which I find myself connected, shall endeavor to estimate them by their real intrinsic worth, according to the amount of happiness or unhappiness which I find them capable of producing, always reserving freedom to change with increasing knowledge; and no further than this will I be governed by the customs and manners which surround me: as I perceive that some of them are merely the production of the most whimsical and injurious practices of my fellow beings, which have been created by the whimsical and injurious circumstances in which they are placed.

J. W.

"Improvement in the Machinery of Law"
(*Free Enquirer*, July 17, 1830, vol. 2, no. 38)

The immense expense with which the making and administering of law has hitherto burthened individuals and nations, suggests the idea of a substitute for law makers and law expounders.

At first thought it may appear to some that the proposal to carry on the business of law by machinery is too novel, perhaps too absurd, for consideration; but let it be remembered that nothing is too absurd to find proselytes.

Let it be considered, that in electing our legislators, we go mechanically to work; we elect them according to old established customs, and at a certain time of the year which is determined by the almanack and the clock. We next go through a certain routine of praises and adulation of our candidates, and a certain amount of abuse of the other parties; this occupies all the time between the nomination and the election, and this time may easily be measured by clock work. The routine of words in praise of our party and in abuse of the others are generally the same, or vary so little, that the advantage of variety when compared with that of performing this expensive, monotonous, and dirty business by machinery, loses all its importance. Therefore, let a number of words and phrases such as "scoundrel," "traitor to his country," "despicable time-server," "heartless demagogue," "Judas," "Infidel," "miserable tool of party," &c., be placed upon the periphery of a wheel, to be turned by the wind or any other power, so that the words would make all due display. Upon another wheel might be placed "hero," "patriot," "defender of his country," "transcendent talents," "the hero and the statesman," "friend to infant manufactures," &c. All these could be as easily and as justly applied to candidates for office by machinery as they now are by the advocates of parties; and when we consider that one machine can be so constructed as to furnish adulation without limit for our candidate, as well as abuse for our opponent, and that a machine so constructed will apply to all parties alike from year to year (only changing the names of the candidates), the inanimate machine, in my view, claims the decided preference on the score of economy; especially when we take into the account that it would save the addling of so much (or so little) brains, the annual consumption of so much good clean writing paper and the setting up and distributing of such vast quantities of types.

We might go through an analysis of the whole business, and show the incalculable advantages of substituting an inanimate machine in each department, but this would be tedious for me and the printer, a bare hint at each must suffice to set the reader fairly on the road to economy, and to show how much has been lost for want of such an improvement.

Think, then, that when the candidate arrives at the legislative hall, the same routine of ceremony, bombast, and sophistry is repeated which has been acted over and over, time out of mind; the same personal abuse of opponents; the same "rising to explain," "rising to correct the gentleman opposite"; and, in fact, the same general routine of words uttered apparently without regard to anything but quantity and sound, both of which we know, by the printing press and the hand-organ, can be produced for at most one twentieth part what they now cost. And as to their effects on the interests of the people, if they do no good they would do no harm, and this we cannot say in favor of the more orthodox common practice.

But last not least, comes the decisions by law, the constructions and applications of these hopeful productions of eight dollars per day.

A citizen has a horse stolen, catches the thief, and seeks redress; where is he to find it? Common sense answers, that the thief should remunerate the citizen to the same amount that he has injured him, in loss of time or property; but law says that law shall decide it. According to which, the thief, the citizen, jurors, judges, lawyers, constables, loungers, ragamuffins, &c., assemble, say to the amount of one hundred, spend perhaps a whole day in discovering that the lawyers on different sides construing these laws in their own way, no one law can be brought to bear so as to decide the case; and that the only way is to search for some precedent among the old relics of monarchical courts, before they can proceed in their republican decision. Referring therefore, to some old musty records of decisions, the very absurdity of which is forgotten in their age, they find authority from my Lord C. or my Lord Q. and proceed to decide that the thief shall be shut up in unproductive idleness for three, five, or seven years; the exact number depending on what the judges ate at the last meal.

Now look at the results. The injured citizen is not remunerated: the hundred days time of the judge, jurors, lawyers, loungers and ragamuffins is entirely lost, viz. 100 days.

Loss of the citizen's and constable's time in catching thief, say 3 days.

Time lost by thief being shut up in idleness, say 825 days.

828 days lost by this method; whereas by the proposed machine, we might save a great part, if not the whole, and stand quite as fair a chance of doing justice.

Thus: Let an index point to the crime "horse stealing." Then place a number of precedents up to the periphery of the wheel, set it going, and when it stops, decide the case by the precedent which stops opposite the index. By this means we could save at least the hundred days time of judges, lawyers, ragamuffins, &c., and we might have one chance of saving the whole thousand eight hundred and twenty five days by putting on the wheel in the place of one of the precedents the suggestion of common sense: that "the thief shall remunerate the citizen and the constables for their loss of time and expense in detecting him." If this decision should happen to stop opposite the index, we should save say about 825 days time in this one case which would be sufficient to raise horses enough to supply all the horse thieves in the county with horses, gratis. Only think of it! for the same expense that we can prosecute one thief!

These views are thrown out to induce reflection. I am not over-tenacious for the fame of an originator: if these suggestions lead to the economy of the public time and money, so that the benevolent may have a little to spare for the erection of houses of punishment for the poor, and that the patriot may spend five dollars at a dinner in honor of a political economist, the very prospect of public improvement and consistency will more than compensate for declining the monopolizing privileges of a patent.

Modern Education

This is essentially an advertising brochure for a school—the Mechanical College—at Modern Times, no doubt printed by Warren, dated December 1861. It's a vision of education for self-reliance and community building. If Thoreau had written an essay on teaching, he would have said much the same (and in fact he did much the same as a schoolmaster). Warren's is a quintessentially American statement, acting as a bridge from Ben Franklin to John Dewey. One feature of Warren's critique of the apprenticeship system was that artisans should not hold specialized knowledge in secret. The incredible range of practical and impractical knowledge that Warren evokes in this rather fantastical curriculum is almost certainly one he felt personally qualified to teach. There is something beautiful about the same man offering to teach you how to make bricks, dance the schottische, and bring about a golden age of peace and prosperity (no doubt, by making, selling, and using these same bricks and dances). The school was evidently meant not only to teach people useful crafts but also to build Modern Times and yield recruits. The touching honesty and extreme prolixity in this advertisement clearly display Warren's limitations as a self-promoter, though there is a strange sort of poetry or music in his words. And it should also be said that a quite serious and systematic philosophy of education underlies this material.

Volumes might be written upon the narrowness, the imbecility, injustice, and cruelty of the prevailing modes of education; but these are now common themes, and volumes are not necessary to portray their defects and deformities. Every newspaper displays to us scarcely any thing but war, fraud, violence, falsehood, crime, and suffering, and the rapid approach toward general confusion.

If the human race is destined to any true civilization, the means of attaining it have yet to be learned by old and young. The problem rests in education.

The knowledge of the philosophy of governments, of laws, of money, being no part of general education, the masses become mere dupes and helpless victims of ignorant and unprincipled politicians, speculators, and impostors of all kinds, who, from deficiency of education are tempted into such modes of preserving their worthless existence.

The present modes of education are generally confined within some one narrow circle of ideas or prejudices, directly or indirectly at war with every other and with human nature. They train the young in and for a life of uselessness and leave them dependent on trickery, fraud, or violence for a living, or confine them to the knowledge of one particular business, which, when it fails in after life, exposes them to poverty, despair, crime, and ruin.

It has been customary for youths to give up two or three, five or seven years of their time and labor to learn a single art or a part of an art or business which might have been learned with the loss of as many days or weeks: and no opportunities are opened to them in adult life for the acquisition of a new business when their old one fails to sustain them, and they are driven to float about upon the sea of accidents or sink.

Those who have not had experience would be surprised at the facility with which adults can acquire a new business; and more so, at the efficiency and productive powers of children when opportunities are opened to them, and when justice is done them. Children can learn five, ten, or a dozen different kinds of business before they are twenty years old, in a sufficiently competent manner for all necessary purposes, besides many more than the ordinary branches of learning and personal accomplishments; and, land being secured from speculation, none need suffer for food, clothing, or shelter, nor to feel through life the privation and mortification resulting from the want of accomplishments which can now easily be acquired and which would qualify them for the pursuits and the society they prefer.

To be sure, it is not always the best economy to attempt to carry on more than one business at a time; but it is good economy to be qualified, when that one fails, to turn to another and to be able to do for one's self that which is indispensable, yet may be inconvenient or impracticable to obtain from others.

It is good economy to attend, first, to that which is first wanted; but not to waste time with satiated, sickly dilletantism that would insist on a certain polish or color to the soles of the shoes while feet are bare and freezing.

There is a vulgar old saying that "jacks of all trades are good at none." The sentiment is worthy of the barbarous age in which it originated. It favors the concealment of necessary knowledge, and discourages and no doubt has prevented the proper development and resulted in the despair and death of many a sensitive nature, which otherwise would have proved the saying to be false, as is already proved by hundreds who can excel in a dozen or twenty different trades, when excellence is a sufficient object to stimulate their powers. He or she who can fill twenty useful departments may prove twenty times as valuable as a citizen who can fill only one.

Opportunities are now being opened at the village of Modern Times by which adults or children can acquire practical knowledge of the following branches of education.

The use of carpenters' and cabinet makers' tools; forging and filing of iron; turning of iron; wood turning; bricklaying; lathing and plastering; white and color washing; paper hanging; cistern building; concrete brick making; type setting; proof reading; printing; tin soldering; shoe and boot making; tailoring and cutting; use of sewing machine; painting and glazing; dress making; ladies' cloak, mantilla, and collar making; ploughing and planting; grafting and budding; culture of fruits, vegetables, and flowers; physiology; gymnastics, geometry; drawing; superior penmanship; reading; arithmetic; grammar; geography.

Dancing—contra dances, quadrilles, polkas, schottisches, waltzing.

History, and the customs, religions, morals fashions, governments, and experiences of different nations. The philosophy of languages, and those portions of French and Latin most useful in this country.

Music: The philosophy or science of the most finished and exact performance, by a simple and expeditious method. Lessons on the violin, clarionette, flute, flageolette, violincello, bassoon, trombones, french horn, guitar, melodian and piano forte; extempore accompaniment; musical composition.

Criticism, public speaking, how to conduct public meetings.

A mode of securing individual homesteads for the homeless without waiting for legislation.

The philosophy of governments, of laws, of morals, of social deportment or manners, of money and its true functions, of a system of commerce and a kind of money which do not degrade human nature and ruin nations.

A military drill with a mental discipline for the sole purpose of preventing all unnecessary violence to any persons or property.

A mode of securing to all labor its just reward (the great problem of the age), and of universal justice, and consequent peace and prosperity.

Instruction in all the foregoing branches is to be obtained (when preparations are complete) at prices so low as to bring them within the reach of adults or children generally; but no uniform or permanent prices can be fixed to all branches, or for all persons alike—some require more instruction and others less; but, as a general rule, the price will be merely that which moderately compensates for the labor actually bestowed in teaching and for contingent expenses of rent of room and tools, firewood, etc., the learners having the whole products of their labor to dispose of at will.

In wood and iron working, bricklaying, lathing and plastering, and several other branches, the products of the pupil will generally pay all expenses, board included.

Those branches which can be taught in classes will be less in price as the number of pupils is large, and the same principle would affect the price of board.

No person is properly educated within the walls of any building, nor under the prescriptions of any theory whatever.

Whatever surrounds, educates us. The university in which we are really and inevitably educated is the town, the city, the circle in which we live and move. The greater our scope of experience in business, the more we mix with different people, the greater the diversity of habits, fashions, tastes, and opinions within the scope of our observation while young, and the more we are called upon to compare the results of all, and to judge each tree by its fruit, to select some and reject others, the more the faculty of discrimination is exercised, the mind expanded, the hands and the judgment strengthened and the better are we prepared for self-government, self-preservation, for citizenship, and for all the contingencies and relations of after life.

Probably nowhere as in the village of Modern Times can be found so much diversity in the above respects, accompanied with that practical toleration, which ensures peace, while each becomes instructive to all, and where so many persons are so well qualified and so ready to assist in educating the young.

The world has suffered more from narrow, crude, and ill-digested theories, than from any other cause; and probably nowhere is this crudity so harmless as in the village of Modern Times, Long Island, New York. And perhaps nowhere else is the remark frequently heard from adults, that the town in which they live "is the greatest school they were ever in."

It is widely known that the atmosphere is exceedingly healthy, and the climate remarkably agreeable.

While reading the foregoing general statements, it should be mentioned, they are not all entirely completed, but the design is to make the preparations keep pace with the sustaining demand for these and any other branches of useful knowledge.

It is well, also, to bear in mind that some branches, such as bricklaying, cistern building, lathing and plastering, framing, ploughing and planting, are more or less favored or retarded by seasons and circumstances, and for this and for other reasons it would be best for persons desirous of securing any of these advantages for themselves or their children, to write and ascertain precisely the facts bearing on their particular wishes existing at the time of application. For this purpose they may address the subscriber at Thompson P.O., Long Island, N.Y., who is alone responsible for any and all the foregoing statements.

Dec., 1861 Josiah Warren

Against Compulsory Education

The following is from "Response to the Call of the National Labor Union for Essays on the Following Subjects," a pamphlet giving one-paragraph responses in the Warrenian manner to such questions as

"Coolie Importation," "Compulsory Education," and "Woman—
Her Rights" (there are twelve in all). The document, dated Boston,
1871, has been supplied by the Labadie Collection at the University of
Michigan.

We have not yet agreed on what constitutes the desired education.
Perhaps the most fortunate children are those who escape education
in the midst of the frauds, falsehoods, violence, and misery growing
out of the barbarian money used in all past time. The idea of compulsory education is as absurd as that of compelling people to maintain
life by means of food.

   Besides, who are to be the educators? When there are as many
plans as there are sects, which one shall be enforced by compulsion?
Who has got the power to properly educate any person by compulsion, when the first and every succeeding step should be taken with a
strict regard to the sacred right of all children to be educated by those
examples and in the habits that they will need to practice when they
have become adults? To educate them by compulsion is to teach them
by example to become tyrants.

Written Music Remodeled

Below are the "preliminary remarks" to Warren's Written Music Remodeled and Invested with the Simplicity of an Exact Science. *The
elements of expression recognized and rendered definite, thereby securing the great object of musical performance everywhere, and abolishing multitudes of ambiguous words adopted in vain to secure that
end. The unnecessary transposition of keys in vocal music dispensed
with, and the principal use and the bewildering study of flats and
sharps thereby abolished. The confusion of clefs abolished. A system
of shorthand accompaniment introduced. No unnecessary innovations made, but the easy transitions from, and to, the common notation are an object of special care. Jewett published the booklet in Boston
in 1860, apparently using Warren's stereotyping technique. This is an
interesting little piece, relating music to politics and economics, and*

pointedly expressing the frustration Warren felt about the difficulty he
had getting an audience for his ideas and inventions. Most of the book
consists of songs in the new notation. I cannot pronounce on the system
itself, since I cannot read music, but I'm told that it is at least con-
structed with expertise, and that it could have been useful if adopted.
Warren had developed his system of musical notation by 1843, when he
published A New System of Notation: Intended to Promote the More
General Cultivation and More Just Performance of Music *at New*
Harmony.

Whoever understands the philosophy of music, that is, the essential
powers of musical sounds, will probably admit that the present mode
of representing them on paper is neither scientific nor reasonable,
and never was adapted to the wants of the public in general. It neither
gives the author power to express his ideas so as to be accurately read
and conceived by the performer, nor can the student obtain by the
present written rudiments any thing that he can call definite or satisfactory knowledge.

The growing taste and demand for such knowledge calls loudly for
a deep and patient consideration of the subject and justify a thorough
and merciless criticism of the causes which lead to the general remark, "I made the attempt two or three times, but my head was too
thick, I couldn't understand it and gave it up, though I would give
almost anything to be able to sing or play an instrument."

The position taken by the author of this work is that the fault is
not with the people, but in the mode of representing music on paper.

But we have great obstacles to overcome. Traditional bias, reverence for authority, vested interests, professional ambition and ego-
tism, all stand in deadly array against any attack on the present system
(or want of a system) and the innovator must be prepared to meet all
the opposition which these adverse influences can wield; and nothing
short of the glaring and positive advantages he offers the public can
justify for a moment the remotest hope for success.

Nothing for the mere sake of innovation. The author yields every
thing to the present system that can be yielded without running into

confusion (which is the evil to be remedied) and proposes only so much innovation as is indispensable to the success of this great agent which is so rapidly becoming one of the necessaries of life.

Some idea of the obstacles to this enterprise may be formed from a few illustrative facts. For twenty years the author had been desirous of finding some music publisher who would take an interest in it but without success. Do you ask why? I will give their own answers.

A very liberal and kind friend of the author, who was a music composer and publisher, was asked by another friend what he thought of the new system proposed. His very frank answer was, "As we have got so much invested in the common music, the less we say about it the better." I do not complain of the man; he was a good, kind, obliging, but the best of men are mere slaves to the unlimited profit making system of business, and can allow no successful rivalries if they can help it. There can be no generosity or public spirit any more than friendship in the present system of trade.

In a controversy with one of the principal musical authorities and publishers in the West in 1844, after the exchange of a few ideas, he said, "Well, I must admit you are right, but we have a living to get, and the present system suits us." He turned away and, sitting down to the piano, commenced playing.

An application was made to one of the principal publishers in Boston, who replied at once, "Yes, we will publish it if you get the sanction of Mr. _____ and Mr. _____. But these gentlemen were precisely the ones from whom the greatest opposition might be expected, as rivals most deeply interested in keeping up the present system.

It is plain then, that music, with all its grand, elevating, and beautifying powers, is made entirely subservient to the one great, all-absorbing object of money making.

The necessities of the public, the necessities of music itself, the immense influence for good or evil which it exerts every where, all weigh nothing in the scale with the profits in trade, and the public are as much puppets (in this respect) of musical wire workers as they are of French milliners and importers of foreign furs or domestic skunk skins.

To understand this item of slavery, let it be considered that music has always been employed as a powerful agency where the object was to subjugate the masses of mankind; it may therefore be employed with equal power for their emancipation.

An English statesman of much note once said "give me the making of the songs of a nation and I care not who make its laws."[1] Perhaps he did not think that however well calculated his songs might be to substitute for laws, to elevate, refine, and harmonise and humanize a people, he could not get them before the public through any of the ordinary channels, in competition with the "established authors" who have other objects in view. To have the market open to every author and their compositions to sell on their own merits would spoil the profits derived from monopoly. It is evident that any great innovation or improvement cannot expect any sympathy or aid from the trade and therefore must take its stand on the unpleasant ground of open contest, and be prepared to let the strongest prevail.

This work must stand or fall on its own intrinsic merits—not at all on its author's name; for, although a professor of music from the age of eighteen, some twenty years, yet he is now entirely unknown to the public and intends to remain so.

Perhaps an apology should be made in advance for the imperfections that may appear in the mechanical execution of the work. It is the production of entirely new mode of engraving, this work being the first ever executed by it. It is but reasonable to expect many imperfections which the older arts have overcome by long experience, which is the only means to conquer them.

The substance of the apology is, that an art was needed by which music, drawings, maps, phonography, and miscellaneous illustrations could be printed by a method less tedious and expensive than by those now in use; and if this work should prove to be the germ of the revolution required for music, the public will excuse the unavoidable imperfections incident to the first attempts to use the instrumentalities by which it was effected.

The copy right has been secured as the only existing means of securing remuneration. But abhorring the principle of monopoly and all the workings and tendencies of copy rights and patents and of an endless and unprincipled scramble after indefinite and unlimited gains, the work and the art by which it is printed (which is equally adapted to printing maps, diagrams, and writing, and which is now a secret) shall be thrown open to the free use of every one, whenever any people or government shall merely remunerate the labor that has been bestowed upon them.

"A Few Words to the Writer in a Paper Called the Circular on the Sovereignty of the Individual"

This is a single page from the Labadie Collection. It is evidently directed at the periodical of the Oneida community, the Circular, *in which John Humphrey Noyes had criticized Modern Times and Warren (as well as Andrews) by name. That would date this published letter in the 1850s. I have so far not located the exact passage that Warren is replying to, but Noyes was quite hostile to and acerbic about the notion of individual sovereignty. It strikes me that the type is Warren's, so I don't think it was published in the* Circular *itself. It may have been distributed at Modern Times as a handbill. It's a lively little statement in which Warren gives a version of one of his favorite arguments: that to deny individual sovereignty is to assert it. The denial of the claim that individuals possess sovereignty over their opinions is a contradiction, so that the claim is true and is therefore entailed by any assertion of opinion. Further, he uses a very direct and compelling argument for individualism, contending that the locus of pain is the individual.*

I am not fond of disputes—I think the time has passed for long, hard-wrought, and far-fetched argumentation, and that the truth and soundness of any propositions must be pretty nearly self-evident to be of much benefit to the public. As there seems, however, to be a good deal of straightforwardness and honesty in your opposition to the sovereignty of the individual, I am inclined to think a few words may be serviceable.

I might legitimately say to you, well, sir, if you do not like "the sovereignty of the individual" as a formula, why, then reject it.

But in doing so you would be acting on that very principle you theoretically reject. You would be practicing the very thing you object to the practice of. You stand upon the very ground you endeavor to undermine. You place yourself in the predicament of the man who stood on that part of the plank which he was sawing off: he did not discover his mistake till he found himself landed in the cellar. Perhaps you and some others may be able to profit from his experience.

I might leave the whole matter here as having said enough, but I wish to put you and others right in regard to several mistakes that are very common and which may as well be corrected here.

I have no right to speak for all the friends of the equity movement without consulting them, yet some of us do not choose to be classed as "reformers." We think that word has become too much disgraced for our purpose; and from what we have experienced, we should expect to be better appreciated by those generally classed as conservatives. Again: Mr. Warren is not "Chief" (in the common and offensive sense of that term) of any "school of reformers"—there is no chief in that sense of the word, where all are sovereigns.

You reason logically from your premises in the main argument, but your premises are false.

You say, in effect, that if one member of my body suffers the whole suffers, and as it is with the individual, so it is with the race: that all humanity suffers for the disease or wickedness of any individual, and then you logically conclude that an individual cannot act in anything at his own cost. Now neither of the premises is true and your conclusion is consequently a fallacy.

It is not true at all that, when I have a toothache, my foot or any other limb suffers. And if this were a fact, it by no means follows that all the people even in the same town will ever suffer or know anything about it.

The absurdity of this reasoning is only equalled by that of the green immigrant who, finding a ten cent piece as soon as he stepped on shore, immediately asserted that the whole country was covered over with money.

As "free criticism" is in so much favor with you I advise the study of A. B. Johnson's *Treatise on Language,* by which you may learn that general propositions, however loud sounding, may have very few and very insignificant applications.

An Individual

"Manifesto"

The Oriole Press reprinted this text in 1952. In the introduction, Joseph Ishill writes, "This Manifesto was originally written & published by Josiah Warren in 1841, and it was incidentally printed by the author on one of his home-made presses. The present reprint is from a photostat copy supplied by Mr. Ewing C. Baskette, for which we gratefully thank him for having discovered this rare historical document. Josiah Warren was undoubtedly the first American anarchist; as such he devoted most of his life towards the betterment of mankind. In spite of his individualistic tendencies which are so characteristic of the spirit of our old American pioneers, he was heart & soul for ALL, and for a society where peace and tranquility would be the dominant factors. It is also true that Josiah Warren was by nature and tradition a born rebel against all injustices & human hardships. His writings have shown the way toward liberation & annihilation of all archaic forms of slavery, and above all, he stood fast on his conviction of the SOVEREIGNTY OF THE INDIVIDUAL. The entire world is today, as never before, under a total eclipse of confusion and disillusionment, due mostly to the manifestation of a perverted 'ism,' which has darkened almost the entire horizon of the universe and which seeks to destroy ruthlessly all democratic principles based on truth & justice. This too, we hope, shall pass into oblivion. As to Josiah Warren's own publications I like to quote here from another great scholar and bibliophile, Dr. Max Nettlau. The following is extracted from an unpublished letter addressed by him to Ewing C. Baskette, dated May 26, 1936,

in which he mentions one of Warren's early publications: The Peaceful
Revolutionist (1833): *'I should like to know who has ever seen it? If there
is a copy anywhere, it should be mostly treasured and removed to one of
the most important libraries in New York or Washington.' Unfortu-
nately, neither of these two libraries have it listed. I shall do my utmost
to reprint other items by this author, as time and effort will permit."*[2]

An impression has gone abroad that I am engaged in forming societies. This is a very great mistake, which I feel bound to correct.

Those who have heard or read anything from me on the subject,
know that one of the principal points insisted on is: the forming of
societies or any other artificial combinations is the first, greatest, and
most fatal mistake ever committed by legislators and by reformers.
That all these combinations require the surrender of the natural sovereignty of the individual over her or his person, time, property, and
responsibilities, to the government of the combination. That this
tends to prostrate the individual—to reduce him to a mere piece of
a machine; involving others in responsibility for his acts, and being
involved in responsibilities for the acts and sentiments of his associates; he lives & acts, without proper control over his own affairs,
without certainty as to the results of his actions, and almost without
brains that he dares to use on his own account; and consequently
never realizes the great objects for which society is professedly
formed.

Some portion, at least, of those who have attended the public
meetings, know that equitable commerce is founded on a principle
exactly opposite to combination; this principle may be called that of
Individuality. It leaves every one in undisturbed possession of his or
her natural and proper sovereignty over his own person, time, property, and responsibilities; & no one is required or expected to surrender any "portion" of his natural liberty by joining any society
whatever; nor to become in any way responsible for the acts or sentiments of any one but himself; nor is there any arrangement by which
even the whole body can exercise any government over the person,
time, property, or responsibility of a single individual.

Combinations and all the institutions built upon them are the inventions of man; and consequently, partake of more or less of man's shortsightedness and other imperfections; while equitable commerce is a simple development of principles, which, although new to the public, are as old as the creation, and will be as durable.

This understanding is very natural; because all attempts at radical reformation known have been founded on combinations, the failure of all these has destroyed confidence, and the public, not being aware of any other principle, conclude that this is another proposal of the same kind and must fail like the rest. I respect their judgment and believe with them, that every attempt to improve their social condition by the formation of societies or any artificial combination (however ingeniously devised, however purely intended or honestly conducted) must and will defeat their own objects and disappoint all who are engaged in them.

The failure of the experiments in the community system in New Harmony during the two years trial from 1825 to 1827, sufficiently proved this to my mind, and led to the conviction that the process of combination is not capable of working out the great objects of society; but, the opposite principle, that of Individuality and the process of disconnection,[3] after much close and severe investigation were found to possess or to lead to all the redeeming and regenerating powers necessary for the complete solution of the great social problem. Indeed they appeared to promise too much to believe, too much to hope; so much, that the discoverer (if we must so call him) dare not communicate his thoughts to his intimate acquaintances for fear of being accounted insane. His only course, therefore, was to prove everything in practice previously to bringing it before the public.

A whole new course of investigations and experiments were then commenced; the first of which was the "Time Store" in Cincinnati which was opened in May, 1827. This was conducted three years, when it was wound up for the purpose of carrying the principles into all the commerce of life; and the interval between that time and the present has been employed (as far as private circumstances would permit) either in further developments or in preparation for them.

The principles have also been applied to the purchase and sale of land and almost all other kinds of property, and to the interchange of almost all kinds of labor including that of merchants, lawyers, physicians, teachers, the conductor of a boarding house, etc., through every step of which the sovereignty of the individual was strictly preserved and invariably respected. No legislation of any description assumed control over the individual in any case whatsoever; and such was the complete individuality of action that hundreds dealt at the Time Store without understanding much of its principles or its objects; but they perceived that it was their interest to do so, thus demonstrating that the business of the community can be brought into this condition by a natural and irresistible process; without combination, without organisation, without laws, without government, without the surrender of any portion of the natural liberty of the individual; demonstrating also that reformation need not wait till the world becomes learned: but the practical operation constitutes a process of re-education which no one can estimate without experience, and which the learned are most backward in acquiring.

Such, too, has been the complete individuality of action throughout all the experiments that although hundreds have taken some part in them, they are in no way distinguished as a sect, a party, or a society; the public in general do not and will not know them; excepting so far as each individual chooses to identify himself or herself with these principles.

Public influence is the real government of the world. Printing makes this governing power; therefore, among the preparations for the general introduction of these subjects are a simplification of printing and printing apparatus which brings this mighty power to the fireside and within the capacities of almost any one of either sex who may choose to use it; thus is this and every other subject of real reformation rendered independent of the common press whose conductors are generally too much absorbed or too much interested in things as they are, too much under public influence or too superficial in their habits of thinking to do this subject justice in its commencement.

The experiments and preparations are now concluded, and the results are on record or in the possession of living witnesses, and are now becoming the groundwork of practical operations in this neighborhood. Those who wish to become acquainted with the subject can obtain the particulars at the public meetings or by reading *The Equitable Commerce Gazette* which is to be published for this purpose; but the following are some of the most prominent features of equitable commerce.

It goes to establish a just and permanent principle of trade which puts an end to all serious fluctuations in prices and consequently, to all the insecurity and ruin which these fluctuations produce; and to build up those who are already ruined.

It tends to put a stop to all kinds of speculation.

It has a sound and rational circulating medium, a real and definite representative of wealth. It is based exclusively on labor as the only legitimate capital. This circulating medium has a natural tendency to lessen by degrees the value and the use of money, and finally to render it powerless; and consequently to sweep away all the crushing masses of fraud, iniquity, cruelty, corruption, and imposition that are built upon it.

The circulating medium being issued only by those who labor, they would suddenly become invested with all the wealth and all the power; and those who did not labor, be they ever so rich now, would as suddenly become poor and powerless.

It opens the way to employment for those who want it, by a simple arrangement which has a natural tendency to keep the supply in rational proportion to the demand.

It solves the great and difficult problem of machinery against labor. On this principle, in proportion as machinery throws workmen out of employment, it works for them; and the way is always open to a new employment, as equitable commerce abolishes profit on misery, disregards the customary apprenticeships, and brings all kinds of knowledge within the reach of those who want it.

The necessity of every one paying in his own labor for what he consumes, affords the only legitimate and effectual check to excessive luxury, which has so often ruined individuals, states, and empires; and which has now brought almost universal bankruptcy upon us.

Equitable commerce furnishes no offices to be filled by the ambitious and aspiring, no possible chance for the elevation of some over the persons or property of others; there is, therefore, no temptation here for such persons; and they will not be found among the first to adopt equitable commerce. It appeals, first, to the most oppressed, the humble, the down-trodden, and will first be adopted by them and by those who have no wish to live upon others, and by those whether among the rich or poor whose superior moral or intellectual qualities enable them to appreciate some of the unspeakable blessings that would result from such a state of human existence.

These are some of the most prominent features of equitable commerce; and it will be perceived that they are precisely the features which a great, redeeming revolution ought to possess: but they are so extraordinary, so out of the common course and current of things that they will be denounced by some as visionary and impracticable. I am prepared for all this, and I am also prepared to prove that all the most important applications of the principles have been made; and have proved themselves sound beyond all successful contradictions; and to show that upon these principles, it is perfectly practicable for almost any person to begin at once to enjoy some of the advantages herein set forth; and by degrees to emancipate himself or herself from the crushing iniquity and suffering of (what is called) civilized society; and this without joining any society or in any other way surrendering any portion of his or her natural and inalienable sovereignty over their person, time, or property, and without becoming in any way responsible for the act or sentiments of others who may be transacting business on these principles.

New Harmony, Nov. 27, 1841

"My Dear Sir"

This is a letter in Warren's bold, flowing hand, dated "Thompson's Station, Long Island, New York [i.e., Modern Times]. March 12, /53." It is

addressed to a person in England, perhaps A. C. Cuddon (at the end of
True Civilization, Warren suggests that people responding in England
address their correspondence to Cuddon). A surprising moment comes
at the end, when Warren says of the spiritualist movement then sweeping
his circle, "It is no delusion." A few of Warren's letters are preserved at
the University of Michigan. All but this one are illegible as a result of
bleed-through.

With much pleasure I received your interesting letter of the 15th Feb.

There is no danger of your "becoming tedious" and if I don't always respond immediately to your valuable communications, I pray you attribute it to a pressure of other matters, or to anything rather than indifference.

Mr. [Stephen Pearl] Andrews was here just in time to see your letter, and sat down immediately and wrote to you, which will render much that I might say unnecessary. I would very gladly enter minutely into the consideration of the points at issue between Antient and Modern Times, but I could not do so with much less space or labor than such as are embodied in the works already printed. One element of society is so connected with another that neither can be detached or abstracted from the other without danger to the whole. One wheel of a coach will not carry us on our journey. We must have the whole coach and the horses too, and all must move together; and I feel a degree of timidity in attempting to move any one part without the others.

Mr. Andrews, who is the publisher of the works on "Equity," will see that you have a supply as early as possible.

Yes "such leaders as Chambers are positively destroying all correct notions of right and wrong." The lead must be taken out of such hands. The order must be reversed—or rather order must supersede disorder. Those who have heretofore been followers must be the leaders—the leaders must become followers—"The last must be first and the first, last."[4] The most astonishing thing to see, since I have understood the world's wants, is the amazing ignorance with which it has been led and governed! and I have found in practice, the very best appreciators and leaders of Equity among those who were in humble positions and who seemed totally unconscious of their superiority. And we have found those who are ambitious to lead to be the most incapable of it, and the most troublesome of any.

You will learn more of my printing inventions now, as I am making them more public than ever; because I have not till now obtained all the results which I aimed at. I wish I could at once put you in possession of them, but this cannot be done by any means short of personal example and instruction. I will from time to time send you proofs that I have attained the means of printing from type without the expensive and tedious process of setting type; and I invite you to take the earliest opportunity of getting the art and the materials among you. I have already a patent half through your English law machinery—this was done more to prevent its being monopolised in that country than for any other purpose. I wonder if some of you could not complete this, and make it profitable, as well as remunerative to me? But some one must come here and learn it practically, or someone must carry it over to you. At present, no person but myself knows the process, nor would they by any quantity of experiments be likely to find out all that is indispensable to the result. I have had these experiments in hand twenty three years!

I see, by your remarks on "land tenures," that you do not fully grasp the whole of our issue with the world's wrong. You would have the land a national interest, a combined interest, a common property. Now the most prominent point we make against all the world's institutions and practices and against all the reforms is that we entirely repudiate all common or combined or partnership interests and consequently all national or state interests; and insist upon it that all interests must be thoroughly individualized before society can begin to be harmonious.

Of course, with us, there can be no such a thing as a nation or state. There should be only the family of mankind—each individual managing his own affairs supremely and absolutely, but equitably, with his fellow man. The ownership of the soil for the sake of order and harmony, for the sake of disposing with legislation, must be absolute in the individual, guaranteed by a public sense of justice, the purchases

and sales of it being conducted upon the cost principle, which remu-
nerates only the labor in the transaction; [this] destroys all landlordism,
profit-mongering, or usury as based upon traffic in the soil. I admit
that land tenures are a fundamental consideration and had we not the
means of completely and harmoniously adjusting them, I should not
now be writing to you from this place [Modern Times] where something like a thousand acres are sold or for sale to settlers, without a
dollar of profit beyond an equitable compensation for the labor of purchasing, surveying, making deeds, &c. I respectfully and affectionately
invite you and your friends to look into this and study it, till you see in
it all that you desire, and more than you expect.

I thank you for the handbill. My blood has boiled and trembled in
my veins at every word of the movements of the noble Kossuth and
Mazzini, but at the same time, at best I could but consider that their
mission was to plough up the soil, to disencumber it of rocks and
trees.[5] The planting and culture is necessarily the mission of others.

In all this I often feel envious to know how the present rulers of
the earth would receive "Equity" were it once made known to them.
It is certainly no more at issue with them, than it is with what is generally called reform. The strongest argument for despotism is
founded upon individuality, which is the first cornerstone of Equity,
and which asserts the absolute right of despotism in every individual
over his own, while despotic governments assert it only for a few, and
this from the absolute necessity of despotic power where there is any
power at all. To have no governmental power at all, there should be
no public interests to manage. All interests must become individualized before we can dispense with governments or despotisms. This
disintegration of interests is a new proposition. It is precisely the opposite in principle to reforms which have failed and been rejected and
opposed by the governments as the elements of disorder and "insecurity." The governments are right in this view of the ordinary reforms
and I therefore feel anxious to know how they treat Equity when it
comes to be made known. It really seems to me to be the platform
upon which rulers and ruled can amicably meet, shake hands, and

weep over the past or look forward to the future with a feeling of inexpressible joy.

I have not yet received the pamphlets, which I much regret. I thank you for sending them and shall be glad to read them, but think you will not need my opinion on them after you have read and understood all our positions, for they seem to be a kind of standing criticism on all reform propositions.

Yes, I believe I have had as good opportunities to examine the spiritual development as any one, the result of all of which is, that I would advise any one to take all convenient opportunities to examine for himself, for no description of other persons can do the subject or the enquirer justice. I would not advise you to incur much expense in this, as it cannot be long before plenty of opportunities will be presented to every one without expense. It is no imposture, nor is it a delusion.

Affectionately,
Josiah Warren
(write again soon)

Open Letter to Louis Kossuth

This remarkable letter, published in the Boston Investigator *on February 17, 1864, was located by Shawn Wilbur. For Kossuth, see the note to the previous selection. Kossuth had gone from resistance fighter to ruler, a success that Warren regarded as no less disastrous than complete failure. He adduces the great revolutionaries of France, and subsequent history has provided many more examples of noble fighters of oppression who mutated into oppressors (e.g., Mao and Lenin).*

Louis Kossuth
Governor of Hungary
Boston, Feb. 1, 1864

Beloved and Honored Man:

When you visited this country years ago, and put forth those heart-stirring appeals in behalf of your bleeding country, my sympathies went out towards you with more than a brother's yearning, with an intensity that no other man in the political sphere ever commanded from me. This almost idolatry, however, was mixed with a tinge of sadness from the fear of your ultimate disappointment from a cause apparently too subtle for ready detection. This was that in resisting tyranny, your national policy might include the mistake which would convert itself into a tyranny. My fears are already confirmed at the very first step taken by your committee in their report of the 24th December. They say, on your responsibility, that they "will know how, and are determined to secure obedience to its (their) orders and the accomplishment of the measures which it (they) must take." Here is, again, the whole issue between the freedom to differ (or the right of individuality) and the demand for conformity; the latter being the very essence of tyranny, against which you would array your country-men, and ask for the sympathies of the civilized world.

That you, with your great heart and deep humanity should fall into this common error, confirms, more than anything else ever did, my standing excuse for Robespierre, Marat, Danton, and despots and ty-rants all over the world, and through all the ages. It is simply a mis-take—a fatal oversight.

The mistake is inventing well-meant systems or theories, and then endeavoring to enforce obedience thereto, by treating involuntary dissent as a crime.

Opinions and preferences are as involuntary in their action as the circulation of the blood; and to threaten dissenters with the "fate of traitors," as your committee have done, is to proclaim that your cause is, for the present, already lost. Remember that the freedom of dissent in subordinates might have saved Gorgey's army—obedience to Gorgey's "orders" lost it, and perhaps defeated your cause at that time.[6]

Look, my brother, at this distracted and already desolate country (America) and behold the consequences of this same fatal error. The people here, in 1776, arrayed themselves against despotism, and re-solved on having "free institutions"; but no sooner are these institu-tions put into words on paper than it is found that no two persons understand them alike. In order to have them administered at all, they must be administered by some one person, according to his particular interpretation of them, which is a return to despotism; and which, as usual, threatens the "fate of traitors" to all who remain faithful to the original idea of American freedom! Are we never to see a prospective end to the blind imitation of barbarian precedents?

You and your committee will soon find grave subjects arising, upon which you will find it impossible to agree, and no external power on earth can make any two persons agree when their mental capacities make them to differ. Difference is inevitable. It grows out of the inherent and inalienable individuality of every person and every thing; and the true statesman, instead of making war upon this diversity, will foster and cherish difference of opinion and preferences as the very balance wheel of society; and will provide for this diversity and its full exercise to the greatest practical extent; and instead of threatening dissenters from political creeds with "the fate of traitors," the true statesman will see that when two parties differ, one is as much a dissenter or traitor (in the vulgar sense in which the latter word is commonly used) as the other.

This word "traitor," so flippantly and ignorantly used in this country just now, against some of its very best and wisest citizens (because they dissent from the policy of our centralized government) has, as it appears to me, no proper application to any person who has not voluntarily accepted some specific, definite trust, and betrayed that trust; and in this sense, it is applicable to those who being entrusted with power in order to promote public peace and prosperity, defeat these very ends, and bring on war and destruction instead; but, as this may happen through incompetency, I do not use the offensive word traitor even towards them.

I entreat you to hesitate in forming any institutions. You cannot form any that will work successfully any more than you can form fruit upon a tree. To be successful they must be allowed to grow, like fashions, customs, or the use of the railroad, according to their demonstrated utility or the preferences felt for them.

A child may lead where a god cannot govern; and Kossuth should be the counsellor—not the governor—of Hungary.

With most respectful and fraternal regard, I give you my particular address.

Josiah Warren
Counsellor in Equity
15 Scollay's Building
Boston, Mass., America

Simplicity

This is an undated note in Warren's hand from the Labadie Collection at University of Michigan.

The only ground of hope for successful civilization is in those who have never strayed from simplicity or those who have returned to it.

APPENDIXES

APPENDIX A

CHRONOLOGY OF WARREN'S LIFE

C harles Shiveley says that Josiah Warren was descended from Richard Warren, who came to America on the *Mayflower*.[1] George Santayana in *Persons and Places* describes the "Brighton Warrens" as "a dissentient family."[2] An early American ancestor, John Warren, was arrested for nonattendance at church and for harboring Quakers.[3] In *Josiah Warren*, Bailie says that "the Warrens of Pilgrim lineage from which he sprang have furnished Massachusetts with many distinguished citizens, of whom the most renowned was General Joseph Warren, the Revolutionary hero killed by the British at Bunker Hill" (1). He describes Joseph Warren as a "distant cousin."[4] Shiveley connects Josiah to a family of mechanics and printers. There is no evidence that Warren had any formal education.

In the chronology below I give important events and publications in individualist, radical reform, and anarchist publications in brackets.

Sources for Warren's life as captured in this chronology include his own writings, in particular narratives of practical experiments; Bailie's biography; Shiveley's honors thesis at Harvard; Ann Caldwell Butler's master's and doctoral theses at Ball State; Wunderlich's *Low Living and High Thinking at Modern Times*; Martin's *Men Against the State*; and Agnes Inglis's archive and rough life sketch at the Labadie Collection, University of Michigan (see bibliography).

1771   [Birth of Robert Owen]

1793   [William Godwin, *An Enquiry Concerning Political Justice*.]

1795   [Birth of Frances Wright]

1798   Born, Boston, Massachusetts.

1803   [Birth of Emerson.]

1805   [Birth of Garrison.]

1809   [Birth of Proudhon.]

1812   [Birth of Stephen Pearl Andrews]

1816–17   Musical engagements in and around Boston; according to Josiah's son George, Josiah and Josiah's brother George played in the Boston Brigade Band, which John S. Dwight said was "a real band, it had clarinets and flutes and oboes, bugles and French horns . . . , and was not the band of brass now used to penetrate the Babel of street noises. Moreover it played good music."[5]

1818   Marries Caroline Cutter.

1819   Economic depression. Moves west with his wife and settles in Cincinnati, Ohio. Later she wrote to Josiah that "when I most willingly consented to be your wife, and came out West, I gave up relations, friends, acquaintances—all, for the (to me) 'greater pearl,' and never do I remember a lingering look behind."[6]

1820   Plays the clarinet in "the first chamber music given in the city" of Cincinnati.[7] Daughter Caroline Maria born in September.

1821 or 1823   Patents a lard-burning lamp. According to his son, George Warren, "The patent documents for the lard lamp were signed by President John Quincy Adams. The patents on the printing presses invented by my father were issued under the signature of Andrew Jackson, and B. F. Butler, in 1835." Fanny Wright describes the key feature of the invention: "This lamp differs from the common one only by having a copper wire adjoining the tube which contains the wick, and connecting with the blaze of the lamp at one end, and with the lard at the other, which being a great conductor of heat, keeps the lard continually in a fluid state."[8]

1825–27   Robert Owen speaks in Cincinnati on June 10, 1825; Warren is among the listeners. Owen purchases the Rappite community of Harmonie and establishes the ideal community of New Harmony, Indiana. Warren moves his family there in September 1825 and establishes himself as the music director. He also teaches at the school and works at the printing facility. The settlement founded by Owen prescribed community of property, possibly under the influence of the Rappites and Shakers. New Harmony was probably the first secular ideal community in the United States. Warren lived there for nearly its entire run. Fanny Wright is also a resident at various points. Some have blamed the community's failure on the fact that some residents were essentially spongers on Owen's wealth, and that agreement on uses of community property could not be arrived at by the extremely various and eccentric inhabitants. These failures gave rise to Warren's doctrines of individual sovereignty and defense of property. Warren builds his own home at New Harmony, selling it to Frances Wright in 1836.[9] Robert Dale Owen (the founder's son) in the *Atlantic* described his delight in the community's musical performances, which featured "an excellent band leader, Josiah Warren. This was a performance of music, instrumental and vocal, much beyond what I expected in the backwoods."[10]

1827–29   Time Store, Cincinnati. In downtown Cincinnati, later at Utopia, at New Harmony (1840s), and at Modern Times (1850s), Warren establishes Time Stores, which employ labor notes as the circulating medium. Each Time Store would become the center of a cooperative, equitable economy. In every case, particularly the first, the experiment was a dramatic success. In fact, Kenneth Rexroth in *Communalism* asserts that the Time Store was "the most popular retail business in the city."[11] Son, George Warren, is born. According to Bailie in *Josiah Warren*, "At four years old the boy was taught to use carpenter's tools. At seven he learned type-setting and composed a tiny book with pages one inch square. . . . He was a musician, and at seventeen began to teach for a living. At eighteen he built an organ, fashioning it from the raw material. It was sold at the current price of such instruments. Being a practical wood-worker, he made the best paling fence in the town. He was also skilled in the use of pencil and brush, and, as one of his sources of income, painted some of the most artistic signs in that part of the country. . . . When he was twenty-one he was noted as a composer of band music, and was an expert performer on the Clarinet, French Horn, Cornet, Violin, and Cello" (31–32).

1828   Visited at home in Cincinnati by Frances Wright. [Alexander Bryant Johnson's *The Philosophy of Human Knowledge* published; read by both Warren and Wright; later revised and republished as *A Treatise on Language*.] The village of Kendal, near the Tuscarawas River in Ohio, originally settled by the Quakers Thomas and Charity Rotch, is a small-scale Owenite community that makes the transition to Warren principles. The Producers' Exchange of Labour for Labour Association formed in Philadelphia on Owen/Warren principles, and soon thereafter markets patent medicines at cost.

1830   Visited in Cincinnati by Frederick W. Evans, later a Shaker elder, who tells him about further Owenite experiments, including a project in New York. Visits Fanny Wright in New York. Robert Dale Owen and Fanny Wright propose an experimental community on Warren principles in New York. This plan comes to nothing as Owen travels to Europe and Wright the next year mourns the death of her sister. Conducts educational experiments at Massillon, Ohio, near Spring Hill and Kendal, with a group of twenty-five children, whom he resolves to treat as autonomous individuals. System of apprenticeships established on a labor-for-labor basis. Warren perfects the continuous-feed printing press (in a letter dated 1853, he says he "has had these experiments in hand for twenty-three years" See "My Dear Sir," p. 244). He was already describing his innovations in printing to the *Free Enquirer* in a communication dated January 10, 1830, and must have been working on the technology through much of the 1820s. Josiah's son George wrote, "Well I remember in 1830, when I was a little chap. I watched my father making type at the same fireplace at which my mother cooked the meals."[12]

1831   Returns to Cincinnati in March.

[Garrison publishes the first issue of *The Liberator*.]

1832   Cholera epidemic in Cincinnati. Warren is able to provide extremely cheap and fast printing of health information, at cost, through use of his typemaking techniques and continuous-feed press.

1833   Warren operates a steam-powered sawmill on a labor-for-labor basis on the Tuscarawas River in Ohio. This is the first venture in the community known as "Equity," to which Warren eventually removes. In *Men Against the State*, Martin terms this "the first anarchist community in America." The *Peaceful Revolutionist* self-published; the plates are cast on the family stove at the Equity community. Warren writes the following poem about Frances Wright's sister Camilla, who died in 1831:

Written on Hearing Unwelcome News
They say 'tis best to be deceived
When sad realities would break the heart:
O would I could be thus relieved
When moral meteors like thee depart.

Ah! vain the thought—We seldom find
A friend like thee in all mankind.
And when thou'rt gone can we caress thee
And think thee here when most we miss thee?

Ah no—Then let the poor, the weak,
The injured, talented and meek
Prepare to hear what I most dread
To tell—their friend Camilla's dead.

O would that death could be controlled
By tears, by reason, or by gold
These in excess thy friends would give—
E'en die for thee, couldst thou but live.

Thy doting sister too, when oft reclined
Fatigued and worn, will call to mind

Thy gentle, soothing, watchful care—
Will call "Camilla" but thou wilt not hear.

She has thee not; but now alone
Feels every moment, thou art gone!
Kind friends around us strive in vain
To place her as she was, again.

She lives now but to haste the day
(and knows her aid can speed its coming)
When, if sweet flowers too soon decay,
They'll leave as sweet, around us blooming.[13]

1835 Warren community established in Tuscarawas County,
Ohio. According to Warren in *Practical Applications*, "The first village
was attempted in Tuscarawas Co., Ohio, in 1835. Six families were on
the ground—24 persons in all. 23 of them had the ague or some other
bileous complaint some portion of the first year! We became alarmed
and dared not invite any friends to join us. We thought we would try
one more year; but these complaints prevailed as before, and in addition to them, the influenza carried off twelve, mostly young, vigorous,
healthy people within a circle of thirty families of the neighborhood,
within two weeks. We now resolved to get away from the locality as
soon as possible, and we did so, at the almost total sacrifice of buildings, furniture, and land, but with the view of concentrating again
when our shattered finances had been recruited" (p. 202).

1836 [Emerson, *Nature*.]

1837 Equity disbands due to disease. Warren returns to New
Harmony.

1840 [Proudhon, *What Is Property?*]

1841 One-off periodical *Herald of Equity* self-published at
Cincinnati.

[Emerson, *Essays: First Series*.]

1842 New Harmony Time Store. According to Warren in *Practical Applications*, "In March 1842 another store (just like that in Cincinnati in 1827) was set in operation in New Harmony, the old seat
of Mr. Owen's communistic experiments. This store worked with an

immense power in revolutionizing the retail trade in that region. It consumed about three years" (p. 202). Publishes the one-off periodical *Gazette of Equitable Commerce* at New Harmony.

1844   New, "mathematical" musical notation published. *The Peaceful Revolutionist* (vol. 2, no. 1) put out as pamphlet. Publicly exhibits a new printing press in New York, a prototype of his later high-speed presses. The principle was so simple that "there was no equitable ground for a patent, and it was given to the public" (Warren quoted by Bailie in *Josiah Warren*, 84). Invents "universal typography," apparently a cheap way of producing type, later used by some commercial printers. Publishes *The Letter on Equitable Commerce* at New Harmony, perhaps the best example of the charms and drawbacks of Warrenian printing processes: it's all in italics and resorts to multiple whole alphabet styles and families, many or all of them no doubt of Warren's design.

1846   First, tiny, self-printed edition of *Equitable Commerce* published at New Harmony. According to Wunderlich in *Low Living and High Thinking*, "On 25 April 1846 . . . the 'first American patent on rubber stereotyping plates' was granted to Warren. This stereotyping device, mixing shellac, tar, and sand, combined with gum arabic, beeswax, stearine, tallow, and oil as a substitute for type metal, was used by the Smithsonian Institution for its first book catalog in 1851" (20).

1847   Third iteration of the Time Store, in New Harmony, is established in February. Establishment of Utopia, Ohio (Clermont County). With some resources derived from printing, Warren bought a village that had previously been a Fourierist phalanx on the Ohio River. Utopia was a small-scale success. In *Men Against the State*, Martin says that in 1852 the population was around one hundred persons. According to Warren in *Practical Applications*, "Mr. E. G. Cubberly, one of the first settlers, in October 1872, while still residing at Utopia, wrote: 'The labor notes put us into a reciprocating society—the result was, in two years, twelve families found themselves with homes who never owned them before. . . . Labor capital did it. I built a brick cottage one and a half stories high, and all the money I paid was $9.81—all the rest was effected by exchanging labor for labor'" (p. 208). This village apparently persisted long after Warren had gone east, and the settlers eventually removed to Minnesota, displaced, like many an ideal community, by land speculation. A village called Utopia still exists at this location.

1848   Visits (moves to?) Boston. Meets William B. Greene and signs his petition to establish a mutual bank. Becomes acquainted with Stephen Pearl Andrews and several other prominent reformers, including George Henry Evans, Joshua K. Ingalls, and Lewis Masquerier.

1849   Second, even tinier, self-printed edition of *Equitable Commerce* published at Utopia, Ohio.

Lectures at Hancock Hall in Boston on Sundays throughout the winter. Pearl Andrews hears him and is converted to his principles, beginning an extended collaboration that is probably the only reason we know of Warren at all.

[Thoreau, "Civil Disobedience" and *A Week on the Concord and Merrimack Rivers*.]

1850   Moves to New York City and conducts "parlor conversations" on his principles. Letters in the collection of the Indiana Historical Society indicate that Warren set up a press operation, including the manufacture of type, for the Boston publisher John P. Jewett. In 1852, Jewett issued the first edition of Harriet Beecher Stowe's *Uncle Tom's Cabin*, which of course raises the possibility that this epochal work was first printed using Warren's apparatus.

1851   Foundation of Modern Times on Long Island, the equitable commerce/self-sovereign community established by Warren and Pearl Andrews (who owned a house there but never lived in it). Warren starts the project by moving alone to a shack in the pine barrens, manufacturing bricks to raise other structures. Lots at Modern Times are sold on the cost principle. As with prior Warren communities, destitute families find themselves able to build homes. Eventually the settlements start attracting anyone whose lifestyle is not conventional, including people living with partners other than their spouses, as well as advocates of free love. Victoria Woodhull is a frequent visitor. A variety of fads are represented, such as spiritualism, nudism, the all-bean diet, the water cure, and the amazing philosophy of Pearl Andrews. In *Periodical Letter*, Warren writes, "Whoever tries what is vulgarly known as 'free love' . . . will find it more troublesome than a crown of thorns: and there is not much danger of its becoming contagious where the results of the experiment are made known" (p. 216).

1851   Stephen Pearl Andrews publishes *The Science of Society*, expounding Warren's ideas with eclectic bits of Comte and Fourier thrown in.

1852   Third (canonical) edition of *Equitable Commerce* published by Fowler and Wells and edited by Pearl Andrews. Also published is its "how-to companion," *Practical Details in Equitable Commerce*, which describes equity experiments ranging from the Time Stores to the foundation of Modern Times. Debate commences in the *New York Tribune* among Horace Greeley, Henry James, Sr., and Pearl Andrews on marriage and free love, focusing prurient attention on Modern Times. This is exacerbated by Thomas and Mary Gove Nichols mailing sex education guides and advocating promiscuity. Within reason, Modern Times was a success, despite the occasional nudist or visitation by malevolent spirits, for some ten years for a hundred people or more. The community seamlessly became the town of Brentwood during the 1860s. Caroline Warren stays behind in New Harmony throughout Warren's later life.

[Lysander Spooner, *An Essay on the Trial by Jury*.]

[Death of Frances Wright]

1854–58   *Periodical Letter* published at Modern Times.

1855   House of Equity established in Boston by Warren follower Keith (first name unknown), who conceived it as an urban community center with equitable stores, lectures, recreational areas, printing facilities, and so forth. Warren helped conceive and execute the plan, which eventually collapsed when Keith's finances did.

1858   It seems likely that Warren was resident in the Boston area, or splitting time between it and Modern Times, by this date. The Dual Commerce Association formed in Boston on Warren principles (though the extent of Warren's involvement is unclear; the proprietor is listed as T. J. Lewis). It was essentially an equitable food store. The wage of the "distributors or merchants" was set at two dollars a day, based on a labor calculation. The project, which was described in a proposal dated July 1, 1858, and then reported on in a tract dated January 1, 1859, is striking for its size and should make us rethink the scale of Warrenian equitable experiments. The January 1 tract is not Warren's writing, but it quotes an earlier advertisement that certainly is. The central store was located in the basement of the Pelham Hotel, with other "stations" in different poor neighborhoods in the city, six in all, each staffed by a man and a woman, with twenty employees altogether. The basic system was consignment: farmers still owned their produce until sold, and price did not vary by quantity. The January 1 report says that "several thousands of individuals have already begun to experience the benefits growing out of the movement." Milk was priced at "five cents per quart in winter, four in summer." The distribution is described as five hundred quarts of milk per day, fifty barrels of flour per week (at fifty cents), six thousand pounds of soap per month, five thousand bushels of Nova Scotia potatoes per month (five cents a bushel "if taken from the boat, or ten cents when delivered at the homes of consumers"), and so on. According to the earlier advertisement by Warren, "'Dual commerce' expresses those commercial relations which result and develope between producer and consumer, instead of being the absorbent of both."[14] It is not known how or when the DCA came to an end.

      [Death of Robert Owen.]

  1862 [Death of Thoreau.]

  1863 Lives in Boston area and; associates with Ezra Heywood and the nascent labor movement. *True Civilization* published. An equitable commerce store established (contact "Nath'l G. Simonds, No. 189 Main St., Charlestown"), apparently on a pretty small scale. (This project identified by Shawn Wilbur in the form of an advertisement, in the *Boston Investigator*, vol. 32, no. 50, April 15, 1863, p. 393.)

1865   [Death of Proudhon.]

1866   Resident at Cliftondale, Massachusetts. According to Martin in *Men Against the State*, Warren "made preliminary preparations for the setting up of [communities] in Jamaica and Central America" (98).

1872   Resident at Princeton, Massachusetts, at the home of Ezra and Angela Heywood. At the spring meeting of the New England Labor Reform League, Warren, Ezra Heywood, William B. Greene, and a young and impressionable Benjamin Tucker are all present in what was possibly the greatest summit meeting of American individualist anarchists. Publication of *Practical Applications*.

1873   Refines *True Civilization*, conceived as a conclusion to *Equitable Commerce*.

1874   At Princeton, Massachusetts, death claims Josiah Warren, individually. Services are held at the Bulfinch Place Unitarian Church, and Warren is buried at the Mount Auburn Cemetery.

AMERICAN INDIVIDUALIST ANARCHISTS
OF THE NINETEENTH CENTURY

This is, all in all, a formidable, if pointedly eccentric, crew, and the greatest figures of this political tradition—Warren, Thoreau, Ballou, Garrison, Spooner, and occasionally Emerson—are persons of substantial accomplishment in a variety of fields.

> Adin Ballou (b. 1803, Cumberland, Rhode Island, d. 1890): Unitarian/Restorationist minister, abolitionist, and absolute nonresistant. In 1842 Ballou founded the religious Hopedale community in Worcester Country, Massachusetts. His book *Christian Non-resistance* (1846) is an under-read but fundamentally influential scriptural argument for pacifism. Ballou corresponded with Tolstoy on this subject. He was one of the few abolitionist nonresistants to condemn John Brown's raid unambiguously and to remain a pure pacifist throughout the Civil War. Ballou's *Practical Christian Socialism* (1854) contained criticisms of Warren and the equity movement.
>
> William Lloyd Garrison (b. 1805, Newburyport, Massachusetts, d. 1879): Like Warren, a printer; publisher of the famous/notorious abolitionist paper *The Liberator*. Leader of the radical wing of American abolitionism, arguing from a radical Protestant perspective for the immediate

abolition of slavery and the secession of the non-slave states. He was also an advocate of feminism and nonresistance, the latter on biblical grounds. From his radical pacifism, Garrison concluded that human governments, all of which rest on force, are entirely illegitimate.

Lysander Spooner (b. 1808, Athol, Massachusetts, d. 1887): A deist, abolitionist, and individualist anarchist. His work *The Unconstitutionality of Slavery* (1845) is an amazingly accomplished exercise in legal interpretation, taking a position rejected by the Garrisonians, who held that the Constitution recognized slavery, and thus that the U.S. government was illegitimate. Lawyer and legal scholar are odd occupations for an anarchist, though Spooner, like Warren, never referred to himself as an "anarchist." In his time, he set up a private competitor to the U.S. Postal Service and tried to organize an incursion to free John Brown after the Harper's Ferry raid. Such works as *No Treason* (1867–70) and *Vices Are Not Crimes* (1875) are classics of libertarian thought. The central idea (as it was not for Warren or the transcendentalists) is the concept of natural rights.

Stephen Pearl Andrews (b. 1812, Templeton, Massachusetts, d. 1886): Andrews moved to Louisiana as a young man and practiced law in Texas, and in the South he became an abolitionist. A scholar of odd accomplishments, he introduced the Pitman shorthand into the United States, in part, to help ex-slaves learn to read, and he supposedly mastered thirty-two languages. Often the spearhead of reform projects (including Modern Times), his commitments were mercurial. His book *The Science of Society* (1851) is presented explicitly as an explication of Warren's ideas. He formed a number of scandalous semisecret organizations, including the League of the Men of Progress and the Grand Order of Recreation. Even as he was promoting Modern Times, he founded the "Pantarchy" near Union Square in New York City, "a Grand Composite Order of Government" on Fourierist/Warrenian lines, with himself as "Pantarch." His *Basic Outline of Universology* (1872) shows remarkable affinities to Charles Sanders Peirce's thought, obsessed as it is with triads and semiotics. He later produced the first American translation of *The Communist Manifesto* for *Woodhull and Claflin's Weekly*.

Henry David Thoreau (b. 1817, Concord, Massachusetts, d. 1862): Among the best-known American prose stylists, he wrote work that was political from the outset. The religious skepticism and anarchism expressed in his first major work, *A Week on the Concord and Merrimack Rivers*

(1849), would have been controversial had the book been widely read. And of course his essay "Civil Disobedience" is a classic of individualist and antistatist thought. One might regard his cabin at Walden as a one-man ideal community. It is to be regretted that, as far as we can tell, Warren and Thoreau never met. Nevertheless, their affinities are remarkable, as they both exhibit pointedly practical activity behind which a profound idealism glows.

William Batchelder Greene (b. 1819, Haverhill, Massachusetts, d. 1878): Originally a Unitarian minister under the influence of Orestes Brownson, Greene introduced Proudhon's ideas into American thought and developed a system of mutual banking. He was also influenced directly by Josiah Warren on such issues as money and institutional forms. Later in his life he wrote about the history of American transcendentalism, the interpretation of the kabbalah, and a proposal for a new version of calculus.

Ezra Heywood (b. 1829, Princeton, Massachusetts (?), d. 1893): After studying for the ministry, he joined up with Garrison as an abolitionist preacher in the late 1850s. After the Civil War, he plunged into labor organizing in Boston, where he met Warren. He wrote a number of pamphlets and essays treating issues of political economy from Warren's perspective. For decades he published the radical periodical *The Word* and was associated with such figures as Victoria Woodhull. With his wife, Angela, a radical feminist and a remarkable writer, he advocated free love and used his press to publish information on birth control and other sexual issues. Thus he ran afoul of the moral crusader Anthony Comstock and was arrested and imprisoned a number of times in the 1880s.

Benjamin Tucker (b. 1854, South Dartmouth, Massachusetts, d. 1939): A well-known publisher and preserver of the individualist tradition. Early on, Warren and Spooner profoundly influenced him; in later life, he was a proponent of the egoism of Max Stirner, whose remarkable 1844 book *The Ego and Its Own* he got translated and published in the United States. His periodical *Liberty* (1881–1908) published the most important libertarians and individualists of its period.

Voltairine de Cleyre (b. 1866, Leslie, Michigan, d. 1912): Among American anarchists, only Thoreau rivals her as a stylist. Born into grinding poverty, de Cleyre was housed as a teenage girl in a nunnery, from which she emerged an atheist. Originally associated with Tucker in the individualist camp, she taught immigrants in Philadelphia and began to incorporate European ideas. She was radicalized by the Haymarket riot and subsequent executions, and wrote a number of feminist essays. Eventually she referred to herself as "an anarchist without adjectives," and showed more and more sympathy with communist anarchists and world revolution, à la Emma Goldman.

AMERICAN UTOPIAS

The following list is compiled from Noyes, *History of American Socialisms*; Holloway, *Utopian Communities in America*; and Hinds, *American Communities*. The division into religious and secular communities is to some extent arbitrary, though convenient as an ordering principle. Noyes's argument throughout *American Socialisms*—which seems to be supported by the historical record—is that communities are more successful when based on common religious commitments. Obviously, this enumeration is far from complete.

Religious

Rhode Island: Founded by dissenters Roger Williams and Anne Hutchinson in 1635 as outpost of female preaching, free speech, and Protestant dissent.

The Woman in the Wilderness: Christian communist community founded near Philadelphia in 1692 by German Pietists.

Ephrata: Founded in 1735 in what is now Lancaster County, Pennsylvania, by Johann Beissel and fellow German Pietists. This community was characterized by extreme austerity and local educational work.

Shakers: Mother Ann Lee, an English woman of peasant stock from Manchester, took a group of schismatic Quakers to New York in 1776 and established a compound at Watervliet. The most successful of the religious utopians other than the Mormons, the Shakers spread widely throughout the United States. Ecstatic dancing, celibacy, and economical design were hallmarks of their organization. Labor for the Shakers was a form of prayer. By mid-nineteenth century they had as many as five thousand followers, and were led for much of that time by Frederick Evans, who had been at New Harmony and knew Warren. It has been asserted that the Shakers' communism influenced Robert Owen.

Rappites (Harmonists): George Rapp, a German prophet, came to Baltimore in 1803 with three hundred families and settled in western Pennsylvania, calling the community "Harmonie." Rapp was more sophisticated than most such religious idealists; in fact, Herder and Schleiermacher greatly influenced his ideas. The community adopted communism for practical rather than idealistic reasons, and it eventually inculcated celibacy, though the doctrine was not strictly enforced. Very prosperous, they sold their land at a profit and removed to Indiana, where they also called their community Harmonie. Eventually, they sold to Robert Owen, who established New Harmony on the site. The Rappites then returned to western Pennsylvania and founded "Economy."

Zoar: A German Protestant sect similar to the Rappites settled this community in the wilderness of Tuscarawas, Ohio (the same county where Warren's village Equity was located) in 1819 with 225 people. The group comprised followers of the German theologian Jacob Böhme.

Mormons: Radical Christian sect founded with a new scripture by Joseph Smith in 1830. Established in upstate New York, the Latter Day Saints eventually moved to Kirtland, Ohio, then to New Jerusalem in Missouri, as they were harassed and expelled from one community after another. Numbered at least fifteen thousand when they settled the town of Nauvoo, Illinois, in 1837. Like many of these groups, the Latter Day Saints experimented with plural marriage and various communistic schemes. Smith was killed in 1844 after a series of problems and persecutions, and Brigham Young led much of the group to Utah, where you can find them still.

Oneida: Founded by John Humphrey Noyes in upstate New York in 1848 on a doctrine of "Christian perfectionism." The group practiced a form of communism and "plural marriage" that eventually mutated into a eugenics experiment by Noyes, who assigned breeding partners. President Garfield's assassin, Charles Guiteau, stayed there a period of time and could achieve no romantic success, even under the auspices of plural marriage (Guiteau was referred to by the women of Oneida as "Charles Gitout").

Hopedale: Founded in 1841 by Adin Ballou, formerly a Universalist minister; like Noyes, he was a charismatic and schismatic Christian. Ballou preached absolute nonresistance consistently throughout the Civil War. The settlement's economy was described as "socialistic," but the polity was based on devotion to the charismatic cult of Ballou. Hopedale had a few hundred members at its height, but it fell to land speculation in 1856.

Amana: "Inspirationist" community near Buffalo settled in 1855 largely by Germans. This was a large, prosperous community that eventually removed to Iowa and began manufacturing appliances.

Secular or "Socialist"

New Harmony: The Scottish industrialist and idealist Robert Owen bought the Rappite village of Harmony in Indiana, and used it to test his theories of property, education, cooperative manufacture, and higher culture. The experiment persisted from 1825 to 1827, when it broke down in factional disputes. Josiah Warren, Frances Wright, and Frederick Evans, later the Shaker elder, were resident. There were other Owenite settlements, notably at Yellow Springs and Kendal, Ohio.

Nashoba: A community for freed slaves and white experimenters founded in 1826 by Frances (Fanny) Wright near Memphis, Tennessee. Wright, one might remark, was peerless in her courage: she seriously contemplated establishing an interracial feminist community in the South in the 1820s. Sensational accusations of miscegenation dogged the community; Wright was, in fact, preaching that the race problem could be overcome by inter-breeding. In 1828 Wright delivered a July 4 address in New Harmony and visited Josiah Warren in Cincinnati. In part because of this association with Wright, Warren remained a staunch feminist throughout his life, though he later rejecting the idea of "free love."

Brook Farm: Transcendentalist community founded by George Ripley in 1841. Adorned by very smart people—including Nathaniel Hawthorne—doing physical labor and playing music and writing poetry. Its proponents included Emerson, Margaret Fuller, and Bronson Alcott. Emerson on Brook Farm: "It was a perpetual picnic, a French revolution in small, an Age of Reason in a patty-pan."[1] Brook Farm made a transition to Fourierism in 1844, after which, like any decent Fourierist experiment, it disintegrated, albeit slowly. A group of "secessionists" from Brook Farm settled at Modern Times in 1857.

Fruitlands: Extremely small transcendentalist community (or house) established in Harvard, Massachusetts, by Bronson Alcott in 1843. It disintegrated after seven months, due in part to the struggles between the English reformer Charles Lane—a fanatic who was pushing a vegan ("Pythagorean") diet, celibacy, and many other ascetic disciplines—and Alcott's wife and daughters. Louisa May Alcott fictionalized the situation in her 1873 story "Transcendental Wild Oats."

Walden Pond: Thoreau's two years (1845–47) at Walden should be considered as continuous with the utopian experiments of the period. It might indeed be easier to form an individualist community when there is only one member.

Icaria: Community established in 1848 at Nauvoo, Illinois—originally settled by the Mormons—by the French utopian socialist Étienne Cabet, The community eventually removed to Iowa, where it persisted in some form until 1898.

Fourierist phalanxes: Fourier had a utopian plan to organize the whole world into "phalanxes" or "phalansteries," grand hotels that looked something like a cross between a palace and a tenement, which would encourage interaction and community. He preached feminism and community of property. The American experiments included La Reunion near Dallas and the North American Phalanx—probably the largest and most successful Fourierist project—in Monmouth County, New Jersey (1841–56).

Capitalist

Early company towns and idealized industrial communities of the nineteenth and early twentieth centuries (e.g., deserve to be mentioned in particular with regard to Warren's projects, since they have some features in common (though not the profit motive).

Oneida, New York: Noyes's industrious community merged after his death into a communally owned maker of flatware. John Humphrey Noyes's son Pierrepont Burt Noyes merged capitalism (e.g., masterful advertising campaigns) with an idealist vision still connected to the original religious ideal. Oneida prospers yet.

Pullman, Illinois: "Model" town founded by the inventor of the sleeping car in 1880 near Chicago. Like a number of enlightened capitalists, Pullman believed that a healthy and educated workforce would be productive and loyal. He was hailed as a visionary. But Pullman ran the town along totalitarian lines, finally culminating in a brutal action to break a strike at Pullman in 1894.

Hershey, Pennsylvania: Milton Hershey's "company town," founded in 1903 and built around his confectionery amid Pennsylvania dairy country, can stand in for many "idealistic" capitalist projects, all of which recall Robert Owen's ideas at New Lanark. Hershey created an architecturally disparate town with many public spaces, free transportation, education, arts programs, and other services. It is perhaps no coincidence that Hershey is located in a hot bed of ideal communities, such as Amish, Mennonite, and Ephrata. It thriveth still.

JOSIAH WARREN: AN ANNOTATED
BIBLIOGRAPHY

A number of people have had a hand in researching Warren's writings, and this appendix is an attempt to summarize the bibliographical work on Warren as it currently stands. Ronald Creagh's bibliography in *L'anarchisme aux Etats-Unis* (Paris: Didier Erudition, 1986) was invaluable. The bibliography below owes a particular debt to Shawn Wilbur, whose research on Warren informs this book throughout. Bailie's research for *The First American Anarchist* remains fundamental. Anne Caldwell Butler's graduate work at Ball State in the 1960s and '70s unearthed new materials. Agnes Inglis collected materials and references for a file at the Labadie Collection, University of Michigan. It is entirely possible that whole books by Warren may exist, waiting to be discovered.

Entries within each section are arranged chronologically.

A New System of Notation: Intended to Promote the More General Cultivation and More Just Performance of Music. New Harmony, 1843. Self-published first statement of Warren's innovations in musical notation.

A Collection of the Most Popular Church Music Written upon Geometric or Scientific Principles. New Harmony, 1844.

Equitable Commerce: A New Development of Principles as Substitutes for Laws and Governments, for the Harmonious Adjustment and Regulation of the Pecuniary, Intellectual, and Moral Intercourse of Mankind, Proposed as Elements of New Society. New York: Fowlers and Wells, 1852. Stephen Pearl Andrews edited this primary source for Warren's thinking. It uses an eccentric typographical/indexing system in which themes are numbered and lettered in a hierarchy and then noted in the margins. The first edition was published in 1846. In his "Editor's Preface" to the 1852 edition, Andrews writes, "The main body of this book was published as far back as 1842. It has now undergone, at my request, a revisal by the author" (5). The work is "signed" "Josiah Warren. New Harmony, Indiana, U.S., 1846" (106). Believe it or not, an 1869 edition was published under the title *The Former Title of This Work Was "Equitable Commerce," but it is now ranked as the first of* True Civilization, a title only Warren, in the whole history of humankind, could have devised. A number of small editions were published in the twentieth century.

Practical Details in Equitable Commerce, Showing the Workings, in Actual Experiment, During a Series of Years, of the Social Principles Expounded in the Works Called "Equitable Commerce." New York: Fowlers and Wells, 1852. I obtained a copy from the Houghton Library at Harvard University. It is mostly in dialogue form, recording what seem to be actual transactions. Something of a miscellany, it features a preface by Andrews in which he sets out the project of Modern Times. There are also theoretical cogitations very much redundant with other writings. But it yields a narrative of Warren's projects between New Harmony and Modern Times, with many detailed records that Warren regarded as the data confirming his theory.

Written Music Remodeled and Invested with the Simplicity of an Exact Science. Boston: John P. Jewett, 1860. An elaboration of Warren's work on musical notation in the 1840s.

True Civilization: An Immediate Necessity and the Last Ground of Hope for Mankind, Being the Results and Conclusions of Thirty-Nine Years' Laborious Study and Experiments in Civilization as It Is, and in Different Enterprises for Reconstruction, by Josiah Warren, Counsellor in Equity. Boston,

1863. This qualifies his anarchism to some extent with a system of arbitration panels, and it also addresses the Civil War. Warren appears to have become a fan of military drilling, an unlikely juxtaposition. The table of contents, rather than running serially through the text, gives page numbers nonsequentially by theme. Chapter 4 reproduces the sections on economics from *Equitable Commerce*.

Practical Applications of the Elementary Principles of True Civilization to the Minute Details of Everyday Life. Princeton, Mass., 1873. This self-published booklet narrates Warren's practical experiments, starting with Tuscarawas. There is a copy in Houghton Library at Harvard University.

PERIODICALS

Warren's periodicals were mostly very small runs of a single or a few issues, printed by himself, and for which he fabricated the type, written entirely by himself. In some cases, the distinction between periodical and booklet is arbitrary.

The Peaceful Revolutionist. Apparently four issues were published in volume 1. I have only located numbers 2 and 4, dated February 3, 1833, and April 5, 1833 (Wisconsin Historical Society, Madison, Wisconsin). There was also a pamphlet published under this title in May 1848 at Utopia, Ohio (vol. 2, no. 1).

Herald of Equity. Dated Cincinnati, 1841 (Working Men's Institute, New Harmony, Indiana).

Gazette of Equitable Commerce. Vol. 1, no. 2, dated New Harmony, September 1842. This issue includes material on the Time Stores and equitable commerce. The contents of vol. 1, no. 1, are not known, nor is it known whether any other issues were published (Indiana Historical Society).

Letter on Equitable Commerce. Dated New Harmony, February 1844 (Indiana Historical Society).

Periodical Letter on the Principles and Progress of the Equity Movement. Dated Modern Times (Thompson's Station), New York, 1854–58. Shawn Wilbur has identified seventeen issues.

The Quarterly Letter: Devoted to Showing the Practical Applications and Progress of Equity, a Subject of Serious Concern to All Classes, but Most Immediately to the Men and Women of Labor and Sorrow! Vol. 1, no. 1, dated October 1867. Consists exclusively of a treatise by Warren, "Labor for Labor," which narrates Warren's experiments up through those at Tuscarawas (New Harmony and Time Store). This source, together with *Practical Applications*, provides the more or less continuous narrative presented in this volume (Labadie Collection, University of Michigan).

ARTICLES, BROADSIDES, AND PAMPHLETS

"Explanation of the Design and Arrangements of the Cooperative Magazine Which Has Recently Been Commenced." *Western Tiller*. Eight communications from September 8, 1826, to July 27, 1827. The *Western Tiller* was published in Cincinnati.

"A Letter from Josiah Warren." *Mechanics Free Press* (Philadelphia). May 10, 1828, 2.

"From 'The March of Mind.'" *New Harmony Gazette*. September 10, 1828, 365.

"Time System for Labor Exchange." *Western Tiller*. Five articles between September and October 1828.

"Reduction in the Cost of Printing Apparatus." Cincinnati, 1830 (broadside).

"To the Friends of the Equal Exchange of Labor in the West." *Free Enquirer* 2 (July 17, 1830): 301–2.

"Improvement in the Machinery of Law." *Free Enquirer* 2 (July 17, 1830): 300.

"Reply to E. C." *Free Enquirer* 2 (August 14, 1830): 332.

"Social Experiment." *Free Enquirer* 3 (February 16, 1831): 137.

"Written on Hearing of the Death of Camilla Wright." *Free Enquirer* 5 (February 23, 1833): 144 (poem).

"Introduction to a New Printing Apparatus, Adapted to the Wants and Capacities of Private Citizens." Trenton, Ohio, 1836.

"Manifesto." New Harmony, Ind., 1841 (leaflet). Reprinted with an introduction by Joseph Ishill, Berkeley Heights, N.J.: Oriole Press, 1952.

Written contributions to the *Indiana Statesman*, New Harmony (February 1, 1845; March 7 1846); and a series of engravings (July 4, August 16, October 11, December 27, 1845; January 31, February 14, 1846).

"Music and the Sciences." *American Journal of Music and Musical Visitor* 4 (February 16, 1846): 147.

"Improvement in Compositions for Stereotype-Plates." US Patent 4,479, April 25, 1849.

"Letter from Josiah Warren." *Boston Investigator* 19 (September 25, 1849): 3.

"Positions Defined." Modern Times, N.Y., 1854 (leaflet).

"Explanation," *Boston Investigator* 23 (February 22, 1854): 2.

"Modern Education." Long Island, N.Y., December 1861 (leaflet).

"Modern Government and Its True Mission, A Few Words for the American Crisis." n.p., March 1862. Signed "A Counsellor."

"On Mobs, I." *Boston Investigator* 33 (September 23, 1863): 155.

"On Mobs, II." *Boston Investigator* 33 (September 30, 1863): 163.

"The Emancipation of Labor." Boston, 1864 (Collection of the Working Man's Institute, New Harmony, Ind.).

"An Open Letter to Louis Kossuth." *Boston Investigator* 33 (February 17, 1864).

"The Principle of Equivalents: The Most Disagreeable Labor Entitled to the Highest Compensation." n.p., 1865 (pamphlet).

"Woman and the Money Question." *Revolution* 4 (July 1869): 29.

"Superficialities." *Revolution* 4 (August 12, 1869): 83.

"Response to the Call of the National Labor Union for Essays on the Following Subjects." Boston, 1871 (pamphlet).

Controversy with Andrews in *Woodhull and Claflin's Weekly*. July–September 1871.

"The Motives for Communism—How It Worked and What It Led To." *Woodhull and Claflin's Weekly* 4 (February 17, 1872): 6. This was the first in a series. The subsequent pieces appeared in *Woodhull and Claflin's Weekly* on the following dates: February 24, March 2, March 16, April 13, April 20, April 27, May 25, June 15, 1872; April 12, April 26, 1873.

"Letter to E. H. Heywood." Princeton, Mass., 1873. Reprinted in *Index* 5 (April 30, 1874); and in Bailie, *Josiah Warren* (127–35), as "Josiah Warren's Last Letter."

"Money: The Defects of Money Are the 'Roots of All Evil.'" Charlestown, Mass., 1873 (pamphlet).

"A Few Words to the Pioneers." *Word.* July 1873. Followed by a series of articles in subsequent issues.

"The Cost Principle." *Index* 4 (December 11, 1873): 504–5.

"Labor the Only Ground of Price." *Index* 5 (May 28, 1874): 260–61.

"A Few Words to the Writer in a Paper Called 'The Circular' on 'the Sovereignty of the Individual.'" n.d. (Labadie Collection, University of Michigan).

"Young America." n.d. (pamphlet) (Working Man's Institute).

LETTERS AND NOTEBOOKS

A set of what are apparently lecture notes, too fragile to xerox. Described by Martin in *Men Against the State* (Working Men's Institute, New Harmony, Ind.).

"Notebook D." A book-length handwritten notebook used by Warren at widely divergent stages of his career (1840, 1860, 1873). It overlaps with *Equitable Commerce* and other writings, but it also contains some previously unknown material. It was edited by Ann Caldwell Butler for a master's thesis at Ball State University in "Josiah Warren, Notebook D," (June 1968). The material used here is based on Butler's version (Working Men's Institute).

Three letters to Stephen Pearl Andrews about stereotype plates and publishing plans (photocopies), 1850–51 (Working Men's Institute).

Letter addressed "My Dear Sir." Thompson's Station, Long Island, New York, March 12, 1853. Addresses various subjects, including Warren's printing experiments (Labadie Collection, University of Michigan; other letters are not legible due to bleed-through).

In *Partisans of Freedom*, Reichert mentions twenty-one letters exchanged between Warren and Stephen Pearl Andrews contained in the catalogues of Charles Coffin Jewitt at the Houghton Library, Harvard University. Reichert characterizes them as showing how close the two men were in their ideas and projects in the early 1850s.

Handwritten document titled "A Scrap of History" ("by the author of TC and EC etc"; thus, late period). A memoir of Owen's New Harmony (Labadie Collection).

MAJOR SOURCES BY OTHERS

Andrews, Stephen Pearl. *The Science of Society*. Weston, Mass.: M&S Press, 1970 [1851]. Explicitly presented as an exposition of Warren's ideas, this book was no doubt greeted with some relief by anyone who had tried to read Warren directly. Nevertheless, in eccentricity Pearl Andrews far outpaced Warren, and he would soon invent a universal language ("Alwato") and attempt to answer all possible questions in his system of "universology." It has often been stated, including apparently by Warren himself, that this book is the best embodiment in writing of Warren's philosophy. As Wunderlich points out in *Low Living and High Thinking*, however, the book was bound to fail in its attempt to reconcile Warren and Fourier, an extremely unlikely project.

Bailie, William. *Josiah Warren: The First American Anarchist*. New York: Herbert C. Roseman, 1971 [1906]. The only biography of Warren, this is a bit on the hagiographic side to be absolutely in good taste. Still, Bailie unearthed much valuable information on Warren's life and ideas.

Butler, Ann Caldwell. *Josiah Warren: Peaceful Revolutionist*. Ph.D. dissertation, Ball State University, July 1978. Rock-solid research on Warren's activities and beliefs. Includes samples of Warren's musical notation and a copy of his will.

Heywood, Ezra. "Yours or Mine? The True Basis of Property." First printed as a pamphlet in Princeton, Mass., 1876. Reprinted in *Essential Works of*

Ezra Heywood, ed. Martin Blatt (Westin, Mass.: M&S Press, 1985), 71–104. Also consult the Heywood essay "Hard Cash," collected in the same volume (103–29). Both are very able expositions of Warrenian economics.

Martin, James J. *Men Against the State*. Colorado Springs: Ralph Myles, 1970 [1953]. This is still the best treatment of American individualist anarchism, and it begins with several chapters displaying serious research on Warren (though his dating of various Warren communities is inaccurate).

Noyes, John Humphrey. *History of American Socialisms*. New York: Dover, 1966 [1870]. See esp. chap. 10. A sharp and fair assessment (characteristic of Noyes) with material from *The Peaceful Revolutionist* and an interview with a resident of Modern Times (probably not Warren or Andrews). Noyes's chapter is based on the A. J. Macdonald Papers on American Communities at the Beinecke Collection at Yale University. This material comes from Macdonald's travels, interviews, and collecting of ephemera from American ideal communities, and contains considerable material on Warren. MacDonald's actual typescript is hard to decipher, but the collection also includes the whole of *The Peaceful Revolutionist*, vol. 2, no. 1, dated Utopia, Ohio, May 1848. There are also some drawings of Modern Times by MacDonald.

Reichert, William O. *Partisans of Freedom*. Bowling Green: Bowling Green University Press, 1976. This text is exemplary in its connection of Warren to Emerson. Reichert calls Warren the "chief architect of libertarianism" (64).

Shively, Charles. "A Remarkable American: Josiah Warren, 1798–1874." Undergraduate honors thesis, Harvard University, 1959.

Stern, Madeleine. "Every Man His Own Printer: The Typographical Experiments of Josiah Warren." *Printing History* 2, no. 2 (1980): 1–20. A delightful and well-researched treatment of Warren's career as a printer and inventor.

Wunderlich, Roger. *Low Living and High Thinking at Modern Times, New York*. Syracuse: Syracuse University Press, 1992. By far the best scholarly work on Warren, it includes many sources no one else consulted. Wunderlich got a Ph.D. from Stony Brook University at age seventy-two and became more or less the official historian of Long Island.

Notes

1. The best sources on American individualist anarchism are as follows: Eunice Schuster, *Native American Anarchism: A Study of Left-Wing American Individualism* (New York: Da Capo, 1970 [1932]). This book is exemplary in connecting American individualist anarchism to radical Protestantism. James J. Martin, *Men Against the State: The Expositors of American Individualist Anarchism, 1827–1908* (Colorado Springs: Ralph Myles, 1970 [1953]). William O. Reichert, *Partisans of Freedom: A Study in American Anarchism* (Bowling Green: Bowling Green University Press, 1976). Martin's and Reichert's volumes represent the most elaborate scholarship on this topic, and I'd like to express my gratitude to both authors for an incredible amount of work for a very small audience, which has been indispensable to my development as a political philosopher and historian of libertarian/ anarchist thought. See also David DeLeon, *The American as Anarchist: Reflections on Indigenous Radicalism* (Baltimore: Johns Hopkins University Press, 1978).

2. Warren, *Equitable Commerce.* See, for example, the Burt Franklin edition of the 1852 text, n.d., p. 40. This is precisely the sort of passages edited out in this volume.

3. PDF files of original typesets of *Equitable Commerce* and *True Civilization* are available at the Anarchy Archives, http://dwardmac.pitzer.edu/ Anarchist_Archives/bright/warren/war ren.html.

4. Conway's article appeared in the *Fortnightly Review* on July 1, 1865, as the author recollected Warren in 1858. Quoted in William Bailie, *Josiah Warren: The First American Anarchist* (New York: Herbert C. Roseman, 1971 [1906]), 69.

5. The main biographical sources are Bailie, *Josiah Warren*; and Roger Wunderlich, *Low Living and High Thinking at Modern Times, New York* (Syracuse: Syracuse University Press, 1992).

6. For the intersection of radical Protestantism, individualism, abolitionism, anarchism, and pacifism, the best sources are Valarie H. Ziegler, *The Advocates of Peace in Antebellum America* (Bloomington: Indiana University Press, 1992); Aileen S. Kraditor, *Means and Ends in American Abolitionism* (Chicago: Ivan R. Dee, 1989 [1967]); and Lewis Perry, *Radical Abolitionism: Anarchy and the Government of God in Antislavery Thought* (Ithaca: Cornell University Press, 1973).

7. Vernon Parrington, *Main Currents in American Thought* (New York: Harcourt, Brace, 1927), 171.

8. Frank Podmore, *Robert Owen* (London, 1906), 404.

9. Ezra Heywood, "Hard Cash . . . Financial Monopolies Hinder Enterprise" (1874), in *The Collected Works of Ezra H. Heywood*, ed. Martin Blatt (Weston, Mass.: M & S Press, 1985), 103–29. This is a very able exposition of Warren-style economic theory.

10. Owen derived his determinism and many political and ethical conclusions from William Godwin. Owen expressed these views, for example, in *A New View of Society; or, Essays on the Formation of Human Character* (London, 1813).

11. Probably the best source on Harmonie (the Rappite community) and New Harmony is William E. Wilson, *The Angel and the Serpent: The Story of New Harmony* (Bloomington: Indiana University Press, 1964). I have relied on this volume for most of the account herein.

12. Kenneth Rexroth, *Communalism: From Its Origins to the Twentieth Century* (New York: The Seabury Press, 1974), 236.

13. Wilson, *Angel and the Serpent*, 151.

14. John Humphrey Noyes, *History of American Socialisms* (New York: Dover, 1966 [1870]), 41.

15. Wilson, *Angel and the Serpent*, 148.

16. Bailie, *Josiah Warren*, 5.

17. Quoted in Wunderlich, *Low Living and High Thinking*, 22.

18. Frances Wright, "Wealth and Money," *Free Enquirer*, October 23, 1830. Quoted in Celia Morris, *Fanny Wright: Rebel in America* (Cambridge: Harvard University Press, 1984), 179n22.

19. On Frances Wright, a good source is Morris, *Fanny Wright*, which portrays Wright as an astonishing synthesis of Jane Austen and Emma Goldman.

20. The publication history of this remarkable book, as set out in the introduction of *A Treatise on Language* (New York: Dover, 1968), is as follows. In 1828 G. and C. Carvill of New York published it under the title *The Philos-*

ophy of Human Knowledge; or, A Treatise on Language. In 1836 Harper and Brothers published a revised and expanded edition, though also with some unfortunate omissions, as *A Treatise on Language; or, The Relation Which Words Bear to Things*. The latter is the basis of the all later editions. In 1854 Appleton published Johnson's restatement, *The Meaning of Words*.

21. Johnson, *Treatise on Language*, 80–81.

22. Ibid., 115.

23. Noyes, *History of American Socialisms*, 42.

24. On Garrison, see Henry Mayer, *All on Fire: William Lloyd Garrison and the Abolition of Slavery* (New York: Norton, 1998); and Horace Seldon, *The Liberator* Files, http://www.theliberatorfiles.com/. On Rogers, see http://crispinsartwell.com/rogershome.htm.

25. Ralph Waldo Emerson, "The Young American" (1844), in *Emerson: Essays and Lectures*, ed. Joel Porte (New York: Library of America, 1983), 214.

26. Ralph Waldo Emerson, "Politics" (1844), in Porte, *Emerson: Essays and Lectures*, 567.

27. Henry David Thoreau, *A Week on the Concord and Merrimack Rivers* (1849), in *Henry David Thoreau: A Week on the Concord and Merrimack Rivers; Walden; The Maine Woods; Cape Cod*, ed. Robert F. Sayre (New York: Library of America,1985), 106.

28. Agnes Inglis, miscellaneous papers on Warren at the Labadie Collection, University of Michigan.

29. Quoted in Madeleine B. Stern, *The Pantarch: A Biography of Stephen Pearl Andrews* (Austin: University of Texas Press, 1968), 74.

30. Stern, *Pantarch*, 76.

31. Wunderlich, *Low Living and High Thinking*, 12.

32. Ibid., 10.

33. Charles Shiveley, "A Remarkable American: Josiah Warren" (Harvard College undergraduate honors thesis, March 1959), 66.

34. "Trialville and Modern Times," *Chambers' Edinburgh Journal*, December 18, 1852, 396.

35. Quoted in ibid., 65.

36. Edgar Allan Poe, "The Literati of New York City," *Godey's Magazine and Lady's Book*, July 1856, 16. Quoted in Wunderlich, *Low Living and High Thinking*, 70.

37. From the self-printed leaflet "Positions Defined," circulated at Modern Times in 1854.

38. Reichert, *Partisans of Freedom*, 74–75. The quotations from Warren are from *Practical Applications*.

39. John Stuart Mill, *Autobiography* (New York: Penguin, 1989 [1873]), p. 191.

40. August Comte to Henry Edger, August 4, 1854, in Richmond L. Hawkins, *Positivism in the United States* (Cambridge: Harvard University Press, 1938), 138.

41. Peter Kropotkin, "Anarchism," *Encyclopedia Britannica*, 11th ed., 1910, reprinted in *The Essential Kropotkin*, edited by Emile Capouya and Keitha Tompkins (New York: Liveright, 1975), 114–15.

42. Madeleine Stern, "Every Man His Own Printer: The Typographical Experiments of Josiah Warren," *Printing History* 2, no. 2 (1980): 1–20.

EQUITABLE COMMERCE

1. Josiah Warren, *Equitable Commerce* (New York: Fowler and Wells, 1852), v.

2. The reference is to Alphonse de Lamartine, *History of the Girondists*, trans. H. D. Ryde (London: Henry G. Bohn, 1854), 3:293. Warren, of course, must have consulted an earlier edition of this book, originally published in French in 1847.

3. Reference is to Lamartine's *History of the Girondists*, 2:337.

4. Ecclesiastes 3:1, King James version.

5. The reference would be to Blackstone's *Commentaries*, part 1, section 2 ("Of the Nature of Law in General"), although it does not seem to be an exact quotation. Of course, any version of social contract theory would have done as well or better than Blackstone here, and one might infer that Warren was not thoroughly acquainted with Hobbes or Locke.

THE PEACEFUL REVOLUTIONIST

1. The two issues from 1833 were obtained from the Wisconsin Historical Society, to which I express my gratitude, as also to the Indiana Historical Society, which supplied the issue from 1848.

2. This is one of the fundamental propositions of Alexander Bryan Johnson's philosophy of language. See, for example, *A Treatise on Language* (New York: Dover, 1968), 47.

3. The quotation is from Jefferson's first inaugural address.

4. Warren heard Robert Owen speak many times and knew him and his sons personally. This quotation is an expression of a thought expressed in all Owens' work, and probably reflects the influence of William Godwin on Owen.

5. Warren refers to Johnson's twenty-eight-page pamphlet *A Discourse on Language* (Utica, N.Y.: William Williams, 1832).

6. Warren refers to Johnson's *The Philosophy of Human Knowledge, or a Treatise on Language: A Course of Lectures Delivered at the Utica Lyceum* (New York: G. and C. Carvill, 1828).

7. One of the only other writers to take note of Johnson's work on semantics was Frances Wright, in the *Free Enquirer*, March 18, 1829, quoted in David Rynin's introduction to Alexander Bryan Johnson, *A Treatise on Language*, 7:

> A work of the highest merit, under the above title, issued from the press of this city [New York] during the past year; and, while calculated to advance human intellect by a full century, in the path of true knowledge and sound thinking, we believe its appearance remains yet unnoticed, and all but unknown. This inattention, however, its enlightened author will know how to interpret.
>
> The diamond of true water is distinguished only by the lapidary; and, unfortunately, in the present state of human knowledge, the brighter jewels of intellectual truth are appreciated only by the philosopher. It is only the reasoner who can appreciate reason, the profound thinker who can appreciate thought, and the scholar who can distinguish the originalities of genius, amid the stores of learning. Such characters may, therefore, be few, but they will not be lukewarm admirers.

8. Legislators have decided that "society has a right to take the life of criminals to preserve itself." Society has left its interests to be preserved by forms of words like this, and gone to sleep, while the causes of crime have remained untouched, and continue to accumulate unseen. [Warren's note]

9. On November 7, 1825, Jereboam Beauchamp killed the Kentucky legislator Solomon P. Sharp, who had fathered an illegitimate child with Anna Cooke and then denied paternity of the stillborn baby. Cooke agreed to marry Beauchamp on the condition that he kill Sharp. This case was quite sensational at the time.

10. The proverbial "hanging judge," George Jeffreys (1645–89) persecuted the opponents of King James II of England with sadistic aplomb.

11. The *Free Enquirer* was the successor of the *New Harmony Gazette*, under the editorship of Frances Wright and Robert Dale Owen.

12. Warren refers to "Social Experiment," *Free Enquirer* 3 (February 16, 1831): 137.

13. Such are some of the reasons for individuality of responsibilities and arranging our affairs within such limits that responsibility may rest unequivocally where it ought, so that every one would be governed by the only gov-

ernment that can safely be trusted, viz., the natural and unavoidable consequences of actions. [Warren's note]

14. Warren is referring to passages such as this, from a letter from Jefferson to James Madison, dated December 20, 1787: "I think our governments will remain virtuous for many centuries; as long as they are chiefly agricultural; and this will be as long as there shall be vacant lands in any part of America. When they get piled upon one another in large cities, as in Europe, they will become corrupt as in Europe." *Thomas Jefferson: Writings*, ed. Merrill D. Peterson (New York: Library of America, 1984), 918.

15. References are to William Paley, *Principles of Moral and Political Philosophy*, first published in 1785 and a standard text on the subject for a century thereafter.

16. "J.P." here may refer to the radical dissenter (and contemporary of Paley's) Joseph Priestley, a scientist and founding figure of utilitarianism. The material appears to be a somewhat Warrenized summary of parts of Priestley's *Essay on the First Principles of Government* (1768). On the other hand, Warren did have an associate with the initials "J.P." at this period (he gives the initials in his papers several times without a name), and perhaps the whole piece on Paley is that person's contribution.

17. Warren alludes to the story of Diogenes of Sinope (as good a proto-anarchist as one could find in antiquity) and Alexander the Great: "Once, while he was sitting in the sun in the Craneum, Alexander was standing by, and said to him, 'Ask any favour you choose of me.' And he replied, 'Cease to shade me from the sun.'" Diogenes Laërtius, *The Lives and Opinions of Eminent Philosophers*, trans. C. D. Yonge (London: Henry G. Bohn, 1853), book 6.

18. The addressee has not been identified.

19. The source of these comments has not been traced.

"NOTEBOOK D"

1. Ann Caldwell Butler, "Josiah Warren, Notebook D" (master's thesis, Ball State University, June 1968). Butler also wrote a fine doctoral dissertation, "Josiah Warren: Peaceful Revolutionist" at Ball State (1978).

2. That is, Warren commenced his experiment in education on the basis of exchange of labor between the teacher (himself) and the two students.

3. "G. W. W." refers to Warren's son, George; the identity of the other boy is not known.

4. The quotation is from Henry St. John, Lord Bolingbroke's essay "On Reticence in Criticism."

5. Lord Bolingbroke, "Letter to Alexander Pope," *The Works of Lord Bolingbroke: With a Life* (Philadelphia: Carey and Hart, 1841), 3:49

6. Ibid., 50.

7. About this entry, though it appears here in the notebook, Butler contends that "it is written in blue ink and seems, from the writing, punctuation, and spelling, to have been written in the New Harmony 1840 period."

8. Warren is referring to the "July Revolution" of 1830, in which Charles X was replaced by Louis-Philippe.

TRUE CIVILIZATION

1. Mark 2:27.

2. Refers to the British educational and postal reformer Sir Rowland Hill (1795–1879).

3. The parenthetical material was originally Warren's footnote. It likely shows the influence of William Batchelder Greene, then writing a history of transcendentalism in America. At any rate, the thought of the divine as the not-human connects Warren to at least moments in Emerson and to Thoreau.

4. According to Valerius Maximus in *Factorum et dictorum memorabilium*, the temple of Artemis at Ephesus was destroyed on July 21, 356 B.C. in an act of arson committed by one Herostratus, "so that through the destruction of this most beautiful building his name might be spread through the whole world." Valerius Maximus, *Memorable Doings and Sayings*, trans. David Roy Shackleton Bailey (Cambridge: Harvard University Press, 2000), 8:14.

NARRATIVE OF PRACTICAL EXPERIMENTS

1. William Maclure (1763–1840) was a Scottish philanthropist and geologist who attempted a geological survey of the United States and was resident at New Harmony for a time.

2. Kendal was an Owen-inspired community located near Canton, in Stark County, Ohio, near the Tuscarawas River.

3. Bridewell was the notorious British prison and poorhouse, originally a palace built for Henry VIII.

4. The Clermont Phalanx was the failed Fourierist community that was superseded by Warren's Utopia in what is now Clermont County, Ohio.

5. That man was Warren, as a number of sources make clear.

6. A *Boston Medical and Surgical Journal* editorial of July 24, 1873, denounced a museum that was "a type of its class," Dr. Jourdain's Gallery of

Anatomy: "It was a collection of anatomical models and dissections, with representations of skin and venereal diseases, most improper for public exhibition, and calculated to excite the morbid curiosity of the young together with it peculiar forms of hypochondria. Vile pamphlets were on hand to induce those having or fearing disease to consult the proprietor. The harm which this single establishment must have done cannot be calculated." See http://www.historycooperative.org/journals/cp/vol-04/no-02/sappol   / index.html.

EPHEMERA AND MISCELLANEA

1. "I knew a very wise man. . . . He believed, if a man were permitted to make all the ballads, he need not care who should make the laws." Andrew Fletcher, Letter to the Marquis of Montrose, collected in *The Political Works of Andrew Fletcher* (London: Bettesworth and Hitch, 1782), 372.

2. Josiah Warren, *Manifesto: A Rare and Interesting Document*, introduction by Joseph Ishill (Berkeley Heights, N.J.: The Oriole Press, 1952), 1–2. Joseph Ishill (1888–1966) was an anarchist author and publisher, often considered one of the best printers and designers of his period. No doubt Ishill connected to Warren's printing and typesetting experiments as well as his doctrines.

3. The great principle of human elevation was perceived to be the sovereignty of every individual over his or her person and time and property and responsibilities. That this was impracticable where these were connected. Disconnection, or individualisation of these, therefore, appeared to be the process required. A habitual respect to this individual sovereignty, it was perceived, would constitute equitable moral commerce. The question then arose, how could this complete sovereignty of the individual over its own time and property be preserved through the process of exchanging them in the pecuniary commerce of society? This great point was settled by the idea of time for time, or labor for labor—disconnecting all natural wealth from labor, each pricing his own by what it costs him; but not overstepping the natural bounds of his individuality by setting a price on the value of his article or labor to the receiver of it. The disconnection of cost from value laid the foundation of equitable pecuniary commerce. This new commerce required a circulating medium disconnected from money of all kinds, and representing labor only; and thus the laborer becomes emancipated from money and tyranny. The principles have been applied to the management and education of children, which go to show the radical mistake and the great cause of defeat on this important subject. [Warren's note]

4. Matthew 20:16.

5. Lajos (Louis) Kossuth (1802–94), a Hungarian freedom fighter and later leader of the country, was a hero to many American reformers. Giuseppe Mazzini (1805–72) was an Italian republican statesman.

6. Artur Gorgey (1818–1916) fought with Kossuth in the rebellion of 1848.

APPENDIX A: CHRONOLOGY OF WARREN'S LIFE

1. Charles Shiveley, "A Remarkable American: Josiah Warren (1798–1874)" (undergraduate honors thesis, Harvard University, March 1959), 9. Shiveley in turn credits Anonymous, *Warren Genealogy* (n.p., 1895), 10–13.

2. George Santayana, *Persons and Places* (New York: Scribner, 1944), 180.

3. Ellery Bicknell Crane, *Historic Homes and Institutions* (New York: Lewis, 1907), 1:130.

4. Shiveley cites John G. Warren, *Genealogy of Warren with Some Historical Sketches* (Boston, 1854), 1.

5. Shiveley, *A Remarkable American*, 10.

6. Caroline Warren to Josiah Warren, October 21, 1855, Labadie Collection, University of Michigan.

7. Harry R. Stevens, "The Haydn Society of Cincinnati, 1819–1924," *Ohio State Archeological and Historical Quarterly* 52 (April–June, 1843): 102.

8. *Free Enquirer*, May 22, 1830, 240.

9. Agnes Inglis, "Josiah Warren's Community-Living Experiments," Labadie Collection, University of Michigan. Inglis put together a series of documents on Warren, including biographical notes. Thanks to the Labadie Collection.

10. Robert Dale Owen, "A Chapter of Autobiography," *The Atlantic*, January 1873, 3.

11. Kenneth Rexroth, *Communalism: From Its Origins to the Twentieth Century* (New York: Seabury, 1974), 236.

12. George Warren, "Josiah Warren," Manuscript Collection of the New Harmony Workingmen's Association.

13. Published as "Written on Hearing of the Death of Camilla Wright." *Free Enquirer*, February 23, 1833, 144. Then as "Written on Hearing Unwelcome News" in *The Peaceful Revolutionist* 1 (February 5, 1833): 7.

14. "The Dual Commerce Association, Its Experience, Results, Plans, and Prospects: First Report" (Boston, 1859).

APPENDIX C: AMERICAN UTOPIAS

1. Ralph Waldo Emerson, "Historic Notes of Life and Letters in New England," in *The Complete Works of Ralph Waldo Emerson* (Boston: Houghton Mifflin, 1911), 10:364.

Index

Italic page numbers indicate where the individual cited is quoted or direct attention to the central treatment of the subject.

AMERICAN PHILOSOPHY
Douglas R. Anderson and Jude Jones, series editors

Kenneth Laine Ketner, ed., *Peirce and Contemporary Thought: Philosophical Inquiries.*

Max H. Fisch, ed., *Classic American Philosophers: Peirce, James, Royce, Santayana, Dewey, Whitehead, second edition.* Introduction by Nathan Houser.

John E. Smith, *Experience and God, second edition.*

Vincent G. Potter, *Peirce's Philosophical Perspectives.* Ed. by Vincent Colapietro.

Richard E. Hart and Douglas R. Anderson, eds., *Philosophy in Experience: American Philosophy in Transition.*

Vincent G. Potter, *Charles S. Peirce: On Norms and Ideals, second edition.* Introduction by Stanley M. Harrison.

Vincent M. Colapietro, ed., *Reason, Experience, and God: John E. Smith in Dialogue.* Introduction by Merold Westphal.

Robert J. O'Connell, S.J., *William James on the Courage to Believe, second edition.*

Elizabeth M. Kraus, *The Metaphysics of Experience: A Companion to Whitehead's "Process and Reality," second edition.* Introduction by Robert C. Neville.

Kenneth Westphal, ed., *Pragmatism, Reason, and Norms: A Realistic Assessment—Essays in Critical Appreciation of Frederick L. Will.*

Beth J. Singer, *Pragmatism, Rights, and Democracy.*

Eugene Fontinell, *Self, God, and Immorality: A Jamesian Investigation.*

Roger Ward, *Conversion in American Philosophy: Exploring the Practice of Transformation.*

Michael Epperson, *Quantum Mechanics and the Philosophy of Alfred North Whitehead.*

Kory Sorrell, *Representative Practices: Peirce, Pragmatism, and Feminist Epistemology.*

Naoko Saito, *The Gleam of Light: Moral Perfectionism and Education in Dewey and Emerson.*

Josiah Royce, *The Basic Writings of Josiah Royce.*

Douglas R. Anderson, *Philosophy Americana: Making Philosophy at Home in American Culture.*

James Campbell and Richard E. Hart, eds., *Experience as Philosophy: On the World of John J. McDermott.*

John J. McDermott, *The Drama of Possibility: Experience as Philosophy of Culture.* Edited by Douglas R. Anderson.

Larry A. Hickman, *Pragmatism as Post-Postmodernism: Lessons from John Dewey.*

Larry A. Hickman, Stefan Neubert, and Kersten Reich, eds., *John Dewey Between Pragmatism and Constructivism.*

Dwayne A. Tunstall, *Yes, But Not Quite: Encountering Josiah Royce's Ethico-Religious Insight.*

Josiah Royce, *Race Questions, Provincialism, and Other American Problems, Expanded Edition.* Edited by Scott L. Pratt and Shannon Sullivan.

Lara Trout, *The Politics of Survival: Peirce, Affectivity, and Social Criticism.*

John R. Shook and James A. Good, *John Dewey's Philosophy of Spirit, with the 1897 Lecture on Hegel.*

Gregory Fernando Pappas, ed., *Pragmatism in the Americas.*

Donald J. Morse, *Faith in Life: John Dewey's Early Philosophy.*